HISTORY OF HARYANA

About the Author

Dr. Aijaz Ahmad is an Associate Professor in History and Principal of YMD College, Nuh, affiliated with Gurugram University, Gurugram. During his service career, he has published 23 research papers in many national and international journals. In the same period, Dr. Ahmad has published twelve books by many reputed publishers. His published books are: 1. *Indian Muslims Against British Rule*; 2. *Sir Syed, Aligarh Muslim University and National Politics*; 3. *Mewati Rebellion of 1857*; 4. *Uprising of 1857*; 5. *History of Mewat*; 6. *Cultural Heritage of Mewat*; 7. *Poorv Aupniveshik Bharat Me Vigyaan Tatha Praudyogiki*; 8. *Triple Talaq*; 9. *Democracy and Discontent in India*; 10. *New Dimensions of Indian Historiography*; 11. *Scientific Development in Islamic Civilization*; and 12. *Religion and Culture under Mughals*.

HISTORY OF HARYANA
Ancient, Medieval and Modern Period

Aijaz Ahmad

CONCEPT PUBLISHING COMPANY PVT. LTD.
NEW DELHI - 110 059

ISBN: 978-93-6344-172-9 (HB)
ISBN: 978-93-6344-470-9 (PB)

First Published 2025

Published and Printed by

Concept
Since 1974

Concept Publishing Company Pvt. Ltd.
A/15-16, Commercial Block, Mohan Garden
New Delhi-110059 (India)
T: +91-11-41101460
E: publishing@conceptpub.com, *W*: www.conceptpub.com

Cataloging in Publication--Courtesy: D.K. Agencies (P) Ltd. <docinfo@dkagencies.com>

Ahamada, Ejāja, 1969- **author.**
History of Haryana : ancient, medieval and modern period / Aijaz Ahmad.
pages cm
Includes bibliographical references and index.
ISBN 9789363441729 (HB)
ISBN 9789363444709 (PB)

1. Haryana (India)--History. I. Title.

LCC DS485.H34A34 2025 | DDC 954.558 23

**To my Mamu Dr. Mohd. Isa Gauhar,
who has always been my source of
inspiration.**

Preface

Although Haryana was established as a separate state on 1st November, 1966, but the existence of Haryana has been recognized since ancient times as a distinct historical and cultural entity. This state or region has been the pivot of Indian culture and civilization since ancient times. There are many references about Haryana in Vedic literature. From the excavations done in this state, it is known that the Indus Valley Civilization and Mohenjodaro culture developed here. According to archaeologists, many evidences of many cultures of the prehistoric period—Pre-Harappan, Harappan, Later Harappan etc. have been found from the excavations of places like Banawali, Siswal, Kunal, Mirzapur, Daulatpur and Bhagwanpura in Haryana.

Centuries before during the *Mahabharata* period, the Aryavanshi Kurus started here the agricultural farming in this region. Therefore, the 48 *Kos* of cultivable land of Haryana was called Kurukshetra in the name of Kurus. It is considered a sacred region of Indian culture even today. The world-famous war of *Mahabharata* was also fought in Kurukshetra region. After the *Mahabharata* period, a blind era began in which there is no evidence of the historical reality. The entire Kuru region was divided into groups and districts without a proper king or absolute ruler. The ruler in these areas known as Ganadhipati was elected by majority vote and he was popularly given the title of Ganapati.

Due to the new discoveries made on the political system of North India during the Buddhist period, a dark chapter of history has come to light. At the beginning of the Buddhist period, sixteen Mahajanapadas have been discussed in detail in Buddhist literature. The regions of modern Haryana were at that time divided into Kuru and Panchal Mahajanapadas. On the basis of ancient coins, seals, stamps, currencies, inscriptions and other historical evidences, it is known that the Yogya Shakti emerged in the fourth century BCE and it maintained its dominance over this land for a thousand years.

Coins of Yaudheyas have been found from many places in the entire Haryana region of Satluj and Yamuna. Even during the Maurya period, the Yaudheyas remained completely powerful and their Bahudhanyak region (Haryana) remained famous in India for its prosperity, while the other tribes of the country had almost collapsed. During the Gupta period, there was a conflict between the Yaudheyas and the Gupta emperors. Emperor Vikramaditya resolved to subdue the Yaudheyas and according to one belief, there was a fierce struggle between the two powers for about a quarter of a century and in the end that huge imperialist power destroyed perhaps the last democratic power (*Gana Shakti*) of the country.

Even during the period of Harsh Vardhana, this entire region was divided into many districts. During this period in Haryana region, this tradition of districts and *Ganas* remained the basis of the political system. He attacked the growing power of the Hunas and drove them away from India. By destroying the power of the Guptas and Gandharas, the Vardhanas established their dominance over all the lands of North India. The most glorious ruler of the Vardhana dynasty was Harsha Vardhana, who established a vast empire. The period of Harsha Vardhana was a glorious era of Haryana state.

After the eleventh century, the tough time for Haryana region started in the form of various invasions. In 1014 CE, Mahmud Ghaznavi attacked Haryana and at that time Tomars were the rulers of Haryana. In the twelfth century, the Chauhans invaded Haryana and defeated the Tomars. This victory made the Chauhans the supreme power of India, because the control over Delhi and Haryana became an indicator of all-India prestige. In this way, the dominance of Chauhans was established over Haryana and Delhi in the 12th century. In 1191, Delhi's Chauhan ruler Prithviraj Chauhan defeated Mohammad Ghori in the first battle of Tarain. However, in 1192 Delhi's Chauhan ruler

Prithviraj Chauhan was defeated and killed by Mohammad Ghori. In this way, Muslim invaders established their control over Delhi as well as Haryana state.

After the death of Mohammad Ghori in 1206, his slave Qutubuddin Aibak laid the foundation of the Slave or Mamluk Dynasty of Turks in India. After the fall of the Slave Dynasty in 1290, the Khilji Dynasty arose. After Khilji, the Tughlaq, Lodis and later Mughal dynasties ruled the entire Haryana region along with remaining parts of India. During the time of Ibrahim Lodi, the estates of Hasan Khan Mewati, Jalal Khan and Mohan Singh Mandhar were the most famous in Haryana at that time. When Babur invaded India in 1526 and defeated Ibrahim Lodi in the First Battle of Panipat, the Mughal rule established in Haryana and many parts of the country. In 1527, Hasan Khan, the ruler of Mewat region in Haryana, died in the Battle of Khanwa and the Mughal rule was fully established in Mewat and Haryana. After the death of Babur, the administration in Haryana remained the same during the rule of his successor (son) Humayun. In 1504, Afghan Sardar Sher Shah Suri snatched this region from Humayun and after the death of Sher Shah, Humayun regained control over his lost kingdom in 1555. After Humayun, his son Akbar ascended the throne and continued to rule over Haryana along with rest of India except a short break of the rule of Hemu or Hemchandra. At that time, Rewari was ruled by Hemchandra (Hemu), who was Akbar's strongest enemy. The Second Battle of Panipat was fought between Akbar and Hemu in 1556 in which Hemu was defeated and killed by Akbar's Mughal forces.

After the death of Mughal ruler Aurangzeb in 1707, the Mughal dominance over Haryana gradually ended. Marathas completely dominated Haryana until 1756-57. After capturing Haryana, the Marathas advanced further and captured Punjab also. The capture of Punjab by the Marathas resulted the Third Battle of Panipat (Haryana) between the Marathas and Ahmad Shah Abdali which put a short break of Maratha expansion in North India.

On 30th September, 1803, Daulatrao Sindhia gave Haryana along with his other occupied places to the British following the treaty of Surji Arjun Gaon. The British were at that time rapidly expanding their power by defeating the newly emerging Indian powers after the fall of the Mughal Empire. In Haryana, the Meos, Ahirs and Gujars of Gurgaon, the Jats and Ranghads of Rohtak, the Vishnoi and Jats of Hisar, the Rajputs, Rodes, Sainis and Sikhs of Karnal and Kurukshetra, strongly protested for a long time against the local chieftains appointed by British. But finally in 1809-10, British control was established over entire Haryana.

During the Revolt of 1857, the British suppressed this revolution very brutally and snatched away the kingdoms of rebellious rulers such as the Nawabs of Jhajjar and Bahadurgarh, Raja Rao Tularam of Ballabhgarh and Rewari. After suppressing them, their kingdoms were either merged in the British Empire or handed over to the rulers of British supporting states such as Nabha, Jind and Patiala. After suppression of this great rebellion, Haryana was made a province of Punjab.

After the establishment of the Indian National Congress, a non-violent fight for independence from the British broke out, in which the warriors of Haryana actively participated. From the nationwide movements of Mahatma Gandhi till the attainment of Independence, the people of Haryana showed indomitable courage and immortalized the name of Haryana in history for ever.

Aijaz Ahmad

Acknowledgements

This text book *History of Haryana* provide a comprehensive overview of the history and culture of Haryana, offering valuable insights into the region's past and societal evolution. This book presents a unique perspective, contributing to a deeper understanding of Haryana's rich heritage. The historical journey of Haryana reflects a blend of ancient civilizations, dynastic influences, and modern developments, shaping the state's cultural and historical significance. The Haryana region has been ruled by various empires and dynasties including the Maurya Empire, Gupta Empire, Mughal Empire, Maratha Empire and the British Empire.

Human presence in Haryana dates back to 1,00,000 years ago with cave paintings and tools found in Mangar Bani. Stone age artifacts have been excavated from the banks of the stream in the region. Haryana holds significant historical importance due to its Neolithic sites like Bhirrana, Siswal, Rakhigarhi, and Kunal. Haryana has many urban and rural sites from the Indus Valley Civilization. During the Vedic era, janapadas like Kuru and Matsaya covered most of Haryana. The Kuru janpada evolved into a mahajanapada, with Kurukshetra being a significant area. The famous *Mahabharata* battle fought on its land Kurukshetra and the epic *Mahabharata* mentions that Haryana was most fertile region is mentioned as the Bahudanayak region. Harshvardhana, the ruler of the Pushyabhuti dynasty was the most famous ruler of Haryana who ruled this area with its capital Thanesar. Haryana came under the Delhi Sultanate after the Second Battle of Tarain. The Mughal Empire's influence in Haryana is highlighted by the battles of Panipat. During the British period Haryana witnessed the Indian Rebellion of 1857, with significant events in Ambala and other regions. Haryana also played important role during the national movement until the independence of India.

This text-book *History of Haryana* covers UG and PG syllabi of universities like Gurugram University, Maharshi Dayanand University, Rohtak, Kurukshetra University, Kurukshetra etc. The contents of this text-book cover the rich and diverse culture and history, spanning various periods and rulers from ancient times to modern period including the Delhi Sultanate to Mughal Empire in medieval period. In completing this text book I consulted various libraries and archives to search the historical facts and applied hypothesis with scientific approach. Most my colleagues, friends, and family members supported me to complete this work for which I will be indebted to them.

Aijaz Ahmad

Contents

1

Sources of History of Ancient, Medieval and Modern Periods of Haryana

The history of Haryana is rich and diverse, spanning various periods and rulers. Haryana is home to several sites from the Indus Valley Civilization, highlighting its early civilization roots. Notable sites in Haryana include Rakhi Garhi, Banawali, Bhirrana, Farmana, Jognakhera, Mitathal, Siswal, and IVC mines at Tosham. During the Vedic era, Janapadas and *Mahajanapadas* existed in Haryana, such as the Kuru Janpada and Matsya Janpada. Haryana played a significant role in Vedic culture and the Kurukshetra region is central to many ancient texts and events. Battles like the First, Second and Third Battle of Panipat marked significant events in Haryana's history, with leaders like Babur, Hemu and Abdali playing crucial roles. Haryana experienced the Indian Rebellion of 1857, with centres of rebellion at various places and key figures like Raja Nahar Singh and Rao Tula Ram leading the resistance.

The history of Haryana is rich and diverse, spanning millennia from ancient civilizations to the struggle for independence against British colonial rule. Established as the 17th Indian state on 1st November, 1966, Haryana was once known as Brahmavarta, Aryavarta, and Brahomoupdesa, owing its names to the emergence of Lord Brahma on its soil and its association with Vedic culture.

Referred to as Bahudhanyaka and Bahudhana, it signifies a land abundant in grains and wealth. Archaeological excavations in Haryana at sites like Naurangabad, Mitathal, Kunal, Agroha, Rakhigarhi, Rukhi, and Banawali have revealed evidence of pre-Harappan and Harappan cultures. Haryana is historically significant as the birthplace of the Vedic Civilization along the banks of the River Saraswati, where the Vedas were composed.

Sources of History of Ancient Haryana

There is a dearth of ancient sources not only in Haryana but in entire India. Therefore, most of the time one has to resort to guesswork. There is no dearth of religious texts and archaeological sources, but there is a complete lack of historical sources. Nevertheless, historians have made a successful attempt to write the entire history by using hypothesis based on many sources. The sources of ancient history include literary, archaeological and accounts of foreigners, which are described as follows.

Literary Sources

A large number of literary sources are available for information about the history of Haryana. Therefore, they can be studied by dividing them into the following points:

(a) Hindu religious literature
(b) Buddhist literature
(c) Jain literature
(d) Historical and Semi-historical literature

Hindu Religious Literature

Vedas, Upanishads, Brahmin literature, Sutras, Puranas etc. are broadly related to Hindu religious subjects. However, despite historical limitations, such texts have been used fruitfully to understand the past.

Vedas

The word *Veda* is derived from the Sanskrit word *Vid* which means "to know" or knowledge. The Vedas are the best of oral literature. They are traditionally considered as *Shruti* or "heard" and defined as revealed texts. A Samhita (code) or Sangraha is also added to them.

Rigveda Samhita: It is the knowledge of praising songs (*Rik*). *Rigveda* is the oldest text of India, which is believed to have been composed in 1500-1000 BCE. It has ten *Mandalas* or chapters, each of which has been composed traditionally by a particular family of sages.

Samaveda Samhita: It contains knowledge of songs or tunes (*Saman*), mostly sung *mantras* from *Rigveda*.

Yajurveda Samhita: The *Yajurveda* contains a collection of sacrificial words (*Yagya* or *Yaju*) for worship rituals.

Atharvaveda Samhita: It contains knowledge of magical formulas (*Atharvan*) and description of diseases and their cures.

The last three Vedas are considered to have been composed between 1000-600 BCE. Vedas are not only religiously important but also reveal the society, economy and to some extent the political system of that period, which helps a lot in writing the history of that period.

Brahmin Literature

The Brahmanas are elaborate treatises on religious topics, particularly commentaries on sacrifices and the practical or mystical significance of sacrificial rites and ceremonies.

Aranyakas (Forest Books and Upanishads)

These contain details of the opinions and statements of forest ascetics and ascetics on God, the world, mankind etc. These contain a good deal of ancient philosophy.

Sutras

Sutras are classified as memoirs or *Smritis*. These were composed by great sages. These texts were written around 600-300 BCE on the basis of rituals.

Srauta Sutras: These contain rules for performing great sacrifices.

Grihya Sutras: These contain guidelines for simple ceremonies and sacrifices of daily life.

Dharma Sutras: These are books of instructions on spiritual and non-religious law. These are the oldest religious law books.

Sutrottar Texts or Smriti

The Sutrottar texts are Smriti texts, which are *Manusmriti*, *Narad Smriti*, *Yajnavalkya Smriti*. They were composed between approximately 200 BCE and 900 BCE. These mention the various classes as well as the duties of the kings and their officials. In these texts, the rules for marriage and property have been fixed. In these texts, there is a provision to punish people for theft, assault, murder, adultery etc.

Epics

The period of the two epics—*Ramayana* and *Mahabharata* is considered to have been composed and written between 500 BCE and 500 CE. *Mahabharata*, which is the oldest among these, sheds full light on the ancient history of Haryana. Its main story is the Kaurava-Pandava conflict of the late Vedic period. This conflict took place in the field of Kurukshetra for Hastinapur kingdom. The sacred religious text *Geeta* is a part of this *Mahabharata*.

Puranas

The total number of Puranas is 18, the compilation of which was completed by 400 CE. The subject matter of these Puranas include *Sarga* (creation of the world), *Pratisarga* (re-creation of *Brahmand*), *Manvantara* (period of various humans and Manu), *Vansh* (genealogical list of gods, kings and saints) and *Vanshanucharita* (chronology of royal dynasties). And the life stories of some selected characters are included in the major Puranas like *Vayu*, *Brahmad*,

Bhavishya, Harivansh, Vishnu etc. There is a lot of information on the ancient dynasties like Haryak, Shishunag, Maurya, Shunga, Kanva and Andhra etc.

Buddhist Literature

Buddhist literature occupies an important place among the non-Brahmanical and non-Sanskrit sources of early India. It was written in Pali and Prakrit languages respectively. The Pali text "*Tripitaka*" (Three Baskets), composed after the death of Buddha, tells us about India during the time of Buddha and 16 *Mahajanapadas*. Of the three books of *Tripitaka*, "*Suttapitaka*" contains Buddha's discourses on various doctrines in the form of stories, poems and dialogues. The second book, "*Vinayapitaka*" describes about 227 rules for Buddhist monks. The third book, "*Abhidhamma Pitaka*" contains summaries, lists and questions related to Buddhist philosophy.

The Buddhist religious text "*Panchsudin*" narrates that Mahatma Buddha had visited many towns and villages of Haryana region. "*Dirgh Nikaya*" has a detailed description of Haryana region. It is known from the text "*Divyavadan*" that Mahatma Buddha propagated Buddhism in Agroha and Rohtak. It is also known from the Buddhist text "*Majjhima Nikaya*" that Buddhism had spread extensively in Haryana. Haryana is considered to be the place of composition of most parts of the major texts of Buddhism, "*Mahanidan Sutra*", "*Majjhima Nikaya*" and "*Bhagandiya Sutra*". All these texts provide us important information about the religion and culture of the then state of Haryana.

Jaina literature

The major Jain religious texts are 12 *Anga*, 12 *Upanga*, 10 *Prakirna*, 6 *Chedsutra*, 2 *Sutra* and 4 *Mool Sutra*. Many Jain religious texts like "*Prishtishtha Parvan*" of Hemchand and "*Kalpa Sutra*" of Bhadrabahu throw light on the history of Haryana of the first, second and third century. Apart from this, "*Bhadrabahhu Charit*" and "*Kathakosh*" also throw light on the religious and cultural history of Haryana. Somdeva's "*Yashastilak Champu*" and

Pushpadanta's "*Jasharacharit*" throw light on the history of Haryana. Agroha and Rohtak were important centres of Jainism in Haryana. In the first century, a scholar named Lokacharya propagated Jainism in Haryana.

Historical and Semi-historical Literature

Haryana region has been the centre of historical events since ancient times. Therefore, in most of the historical texts, many places and events of this region have been described in detail. Although there is a lack of texts in ancient times, "*Harshacharita*" written by Harshvardhana's court poet Vanbhatta gives adequate information about the history of Haryana. In this text, not only the political history of Harshvardhana but also adequate and satisfactory information is obtained about Harshvardhana's dynasty, status of Thanesar, governance system, wars and conquests, and social system.

Apart from the historical literature, there are many texts which indirectly throw light on the history of Haryana. These texts are kept in the category of semi-historical literature. These semi-historical texts have been written on religious, cultural, social, economic and imaginary subjects. In this field, Harshvardhana's works like "*Nagananda*", "*Ratnavali*" and "*Priyadarshika*" are prominent. These plays give a suitable glimpse of the society and culture of Haryana region of that time.

Archaeological Sources

Archaeology studies the physical materials to understand the past. There are remains of statues, pottery, bone fragments, remains of houses, temples, buildings, monuments, grains, coins, seals, inscriptions etc. which are in front of us as the subject matter of archaeology. Archaeologists study these materials and create history based on unbiased and truth. There is no possibility of any kind of bias in this? Archaeologists also provide information about the age of archaeological objects and the history of a particular era through carbon dating and uranium dating methods. Archaeological sources are very important from historical and scientific point of view. These can be understood properly by dividing them into the following points.

Buildings and Monuments

By studying buildings and monuments, the detailed information about the design, construction and architecture of that particular object is obtained. The size of a building gives information about its status, political importance, even the status and greatness of the ruler related to it. The construction style of many ancient buildings astonishes even today's architectural scientists.

In this regard, excavations were carried out at many places in Haryana, like Mitathal, Dholpur, Bhagwanpur, Karna's Mound, Agroha, Banawali, Rakhigarhi, Balu, Mirzapur etc. From these archaeological sites, many remains of Harappan culture have been found. The structure of the buildings here matches closely with other cities and settlements of the Harappan period. Apart from this, the mounds of Harsha and Karna in Thanesar, the temples of Pinjore and Kalayal are quite important from the historical point of view.

Inscriptions

The detailed information about the society, language and religion of various dynasties of that time is obtained from the inscriptions. These inscriptions are specially engraved on rocks, copper plates, pillars and columns. The oldest inscription found in Haryana has been found from Topda area of Ambala district. This is a pillar inscription. It was uprooted and installed in Delhi by the ruler of Delhi Sultan Firoz Shah Tughlaq. Two similar inscriptions have been obtained from Tosham. These provide information about the history from the Mauryan period to the Gupta period of the fifth century. Apart from this, another inscription has been obtained from the sand of Jagadhari.

Other inscriptions include inscriptions in Kharosthi language obtained from Karnal. Eight inscriptions are written on pillars in the fort of Hisar which are believed to be of the fifth century. Copper inscriptions obtained from Sonepat, inscriptions of Pratihara period from Pehwa and Sirsa, Mahendrapala's inscription from Pehwa etc. are very important from the historical point of view. The genealogy of the Tomara rulers is mentioned in the inscription of Mahendrapala of Pehwa. The Shivalik inscription describes Chauhan king Vigraharaj IV who defeated the Tomars. Three inscriptions from Pinjore and one from Agroha are very important from the historical point of view. The inscriptions obtained from Hansi provide important information about Prithviraj II.

Coins

Coins are important sources of historical information. A lot of coins have been found in excavations at many places in Haryana, which are related to various kings and dynasties. These coins provide ample knowledge of the names, titles, language, reign, system, trade status, religious status etc. of the kings or rulers. Apart from this, the cultural life of the rulers, the geographical expansion of the kingdom can also be estimated. Finding a coin of a region in a distant area indicates its trade relations, while finding it in a nearby area indicates its kingdom expansion or administrative area. The metal of the coin and the abundance of coins assess the economy of the kingdom. The image engraved on the coin shows the religious, cultural activities, and interests of the king.

In Haryana, many coins have been found from Sandh, Naurangabad and Agroha. Panchmark coins have also been found from various places in Haryana. Indo-Greek coins belonging to the second and third centuries BCE have been found in abundance from Khokharakot. Many coins related to Youdheyas have also been found. Along with coins, many moulds for minting coins have also been found here in Haryana. From which it can be assumed that there must have been a mint of Youdheyas. Coins of the Kushans and Harsha period have been found from Khokharakot itself. Coins of the Pratihara, Tomar and Chauhan dynasty have been found from different parts of Haryana. Kushana coins have been found in abundance from Naurangabad. Coins of the Tomar, Pratihara and Chauhan dynasty have also been found from Hansi and Hisar. Similarly, coins of the Gupta rulers have been found from places called Karnal, Jagadhari and Budhiya.

Sculptures

Idols or statues belonging to many religions have been found from many places in Haryana. From the study of these sculptures, we come to know about the religious situation of that period, the quality of sculpture, metallurgy and the technical development related to it. The sculpture gives complete knowledge of the beliefs and folk traditions of the local people. Some idols found from Haryana are made of metals and most of them are made of stone and baked clay. Statues related to Buddhism have been found from Rohtak, statues of Jainism have been found from Hansi and Hisar and statues related to Vaishnavism have been found from all over Haryana.

Accounts of Foreigners

In ancient and medieval times many foreigners came to India and after spending a long time, they wrote down whatever they saw, heard, thought or felt. The books written by these travellers prove to be very important source in the history writing of Haryana.

Greek Travellers

In ancient times, many travellers and diplomats from Greece came to India and recorded the history of India and Haryana region. The name of Megasthenes is prominent among these travellers. During the period of Chandragupta Maurya, his capital was Pataliputra and a book named '*Indika*' was composed. Today this book is not in existence and some parts of it have been found described in other texts. It is believed that this book has also thrown light on the history of Haryana.

Chinese Travellers

The first Chinese traveller was Fa-Hien who came to India during the time of Chandragupta II and wrote a book called '*Fo-Ko-Ki*'. Some areas of Haryana are described in this book.

Sources of History of Medieval Haryana

There are many sources available related to the history of Haryana in the medieval period. Apart from this, archives, museums and libraries are filled with archival material, literary and archaeological sources related to this subject. The court writers of the rulers and the autobiographies of the rulers have proved to be very important in writing and understanding the history of the medieval period. It can be described as follows.

Archival Material

Sources related to the medieval history of Haryana are available in various archives of Haryana and other states. The material available in the State Archives of Rajasthan, Bikaner, throws important light on the economic and social life of the Haryana region. Many documents of pre-medieval period are also available from Punjab State Archives Patiala, and National Archives, Delhi.

Farman, *Nishan*, *Parwana*'s etc. of all the rulers of the Mughal period are preserved in Delhi and state archives. By studying these documents, a factual history can be composed, which will prove helpful in writing the history of Haryana. The other materials preserved in these archives also help in writing history. Apart from the National Archives of Delhi, the provincial archives of Chandigarh, archives related to princely states, district level archives etc. are also very important in writing local history. Factual and true history can be written from the material obtained from the archives, which will be acceptable to all in every way. Materials related to the Mughals and Sikh states are available in the archives of Haryana and Punjab.

The documents related to Marathas from 1789 to 1803, are available in the state archives of Madhya Pradesh which have a significant impact on the economic, social, religious and political life of Haryana. "*Akhbarate Darbare Mualla*" of Raghuveer Singh Library of Sitamau mentions the events of the reigns of Aurangzeb, Bahadur Shah, Jahandar Shah, Farrukhshiyar and Mohammad Shah, from which important information about the contemporary history of Haryana is obtained. A lot of documentary materials related to the late medieval history is also available in the National Archives of India in New Delhi. Although there is very little material in the Haryana State Archives, however, whatever is available are very important for writing the medieval history of Haryana.

Some old documents were carried to Pakistan by some Muslim families at the time of India-Pakistan partition. One of these families published a document in the name of "*Muasire Ajdad*", which is very important. Some of the Mughal period records are available to some individuals and families in Mewat. The "Settlement Reports" of some villages, parganas, and tehsils, which are available in the record rooms of the districts, provide important information for the medieval history of Haryana.

Materials related to the old princely states of Jind and Rewari are also very important. Some documents of Jind are preserved in the Punjab Archives and those of Rewari are preserved with Rao Vijaypal Singh, which are from the Mughal period and are very important to write the late medieval history of Haryana.

Literary Sources

Many texts were composed in the medieval period, some of which were composed in Arabic, some in Persian and other languages. These texts provide important information about history and more especially the history of Haryana. Exaggeration has also been used in some texts. Therefore, scientific analysis of these texts also holds great importance. Some texts written in the early medieval period, which are also very important from the point of view of history, are as follows:

Kitabul Hind: This book was composed in Arabic language by Alberuni. Alberuni came to India with Mahmud Ghaznavi. He studied Hindu religious philosophy, astrology, Sanskrit language and history in India. His book "*Kitabul Hind*", which is also known as "*Tahqiq-e-Hind*", is a valuable source to know the Hindu society, philosophy, religion, economic and political life etc. of North India, especially the Haryana region of the eleventh century.

Tajul Maasir: This book written by Sadaruddin Mohammad Hasan Nizami, is an important source of history from Mohammad Gauri to Iltutmish. Although, he was a court writer, he has emphasized on the truth of facts and the style of Persian language. It has considerable importance as a source of the history of Haryana.

Tabaqat-e-Nasiri: "*Tabaqat-e-Nasiri*" was written by Minhajuddin Siraj. This book describes the events from the war of Mohammad Gauri to 1260. It is the best book of knowledge of history written in Arabic language. A lot of information about Haryana is obtained from this book.

Tarikh-e-Firozshahi: It was composed by Ziauddin Barani, which contains a detailed analysis of the events related to Haryana and Mewat. In this book, Barani has presented the history from the period of Balban to Firozshah Tughlaq.

Tarikh-e-Firozshahi: It was composed in Persian language by Shamsh Siraj Afif. This book describes the life, administration and public welfare works of Firoz Shah Tughlaq. It also describes the social and economic life of Haryana and Mewat region.

Kitab-ul-Rehla: The author of this book was Ibn Battuta, who came to India from Morocco during the reign of Mohammad Tughlaq. This book also contains details of Battuta's journey. It contains a treasure trove of history of North India. But this book also has an abundance of negative aspects.

Tarikh-e-Mubarakshahi: The author of this book is Yahya bin Ahmad Sirhindi. This book contains the history of the period from Mohammad Gauri to Sayyad ruler Mohammad Shah. In this book, Sirhindi has given an eye-witness account of the reign of Mubarak Shah.

Baburnama or Tuzuk-e-Babri: *Baburnama* was written by Emperor Babur during the early period of Mughal rule. Actually, this is the autobiography or Memoir of Babur which was written in Turkish language. In this book, Babur has described all the day-to-day events in detail and is completely based on the truth without resorting to any exaggeration. This provides evidence of the political, social and economic condition of Haryana. Mewat's ruler Hasan Khan Mewati and his son Nahar Khan have been mentioned extensively in this Memoir.

Akbarnama: Abul Fazal, one of the nine jewels of Emperor Akbar, composed this book which is in three volumes. *Ain-e-Akbari* is the third volume. It provides important information about the social and economic history of Haryana. The people of Mewat in Haryana have also been mentioned in this book.

Humayunnama: Emperor Humayun's sister Gulbadan Banu Begum composed this book on the basis of her memoirs on the request of Akbar. It contains information about Babur and Humayun.

Tarikh-e-Shershahi: This book was written by an Afghan Amir Abbas Khan Sherwani. Almost all the information related to Sher Shah is present in this book.

Shahjahannama: This book was written by Mohammad Sadiq on the basis of reliable sources. Another book named "*Shahjahannama*" was written by Mohammad Tahir (Inayat Khan). A lot of information related to history is also found in this book.

Padshahnama: It was written by Abdul Hameed Lahori. It describes the period from Timur to Shahjahan. Undoubtedly, this book also sheds a lot of light on the history of Haryana.

Muasir-e-Alamgiri: This book was written by Mustaid Khan. It mentions the events that happened during the time of Aurangzeb.

Muntakhib-ul Lubab: This book was written by Khafi Khan. It describes in detail the events from the rebellion of the Satnamis in Haryana to the activities of Banda Bahadur.

Apart from all the above mentioned books, the writers from Haryana have also thrown a lot of light on the history of this place.

Information about the literary and cultural history of Haryana is available from the writings of Jain scholar Jin Vallabhsuri, the book of Sharafuddin Panipati, and *Mohammad Afzal ki Vikat Kahani.* Ample information on the Satnami movement is also available on the works on Birbhan, the hero of Satnami revolt.

Archaeological Sources

Buildings and monuments were built in large numbers during the medieval period. Therefore, archaeology also holds great importance in the history of this period. Although there is a plethora of historical texts on this period. Still, archaeological sources can never be ignored.

Buildings and Monuments

The buildings and monuments in Haryana in the form of forts, mansions, mosques, temples, tombs, gardens, stepwells and inns are present in almost every city and town across Haryana. At that time, seeing their design, art style, grandeur and beauty, history spontaneously starts forming in the mind, which has been written in thousands of books. Among the oldest buildings is the Hansi Fort. It was built by the Chauhan kings. It was rebuilt by later Pathan rulers and by George Thomas in the 18th century. Deeni Masjid of Rohtak and many buildings of Hisar were built by the Pathan rulers during that time.

The buildings of Narnaul, including Jalmahal, Chhatta Mukund Das etc. are extremely magnificent. The Tomb of Ibrahim Suri, built by Sher Shah Suri of Narnaul itself, is a beautiful specimen of the architecture of that time. The Tomb of Shaikh Chehli of Thanesar, which was built by Dara Shikoh in the memory of *Sufi* saint Shaikh Chehli, is an unmatched specimen of the architecture of the Mughal period. It has been called the Taj Mahal of Haryana. The Tomb of Sheikh Bulli Kalandar Shah of Panipat and the bridge of Yamuna canal near Karnal, which is called Mughalpul, depict the beauty of architecture. Kabuli Bagh of Panipat, Shah Quli Khan's garden of Narnaul, Mughal Garden of Pinjore are other major archaeological heritages of medieval Haryana. From all these buildings, we get great success in getting information about the history of medieval Haryana.

Coins

Like the coins of ancient times, the coins of the medieval period are also present in large numbers in Haryana and are kept safe in museums and archives. The quality of their metal, inscriptions and spread describes the social, economic and religious life of that time. Mughal and Sultanate period coins have been found from many places in Haryana. But similar coins have been found from places other than Haryana as well. From which a lot of knowledge can be gained especially on the history of Haryana. This also throws light on the prosperity and economic condition of the Haryana region.

Inscriptions

The inscriptions on many buildings, monuments etc. prove to be very helpful in research and the history writing of the Haryana region. Through inscriptions on the buildings, a lot of detailed information can be obtained about that building without doing any scientific study or survey. These records are living evidence of the creation of local history, policies of kings and welfare works. The abundance of buildings in Haryana of the medieval period, the number of inscriptions and the detailed descriptions written on them prove to be very helpful in writing history. Historians provide veracity and authenticity to their work by taking these records as their base. Inscriptions found on mosques, tombs, inns etc. throughout Haryana of the medieval period are still found in abundance. These inscriptions are written in Arabic and Persian languages. These records throw light on various aspects of the history of Haryana.

Sources of History of Modern Haryana

During or after the arrival of the British in India and the establishment of their reign in Haryana, many books, magazines, reports and gazetteers were published which are quite important from the historical point of view.

Archival Sources

Archives are the places where old records and documents are kept safe. Documents related to the modern history of Haryana are available in National Archives, New Delhi, Haryana Archives, Chandigarh, Punjab Record Room, Lahore, Commonwealth Relations Office, London etc. In the National Archives, New Delhi, we have the original government documents available after 1748. These have been divided as follows:

- (i) Pre-Mutiny Record Series.
- (ii) Post-Mutiny Record Series.
- (iii) Punjab State Record Series.

Apart from this, important news in 72 volumes published by the Home Department is available in National Archives. A lot of material related to Haryana has been provided in these volumes. The Delhi Division Records, Hisar Division Records, Ambala Division Records, records related to revenue, justice and other administrative matters of Rohtak, Hisar, Gurgaon, Karnal and Ambala districts in Persian language are available in Haryana State Archives, Chandigarh.

Important material related to every department of Haryana is available in Punjab Record Room, Lahore. Commonwealth Relations Office, which was earlier called India Office Library, has documents related to revenue, justice, education and press related to Princely States of Haryana.

Materials Received from Offices

Very important historical material is also available in the district record offices and tehsil record offices. This includes revenue reports, village records prepared by the Patwaris, instalment-wise *Khatauni* and usage reports, *Jamabandi* and diary etc.

Newspapers and Magazines

Some newspapers started to be published in Haryana in the last phase of the 19th century, among them "*Rifaay Aam*" was published by Pandit Deen Dayal from Jhajjar. "*Khair Sandesh*" was published from Ambala in 1899. "*Jat Gazette*" was published in 1916 and "*Haryana Tilak*" in 1923 in Rohtak. Very important material related to the history of Haryana is found in these newspapers. "*The Tribune*" and "*Civil and Military Gazette*" were also having important information related to Haryana.

Among the magazines, "*Haryana Shodh Patrika*" and "*Journal of Haryana Studies*" were very important. A lot of material related to the history of Haryana region is available in these magazines. "*Haryana Journal of Education*", "*Sapt Sindhu*" and "*Jan Sahitya*" also throw important light on the modern history of Haryana.

Government Reports and Gazetteers

Haryana was a part of Punjab state till 1966, hence government reports were published by the Punjab Government. Among these reports, economic and social surveys of many villages have been published in "*Punjab Administration Report*", "*Session Report*", "*Land Settlement Report*" and "*Punjab Board Block Economic Inquiry*". In addition, "*Proceedings Government of India Home Public*", "*Moral and Material Progress Report*", "*Punjab Government Indian Famine Commission Report 1889*", "*Famine Relief Commission Report 1899*", "*Punjab Evidence 1889 & 1919*", "*Indian Industrial Report 1916-18*", "*Royal Commission Report 1928*" etc. throw important light on history of Haryana.

Apart from government reports, gazetteers are also considered very important sources of history. Hunter and Thornton's "*Imperial Gazetteer of India*", "*Punjab District Gazetteer*", "*Haryana State Gazetteer*", "*Delhi Gazetteer*" etc. throw a lot of light on the history of Haryana region. Apart from these gazetteers, the district gazetteers which were published in almost every district describe the entire region of Haryana in detail. For the knowledge and writing of history of Haryana, these sources not only provide information but also prove to be a boon.

Modern Books

Many books related to Haryana region were written in the nineteenth and twentieth century which are still important sources of history. Among the early written books, Denzil Ibbetson's "*Punjab Castes*" and H.A. Rose's "*A Glossary of Tribes and Castes in Punjab*" are prominent. In this series, "*Tarikh-e-Zila Rohtak*", "*Tarikh-e-Zila Gurgaon*", "*Tarikh-e-Jhajjar*" written in Urdu language are very important from historical point of view. Charles Ball's "*The History of Indian Mutiny*", K.C. Yadav's "*Revolt of 1857 in Haryana*", Jagdish Sharma's "*Freedom Struggle in Haryana*", Shriram Sharma's "*Haryana Ke Swatantrata Senani*", Aijaz Ahmad's "*Mewati Rebellion of 1857*", "*Heritage of Mewat*", and "*History of Mewat*" etc. books are important sources related to the history of Haryana.

In this chapter we studied that among almost all the states of India, Haryana state is the most historical. Therefore, the importance of this region is paramount in the history of India. Haryana is a state where most of the historical events took place. From the events of *Mahabharata* to the battles of Tarain, the battle of Panipat, the battle of Karnal, many events make the history of Haryana important. Records, inscriptions etc. mention the social and economic condition of the Princely States of Haryana. There is a large amount of literary and archaeological sources available for the events happened in Haryana. By studying them we discover the truth and with the help of some hypotheses we can write a complete history of Haryana.

2

Harappan Civilization

Although the Harappan sites were began to be excavated from 1921, but after the partition of India these sites were also divided between two nations. After the partition of India, the Government of India excavated the Harappan Civilization sites in India and found that this civilization was developed at many sites in many states of India like Punjab, Haryana, Rajasthan, Gujarat and Western Uttar Pradesh.

Discovery of Harappan Civilization

In 1856, work was underway to lay a railway line between Karachi and Lahore under the supervision of two English engineers, John Brunton and William Brunton. When bricks and stones were required to build the base of the railway line, the villagers suggested the mounds of Harappa from where they themselves extracted bricks and stones to build their houses. According to William Brunton, a 93-mile (150 km) rail road track was built between Karachi and Lahore with these bricks. General Alexander Cunningham, who founded the Archaeological Survey of India (ASI) in 1861, also visited the area. But the biggest success was achieved in 1921-22 under the directorship of ASI, Sir John Marshall, when the Harappa site was excavated by Dayaram Sahni in 1921 and the Mohenjodaro site was excavated by Rakhaldas Banerjee in 1922. From 1931-1944, Mortimer Wheeler conducted continuous excavations of those sites and the other sites associated with them, which revealed a vast history of this civilization. Many sites were excavated in Haryana which revealed that there was a very large population living during the Harappan period.

Extent and Period of Harappan Civilization

As the excavation of Harappa is going on, its extent is continuously increasing. At present, the area of expansion of Harappan civilization seems to be spread in Suktagendor in Baluchistan in the west, Shortugard on the banks of Abu Darya in North Afghanistan, Alamgirpur in Uttar Pradesh in the east, and Malwan near Surat in Gujrat in the south.

Different historians have different opinions about the period of this civilization. But R.S. Sharma, after studying the dates of Sir John Marshall and Mortimer Wheeler, has determined the date of this civilization as 2500 BCE to 1500 BCE. Most of the Indian historians and archaeologists agree with the dating of Professor Sharma.

Harappan Civilization Sites in Haryana

Haryana region is rich in Sothi-Siswal culture which was excavated in 1955 and 1970 respectively. Apart from Siswal, this phase has been found in Kunal, Balu, Banawali, Mitathal, Rakhigarhi and Bhirrana.

Rakhigarhi

Rakhigarhi is located in Hansi tehsil of Hisar district in Haryana. It is the most extensive Harappan site in Northern India. Situated on the banks of the extinct Saraswati river, this city was discovered by archaeologist Amarendra Nath of ASI in 1962 and its origin is believed to be 3000 BCE, which is 500 years older than Harappa and Mohenjodaro. According to Dr. Phadke, looking at the location and vastness of this site, it seems to be the former capital of the

Harappan people. Its area is also the largest at 300 hectares and it has a total of seven mounds, out of which a village is settled on three and excavation is possible on only four mounds.

Like other big cities of Harappan civilization, this city was also divided into two parts, eastern and western, around which a secure wall was built. The roads and lanes of this city also cut each other at right angles. Bricks of size 65×13×26 cm and 12×24×48 cm have been found here. The utensils, furniture, agricultural equipment, stoves, tandoors, jewellery, toys and bone pinchers of humans and animals and birds found here testify to the grandeur of the city. The seals found in abundance from here demonstrate the commercial and political importance of the city.

Banawali

Houses in Banawali were normally spacious with multiple rooms and a courtyard, at times connected by corridors. In one instance, a sitting room was paved with mud bricks. This house had a toilet with wash basins placed on a high place in a corner near the drains, which carried wastewater into the soakage jar. The famous Harappan seal with a horned tiger was found in this housing complex. Another house, which was bigger in size, yielded a large number of beads made of Lapis Lazuli, etched carnelian, gold and other artefacts such as weights. The findings led the excavator to label it as a jewellery dealer's house. Some houses also had a square-shaped fireplace, similar to those found at Kalibangan.

Situated on the banks of the extinct Saraswati river, Banawali city has been found in Fatehabad, Haryana. This city was discovered by R.S. Bisht in 1974-77. Banawali was fortified and its origin and development is believed to be from 2500 BCE to 1500 BCE. The Banawali site mound is spread over 1.25 kilometres and is about 10 metres higher than the surrounding area. The entire city was enclosed by a massive defence wall with bastions estimated to be around 275×130 metre along the north-south and east-west axis. The walled city is then divided into the citadel and lower town. And both are fortified, each presenting unusual formations—an apsidal citadel and a trapezoidal town (lower town). The roads intersected at right angles and there were mud-built houses on both sides of the streets. The size of bricks used in them were 10×12×24 cm, 10×20×40 cm and 12.5×25×50 cm and their ratio was generally 1:2:4.

During the excavation of Banawali, bronze and earthen utensils, stoves, tandoors, mortars, agricultural implements, food items, tongs, jewellery, toys, bangles, garlands, beads, gold and copper pieces etc. have been found. Red and gray coloured earthen pots and scales are the main attractions of this place. The seals found here have pictures of various animals like goat, hippopotamus etc. The picture of animals found on a seal has the body of a lion and the horns of a bull and also bear some writing that has not yet been deciphered. In the excavations from Banawali, huge amount of evidence of animal husbandry and agriculture has been found. Bone pincers of animals like cow, buffalo, sheep, goat, bull etc. have been found and evidence of plowed fields is also found. Barley, sesame, mustard etc. were also cultivated in Banawali site of Haryana.

Mitathal

Mitathal is located in Bhiwani district of Haryana. Its excavation was done in 1968 under the leadership of archaeologist Dr. Suraj Bhan. There are two mounds here. The high and prominent mound is situated in the east direction and the low mound is situated in the west direction. The area of the main mound is 150×130 metres and the height is 5 metres. The area of the second mound is 150×130 metres and its height is 3 metres. There is an erosion of 200 metres in the east of the mound, which is indicative of the river flowing here in ancient times.

Even before the excavation, a collection of coins of the Gupta period was found here in 1915-16 from Mitathal. Two copper harpoons were found in 1965 and 13 rings were found while digging a canal near the mound in the same year. The population here was also settled like a chessboard same as Harappa. The roads of this city were 1.5 metres to 3.10 metres wide. There were houses on both sides of the streets, for which unbaked bricks were used. Most of the bricks found here are of the size of 10×20×30 centimetres. During the excavation, food items, earthen utensils, furniture, jewellery, many types of bangles, many types of seals etc. have been found at Mitathal.

Balu

Balu city, located in Kaithal district of Haryana, was excavated by Dr. Udaiveer Singh and Dr. Suraj Bhan in 1977-1982. The urban structure here was similar to Harappa. Excavations here have yielded paved roads, proper drainage, painted and non-painted pottery, clay seals, statues, copper-tipped ploughs, barley, cotton etc.

Daulatpur

Daulatpur site was found on the banks of the extinct Saraswati river near Pipli crossing in Kurukshetra district of Haryana. The excavation of this city was done by the Department of Archaeology of Kurukshetra University from 1868-1878. This city, settled on a chessboard, is believed to be from 2000 BCE to 1500 BCE. Wide roads and lanes have also been found in this city which cut each other at right angles. The houses are made of baked and unbaked bricks which are of the size of 10×30×52 centimetre and 10×32×42 centimetres. Buildings, agricultural tools, machinery, brass and earthen utensils, various types of bangles made of different metals, children's toys, earthen pots for cooking, jewellery and food items have been found from Daulatpur excavation. A humped bull made of baked clay, bullock cart wheels, and other toys, bone bangles are the main attractions of this place.

Bhirrana

The Harappan site in Bhirrana village in Fatehabad district of Haryana was discovered in 2003-2006 under the leadership of S.L. Rao. This site is a 6 metre high mound spread over an area of 5 acres, 190 metre north-south and 250 metre east-west. This site is considered to be on the banks of the extinct Saraswati river. Bhirrana site is pre-Harappan because pit houses have been found in abundance. For this reason historians believe its period to be 7500 BCE to 1500 BCE. A lot of evidences of the mature Harappan period have also been found. Among the remains found in Bhirrana, these are earthen pots, raw and baked bricks, gold and copper ornaments and beads, bangles, seals, tandoor etc. The most important material found here is the picture of a dancer on a vessel which is very similar to the dancer of Mohenjodaro.

Kunal

Kunal site was discovered in 1998-99 in Kunal village in Fatehabad district of Haryana. Its period is considered to be 4000 BCE. Like Bhirrana, pit houses have been also found at Kunal. Pictures of *peepal* leaves and humped bulls on the utensils are the main features of this place. Some button seals have been found here, with images of two deers on one side and geometric patterns on the other side. From here, two silver crowns along with gold and silver jewellery kept in an earthen vessel have been found. Other materials found here include seals, clay tools, blades, hooks, arrow heads, copper rods, rings, pieces of bangles, baked clay toys, bullock cart frames etc. Remains of rice have also been found from Kunal.

Agroha

The Harappan site has been found from the excavation of Agroha in Hisar district of Haryana. Coins, stone statues, baked clay seals, iron and copper materials and many tools have been found from the excavation in Agroha. This was the latest site of the Harappan period where the confluence of Bronze and Iron Age is considered.

Bhagwanpur

The Harappan site at Bhagwanpur was excavated in Kurukshetra district of Haryana in 1975-76. Bhagwanpur site is believed to be of around 1700 BCE to 1000 BCE. In this way, this site was the confluence of two great civilizations, Harappan and Vedic. The structure of this city was also like other Harappan period cities.

Pucca buildings, stoves, *tandoors*, clay and bronze vessels, food items, spice boxes etc. have also been recovered from Bhagwanpur.

Urban Life

Like the various cities of the Harappan Civilization, all the sites from Haryana confirm that this civilization was urban. Most of the cities are located on the banks of the ancient rivers Saraswati and Drishti of Haryana, which were very important from the trade point of view. The concrete houses, essential items related to trade etc. of various cities found from Haryana sites like Rakhigarhi, Mitathal, Banawali, Bhagwanpur, Daulatpur, Balu etc. indicate that these places were urban.

Town Planning

The most important feature of the Harappan civilization is the high quality city planning obtained from the sites excavated in Haryana. The planning of almost all the cities in Haryana was similar to the city planning of distant Harappa and Mohenjodaro. The city sites excavated in Haryana are like Harappa and Mohenjodaro, who were fortified on all sides with a thick wall which had many big doors. The entire fortified city was then divided into two parts by a wall. The first was the western part in which the rich and the officials resided. Common people lived in the eastern part because its buildings were smaller, simple and underdeveloped as compared to the western part. One special thing about the cities of Haryana was that there was a bathroom attached to all the residential buildings.

Roads

There was a network of roads and lanes in the Harappan cities of Haryana. The width of the roads varied according to the need and plan. The average width was 18 feet to 20 feet, but less wide roads have been found in Mitathal and Rakhigarhi. The lanes were also generally 5 feet to 10 feet wide. Buildings and houses were built according to the design of the roads and lanes, which looked like a chess board. All the walls of the houses were similar according to layout map. The windows and doors of the buildings also did not open towards the roads. There were no turns in the roads and lanes and they were straight and cut each other at right angles. Shops attached to the buildings have also been found on the roadsides of many cities, which gives the impression that people used to buy the items for their use from these shops.

Buildings

The buildings in the Harappan period sites of Haryana were very beautiful, big and strong. These buildings, full of facilities related to daily life, are the finest example of that period. While constructions of these buildings, the foundation was first dug according to a certain plan, then thick walls were built using mud, mortar and lime, and plaster was also applied on them for strength and beauty. Mud plaster was applied on the walls of *kutcha* buildings. The roofs were made of bricks and mud and gargoyles and pipes were used to drain water during the rainy season.

Two-storey residential buildings have been found in Bhirrana, which are indicative of the prosperity and wealth of the people residing there. Apart from residential buildings, big buildings built on high platforms have also been found which may have been for government or general use. A 60×80 feet room has been found in Rakhigarhi which might have been used as a living room. Bricks of different sizes were made and baked to build buildings. The size of some bricks were 12.5×25×50 centimetre and 10×20×40 centimetre. Generally, bricks of that time were used in the ratio of 1:2:4. In this way, a very beautiful example of the urban life of the people can be seen from the buildings found in the sites found in Haryana during the Harappan period.

Drainage System

In the Harappan period sites in Haryana, water from inside of the house to outside easily went out through drains. The drains from every house merged into the drains of the streets. And in this way all the dirty water of the city was taken out. The drains in the streets were up to half a foot deep. The drains on the roads were 3 to 11 inches wide and one and a half feet deep. The big drains that connected the ponds and rivers outside the city were 5 feet deep and 2.5 feet wide. The drains of the streets were open while the bigger drains were covered. Big drains had big holes (manhole) at various places for cleaning. These drains were open outside the city. Foreign historians were stunned to see this drain system and had to say that this system is better than the drain system of London and Paris.

Economic Life

The Harappan economy in the sites found in Haryana was largely based on agriculture and animal husbandry. They grew a variety of crops, including wheat, barley, cotton, cereals, dates etc. They were the first to cultivate cotton. They also domesticated animals like cows, buffalo, sheep, goats, dogs, cats etc. It was economic life of the people by which the society was classified.

Agriculture

Like other areas of India, agriculture was the main occupation of the people of Harappan Civilization in Haryana. Excavations at Banawali, Mitathal, Daulatpur, Balu etc. have revealed remains of many crops like jowar, wheat, dates, gram, maize, sorghum, jute, sesame, watermelon, mustard etc. Remains of related equipments like ploughs, flails, spades, bullock carts, sickles etc. have been found. Some granaries have also been found from excavations at various sites in Haryana. This shows that the people of those period used to store grains for difficult times. Agricultural work was done with the help of ploughs pulled by oxen. Most of the flails were made of wood and some were made of metals. Bullock carts were used to bring and take grains, which were even older than bullock carts of Egyptian civilization. Stone mills were used to grind grains.

Animal Husbandry

People of Harappan civilization in Haryana domesticated many types of animals. The people of the Harappan civilization used these animals for carrying loads, pulling vehicles, ploughing the fields, for protection and for eating moss. Evidence of animal husbandry has been found at many places like Bhagwanpur, Daulatpur, Mitathal, Siswal, Banavali etc. People of the Harappan period reared many animals like buffalo, sheep, goat, cow, bull, elephant, dog, camel, pig, donkey, cock, cat, peacock, duck, rabbit, deer etc. for their use. No evidence of horses has been found from here. Pictures of humped bull have been found mainly from Harappan sites in Haryana. At that time people were familiar with wild animals like tiger, lion, bear, rhinoceros etc.

Industry

Many types of industrial tools like copper knives, arrows, spears, axes, fishing hooks, razors etc. have been found from almost all the sites of Harappan period. Statues and utensils have been found in abundance among bronze objects. Weavers, goldsmiths, potters, cobblers, carpenters, blacksmith etc. related to cottage and handicraft industries lived in almost every town and village of Harappan sites in Haryana. Textile industry was the largest and famous industry among the Harappan period industries. Both cotton and woollen clothes were made during those period and these were also exported to foreign countries. Needles made of cotton and ivory were used for sewing clothes.

In Haryana, extensive evidence of various industries has been found from places like Banavali, Bhagwanpur, Mitathal, Rakhigarhi, Bhirrana etc. Apart from the textile industry, the pottery industry was also quite prominent. Earthen pots, pitchers, jars, cups, saucers, bowls, fruit bowls etc. were widely manufactured in every city and village of Harappan sites in Haryana. These utensils were painted with red, black and gray colours and baked in fire. Many types of jewellery were made from different types of metals like copper, brass, gold, silver etc. which were very popular at that time. Manufacturing of different types of bricks was also prominent in Haryana during the Harappan period.

Trade and Commerce

In the cities of the Harappan period, all the things were not manufactured at one place, hence trade had great importance to fulfil everyone's needs. It is believed that the goods manufactured from the cities of Haryana were exported to big cities of Harappan period and also to foreign countries. The goods manufactured and agricultural products were carried from one place to another through carts, donkeys etc.

Measuring yards and weighing tools and weight have been found from many cities like Banawali, Mitathal etc. The smallest weight is 13.64 grams. All the weights were in the ratio 1:2:4:8:16:32:64. Apart from these tools, metal scales have also been found in excavations in Haryana. At that time people used to divide one *Seer* into 16 parts. The measuring yards were divided into 9 equal parts.

The people of Harappan Civilization in Haryana had foreign trade with countries like Sumer, Egypt, Mesopotamia, Iran, Syria, Afghanistan etc. Harappan cotton cloth, jewellery, ivory items, grains and utensils were exported to these countries. Monkeys, langurs and peacocks were also exported. Gold, silver, jewellery and precious stones were imported from foreign countries. Deodar or cedar wood and *Shilajit* were imported from Kashmir, marble from Rajasthan and gold from the south. All trade was probably done through barter because there is no evidence of currency usage anywhere during that time.

Social Life

Excavations of Harappan period cities in Haryana provide evidence of the prosperous and advanced social life of the people of that time.

Social Classification

Many cities like Banawali, Mitathal, Rakhigarhi, Bhagwanpur, Siswal etc. show that the people of these sites during Harappan period were mainly divided into two classes because each city was divided into two parts. In one part or eastern part the rich and the official class were residing and in the other or western part the common people were residing. Remains of some mud houses have also been found outside the cities. This shows that the working class lived separately. In this way it can be estimated that generally the people of that time were divided into three classes—1. King, priest, rich and official, 2. Ordinary traders and businessmen, and 3. Lower class (farmers, labourers and other common people).

Meal

On the basis of the remains obtained from many sites, it can be inferred that the food habits of the people of Harappan civilization in Haryana were simple and straightforward. Their main food was wheat, barley, gram, maize and rice. Apart from this, they consumed peas, beans, various types of pulses, lemon, milk, curd, butter, ghee, spices, dates, coconut, pomegranate, banana etc. They also ate meat of sheep, goat, cow, pig, deer, chicken and fish.

Finding of fishing hooks and lots of date kernels (seeds) shows that the people of Harappan period were very fond of fish and dates. At that time people used to eat cooked food and serve it in utensils and used spices to make the food tasty. Under their influence, mortars for grinding flour, tandoor, stove, spice jars and utensils made of clay and coir have also been found from various places.

Garments

The garments or the dress of the people of Haryana during the Harappan period was very simple. Cotton clothes were mainly worn. Wealthy people used to wear woollen clothes. Women used to wear *lahenga* in the lower part and cover the upper part with a sheet. Men also used to wear *dhoti* in the lower part and wrap a sheet on top. Many types of clothes such as colourful, printed and plain were used. At that time people used to spin yarn from cotton with the help of spindles and later weave. Needles made of copper and brass found from places like Banawali, Mitathal, Balu, Rakhigarhi etc. shows that people used to wear stitched clothes as well. The rich and ruling class used colourful and printed clothes and woollen clothes in winter.

Jewellery and Makeup

Both men and women of Harappan civilization in Haryana were fond of jewellery and adornments. Jewellery and adornment items have been found from places like Mitathal, Rakhigarhi, Dolatpur, Balu, Bhirrana etc. Their main ornaments were necklaces, bangles, bracelets, rings, armlets, nose rings, anklets, earrings, waistbands, *jhumkas*, *hasli*, garlands, amulets etc. The ornaments of rich people were made of gold and silver and precious stones while poor people used to wear ornaments made of copper, bronze and bones.

During excavations, jewellery boxes, copper mirrors and ivory combs have been found at many places, which shows that both men and women used to adorn themselves at that time. Women were fond of having long hair and making different types of braids. These women used *kajal*, lipstick, different types of powders, scented oils and vermilion etc. There was a custom among men to keep beard and mustache and some people even got them cleaned.

Entertainment

The people of the Harappan civilization used to entertain themselves in various ways during their leisure time. Their main means of entertainment were hunting, dancing, singing, playing chess, wrestling, fishing, fighting between animals and birds etc. Children entertained themselves with various types of toys like bullock carts, rattles, toys in the shapes of animal, birds and humans.

Rites of the Dead

The people of the Harappan civilization in Haryana had three means of immersing dead bodies. According to the first method, the dead body was completely burnt. The dead body was buried according to the second method. According to the third method, the dead bodies were left in the open for animals and birds to eat and later they were buried.

Political Life

There is a lot of disagreement among historians about the political life of the people of Harappa civilization. The reason for this is that the scripts cannot be read. According to Hunter, the Harappa era governance system was democratic. According to Wheeler, the governance in Harappan perion in Haryana was based on religion and priests ruled. Bongard Levin has described the governance system as aristocratic. Many such ideas have been presented by historians and archaeologists. But no idea is based on clear evidence.

Whatever the government system may have been at that time, it was a good government system and the system was similar in all the areas of Harappan civilization including Haryana. The study of building plans, roads, drainage system, lighting, sanitation and weights and measures proves that there was political unity in all the areas which were ruled by two capitals, Harappa and Mohenjodaro.

Religious Life

From sculptures, paintings, buildings and burial system found from the sites of Harappan civilization in Haryana, it is estimated that the people of those times had deep religious faith.

Worship of Mother Goddess

On the basis of many idols of Mother Goddess excavated from various places of Haryana, her pictures depicted on seals and talismans, it can be estimated that the people of that time worshipped Mother Goddess the most. The picture on a seal shows that people also used to sacrifice men to please the Mother Goddess. Mother Goddess was worshipped as a symbol of power and mother. The smoke stains on many statues show that people used to worship the Mother Goddess with incense and lamps etc.

Worship of Shiva or Pashupati

On many of the excavated seals, there is a picture which has three mouths and two horns. He is sitting in *yoga* posture and animals like deer, humped bull, rhinoceros are sitting around him. It is called animal god or Pashupati. Due to Shiva's love for animals, this picture has also been called Harappan Shiva. In another idol, there is a snake wrapped around the *yogi*, which proves that Shiva was worshipped at that time.

Worship of Animals

Many seals found from excavations show that people used to worship animals at that time. The most prominent of these animals was the humped bull. Other revered animals were elephant, tiger, buffalo, bull, rhinoceros, deer, crocodile etc. Figures have also been found on many seals which were a mixture of human and animal. Many birds like peacock and eagle etc. were also worshipped at that time.

Worship of Trees

The Harappans worshipped many trees as gods who gave knowledge and life. *Peepal* was the most prominent among the worshipped trees and it was given special religious importance. Apart from *Peepal*, trees like *Neem*, Date Palm, *Babul*, *Sheesham* etc. were also worshipped.

Worship of Linga and Yoni

In the Harappan era, people used to worship *Linga* and *Yoni* as creative powers. During the excavation, many such symbols made of stone, clay and shells have been found which are symbols of penis and vagina. Considering small penises as auspicious, people always kept them as talismans.

Worship of Water

It is assumed from the bathhouses found during excavation that people used to worship water at that time. Rivers were also worshipped and on religious occasions the people also took bath in them.

Worship of the Sun

Since the *Swastik* symbol is imprinted on many seals of the Harappan period, it is assumed that the Sun was worshipped at that time as the *Swastik* is considered to be the symbol of the Sun.

Worship of Snakes

Many seals recovered from the excavations depict a snake with its hood spread over a deity. Another seal depicts a man feeding milk to a snake. This proves that people at that time worshipped snakes.

Decline of Harappan Culture

The facts found in the excavations, their analysis and conjecture, historians have given many reasons for the decline of the Harappan civilization such as:

Aryan Invasion

Many historians like Garden Child, Mortimer Wheeler, Stuart Piggott etc. are of the opinion that the Harappan civilization was destroyed due to the Aryan invasion. Historians believe that the people of the Harappan civilization were peace-loving and did not have good warfare weapons, whereas the Aryans who defeated them had high quality weapons and horses. There is also evidence from the *Rigveda* that a prayer was made to Lord Indra to destroy the *Linga* worshippers. Indra is called Purandhar because he destroyed this great civilization. Apart from this, 38 bone skeletons have been found from Mohenjodaro and there are marks of sharp edged weapons on them. From this point it is believed that some major attack must have taken place here. But many historians do not accept the theory of Aryan invasion. R.S. Sharma believes that a few Aryans could not destroy the civilization spread over such a vast area.

Flood

According to M.R. Sahni, Dallas and Raikes, the reason for the fall of Harappan civilization was the annual floods in Indus and its tributaries and other rivers. Due to floods, agriculture, trade, transportation, animal husbandry etc. were adversely affected. Hence, people were forced to move to other places.

Earthquake

Some scholars believe that the Harappan civilization collapsed due to an earthquake. The earthquake destroyed all traces of the cities and many rivers also changed their course and destroyed settlements.

Pandemic

Some scholars believe that the downfall of this civilization happened due to an epidemic, which caused the death of a large number of people. Since science and medicine were not so developed at that time, the entire civilization was destroyed by a terrible disease.

In this unit we studied that the fortified cities, town planning, systematic system and mature life found in the Harappan civilization in Haryana which are rarely found in other cultures of the world. Its area of expansion is very wide. The Harappans were able to maintain remarkable uniformity for about 500 years. From 1800 to 1500 BCE, changes started appearing in the archaeological data. The urban system started ending. Smaller and less prosperous cultures were named as later Harappans. But around 1500 BCE, when the Aryans arrived in India, this greatest civilization of the world collapsed.

3

Vedic Culture

Kuru Dynasty and Historicity of *Mahabharata*

The people of Vedic civilization used the word 'Aryan' for themselves which means 'superior' because they considered themselves more civilized, superior and virtuous than others (non-Aryans). The entire Vedic period is considered to be from 1500 BCE to 600 BCE. During this period, the Aryans came to India and spread their civilization throughout North India and later it spread to South India also. During these periods, apart from the four Vedas, they composed almost all the scriptures of Hinduism. The famous Epic *Ramayana* and *Mahabharata* are amongst them. In this chapter the arrival of Aryans, development of Kuru dynasty and the war of *Mahabharata* and its historicity has been very logically described.

Brief Description of the Vedic Aryans

When the Aryans came to India, they first came to Haryana and settled in its region. The green land irrigated by Saraswati, Drishadvati and Yamuna was more suitable for the agriculture production for the Aryans. But there is a lot of disagreement among scholars about where the Aryans came from. Some people consider the Aryans to be residents of India, some believe that they were migrated from Tibet and some believe that they were migrated from polar regions. However, based on research and historical facts, many scholars consider them to be from Central Asia. The Aryans were nomads and brave people who first spread to the Sapt-Sandhav region, then Haryana and later to the whole of North India and then to the whole of India. B.B. Lal's research on painted pottery proves that the Aryans lived in the whole of Haryana.

Arrival of Vedic Aryans in Haryana

There is no universally accepted date for the arrival of the Vedic Aryans in Haryana. But most of the people believe that between 1500 BCE and 1000 BCE, when the Aryans settled in the Sapt-Sandhav region, they also settled in many areas of Haryana during the same period. Because the Saraswati river, which was the most sacred and revered at that time, flowed in the Haryana region only. Saraswati and Drishadvati rivers were more suitable for the agricultural life of the Aryans and irrigated the entire Haryana region. Evidence of the residence of Aryans has been found from places like Kurukshetra, Jind, Narwana, Hisar, Fatehabad, Hansi, Karnal, Panipat, Gohana, Sonipat, Rohtak, Jagadhri etc. So far, more than three hundred settlements have been discovered in Haryana, from where apart from the painted gray pottery used by the Aryans, a large quantity of items used daily in agriculture have been found.

After the entry of Aryans in Haryana, there were wars between Aryans and non-Aryans for supremacy. Most of the historians accept that almost all the wars between Aryans and non-Aryans mentioned in Vedas were fought in Haryana region. After these wars, the supremacy of non-Aryans ended completely. According to K.C. Yadav, "... At that time, the tribals of this region, especially the Indus people were going through the process of disintegration. The main reason for this was the social contradiction in their lives. ...Probably, at this time, due to the invention of iron by the Aryans, their condition improved a lot. ...From here, the true Vedic civilization begins."

Life of People During Vedic Period

The main sources of the life of Vedic period Aryans are the four Vedas and other texts written by the Aryans. Most parts of *Rigveda, Samveda, Yajurveda* and *Atharvaveda* were composed in Haryana region. Therefore, every incident described in these texts describes the history of Aryans of Haryana region. Apart from this, information about the early life of Aryans is also available from areas like Daulatpur, Banavali etc.

Social Life

The basic unit of social organization of the Aryans was the family and its head was called *Kulap*. The higher organization to the family was village and highiest unit of the Aryan social system was *Jana* or tribe. These *Jana* or tribes joined together and formed another political unit *Janapadas* and many *Janapadas* formed *Mahajanapadas* or big states by joining together in the same way. The society was divided into four parts on the basis of *Varna* or colour. Amongst the four the knowledgeable were called Brahmins, the brave were called Kshatriya, the farmers and traders were called Vaishya and the non-Aryans were called Shudra. Shudras used to serve the first three parts of the society.

Human life was also considered to be of 100 years and divided into four parts called *Ashrams*—first *Ashram* was *Brahmacharya* (student life), second *Grihastha* (household life), third *Vanaprastha* (retirement life) and fourth *Sanyas* (hermit life). In the household life, man used to get married which was considered a sacred ritual. There were three purposes of marriage: first—religious act, second—procreation, and third—fulfilment of sexual desire. At that time there were a total of eight types of marriages—Brahma, Daiva, Arsha, Prajapatya, Asura, Gandharva, Rakshasa and Pishacha. Out of these, the first four were more accepted while the last four were considered inappropriate. Generally, marriages took place within the same caste but some marriages were inter-caste as well. The marriage between a groom of a higher caste and a bride of a lower caste was called *Anulom* and the marriage between a bride of a higher caste and a groom of a lower caste was called *Pratilom*. *Anulom* was permitted in the society but *Pratilom* was not considered right.

The status of women was respectable in the Vedic period. They had the right to receive education. Many women like Apala, Ghosha, Lopamudra, Vishwavara etc. even composed Vedic *mantras*. Giving respect to the bride, it is written in a mantra of *Rigveda* that "O bride! May you have a good arrival in your husband's house and may you bless our house or animals ... You live like a queen among your mother-in-law, father-in-law, brother-in-law and sister-in-law." There was a provision for men to receive education in *Gurukuls* or *Guru Ashrams* in the forests or outside the populated place.

The main food of the people of the Vedic period was vegetarian in which wheat, rice, barley, pulses, *urad*, *moong*, milk, *ghee*, butter, buttermilk, fruits, green vegetables, honey etc. were consumed. Meat was also consumed but it was only on festivals and other festive occasions. Someras was a very popular beverage of the Aryans. Aryan people used to wear clothes of wool, cotton and silk. The clothes worn on the lower part of the body were called "*Nivi*", the clothes worn on the middle part were called "*Vas*" and the clothes worn on the head were called "*Adhivas*". At that time both men and women were fond of makeup and wore jewellery.

Religious Life

The life of the Vedic Aryans in Haryana was simple and ritualistic; neither any idol was worshipped nor there was any temple. The Aryan people of that time worshipped many natural powers in the form of gods and goddesses. The method of worshipping God was "*Yagya*" (ceremonial prayer) and sacrifice. The Aryan people worshipped many gods and goddesses in the form of different powers considering that only one God is in different forms.

Varuna: Varuna was considered to be the greatest god on earth. It was generally believed that from the creation of the world to every event happening in the world was according to Varuna's wish. In a mantra of *Rigveda*, it is written, "O Varuna, I ask you with eager mind about my sins. I have gone to a Brahmin for this. Everyone said that Varuna is angry with you." Aryans believed that Varuna destroys sinners and when pleased with humans, he provides them happiness and prosperity.

Indra: Indra was considered the second biggest god and the god of rain and war. It is written in a mantra of *Rigveda*, "O Indra, you are the thunderbolt. You have shown us immense kindness by showering rain. You never rejected our prayers." It is written in another mantra, "O Indra! We have enough strength to fight because you are our protector. With your help we will conquer the enemy."

Agni: On the basis of utility, Agni (fire) had the third place among the gods and goddesses. No religious work could be accomplished without fire. In all big and small *Yagyas*, offerings were made to the Agni. To these offerings the Agni god used to take to God. Food was cooked with the help of Agni and after death the dead body was thrown into the Agni. Agni was considered the messenger and ambassador of almighty God. It is in a mantra of *Rigveda*, "O Agnidev! The person who performs *Yagya* becomes the moon in heaven."

Sun: Aryans worshipped the Sun to escape from cold and to ripen crops. Aryans considered the Sun god to be the face of all gods and a friend of Varuna and Agni.

Tridev: In the later Vedic period, worship of three other gods—Brahma, Vishnu, Mahesh had started. During these periods, Brahma was recognized as the creator of the universe, Vishnu as the preserver and Shiva as the destroyer. In the later Vedic period, recognition of other gods of *Rigveda* except Agni was decreased.

Origin and Development of Kuru Dynasty

About the Kuru dynasty, we get information from *Rigveda* that a tribe named Bharata ruled around the Saraswati and Drishadvati rivers. The main king of its clan was Divodas who belonged to the Tritsu dynasty. Divodas had fought with people named Pani to expand his kingdom. After the death of Divodas, his son Sudas became a powerful king who defeated the alliance of ten kings on the banks of river Yamuna. After this grand victory Sudas became the sole ruler of the entire Sapt-sandhav region. Another tribe Puru, who ruled on the other side of Saraswati, joined the Bharatas and both were called Puru-Bharat. He took the Vedic civilization to its heights. After some time, a powerful tribe named Kuru drove them away from this region and established their own kingdom. *Vamana Purana* reveals that the Kurus cleared the forests of the Saraswati and Yamuna river valleys and started farming with the plough and made this region agriculturally rich. Through agricultural and political supremacy, the Kurus became economically prosperous and Vedic civilization developed significantly during this time.

According to the Puranas, the first king of the Kuru clan was the ruler Kuru, after whom the kingdom was named Kurukshetra. After Kuru, rulers like Parikshit I, Jah, Surath, Vidurdha, Sarvabhauma, Jayatsen, Aradhin, Mahatsava, Ayutyus, Akrodhan, Devatithi, Daksha Bhimsen, Pratisara Vansh, Pratipa, Shantanu, Vichitravirya, Dhritarashtra etc. ruled Haryana and adjoining regions. Shantanu had two wives, Ganga and Satyavati. The legendary character Bhishma was born to Ganga. Satyavati had two sons, Chitrangada and Vichitravirya. It is said that Satyavati married Shantanu on the condition that her son would become the king. Therefore, Vichitravirya became the ruler, but due to his untimely death his wife perform *Niyoga* (temporary marriage with near relatives to get a son) and gave birth to two sons, one Dhritarashtra and the other Pandu. Since Dhritarashtra was blind, Pandu got the kingdom. Dhritarashtra had 101 sons and Pandu had five sons. Dhritarashtra's sons including Duryodhana were called Kauravas while Pandu's five sons were known as Pandavas. A fierce war took place between the Kauravas and Pandavas over the division of power which is known as *Mahabharata*.

War of Mahabharata

The war of *Mahabharata* is full of contradictory statements of scholars. There is a lot of disagreement among historians regarding the events and their authenticity. Apart from historians, theologians, logicians and litterateurs also consider the war of *Mahabharata* as a subject of analysis. According to *Mahabharata* story, Pandu ruled the entire Kurukshetra kingdom from the capital Hastinapur for about ten years as his elder brother Dhritrashtra was blind. Pandu had two queens and five sons known as Pandavas. Dhritarashtra had many queens including Gandhari and 101 sons known as Kauravas. All the princes were looked after under the leadership of Guru Dronacharya.

After the death of Pandu, power came into the hands of Dhritarashtra although he was blind. When Duryodhana became an adult, Dhritarashtra handed over the power to him and gave half of the kingdom to the Pandavas. The capital of the Kauravas remained Hastinapur but the Pandavas made Indraprastha their capital. On one occasion, the Pandavas lost not only their kingdom but also their joint wife Draupadi to Kauravas in gambling. Meanwhile, the incident of Draupadi's disrobing also took place. The Kauravas said that they would return the kingdom to the Pandavas after 12 years of exile and one year of incognito. But even after the time limit was over, Duryodhana did not return the kingdom. In the end, a terrible war was fought for 18 days within the 48 *Kos* perimeter of Kurukshetra, which is called the war of *Mahabharata*. In this war, the Padavas won.

In this war, Arjuna refused to fight after seeing his relatives against him but Arjuna's charioteer Krishna preached the *Gita* to Arjun. This preaching is known as the holy book "*Gita*". Initially, the war remained indecisive for nine days but after the death of Bhishma on the tenth day, the Kauravas suffered a great loss. Dronacharya took Bhishma's place and formed a formation (*Chakravyuh*) in which Abhimanyu was killed on the thirteenth day. On the fourteenth day, Bhurishrava and Jayadratha were killed. On the fifteenth day, the Pandavas killed Dronacharya by deceit and on the seventeenth day, Karna was killed. Finally, after the death of Duryodhan on the eighteenth day, the terrible war ended in which thousands of people were killed from both sides.

Historicity of Mahabharata War

Many scholars doubt the historicity of this war. First of all, there is no universally accepted date for it. B.B. Lal gives the date of this war as 836 BCE. Max Muller has given its date as 422 BCE. C. Roy Chowdhury gave its date as 900 BCE. K.C. Yadav gives more contradictory dating of the *Mahabharata* war as 1400 BCE. The contradiction of all these dates casts doubt on its historicity.

The second doubt is that if this war was fought in the Vedic period, then why is it not described in any Vedas or other texts. The third doubt is that the Kuru clan or kingdom was not as large as described in that epic. In such a situation, the role of millions of people (Kauravas—2,40,570 Chariots, 2,40,570 Elephants, 7,21,710 horses, 12,02,850 foot soldiers; Pandavas—1,53,090 Chariots, 1,53,090 Elephants, 4,59,270 horses, 7,65,450 foot soldiers) raises more doubts. At that time, there would not have been such a population in the whole of India. It is also doubtful that this war was fought in Kurukshetra and the 48 *Kos* radius around it. In such a situation, a lot of remains of skeletons and war material should have been found in the excavation on that site. But apart from some earthen pots, nothing was found on that place. Apart from this, the literary sources testify that the role of various names, dynasties and places shown in this war are not contemporary. In such a situation, the attempt to see them together weakens historicity and promotes imagination.

As far as it is being considered true on the basis of the chronological description of the events, the names of the characters, families and places, then it proves the high intellectual level of the writer that he wrote a story or poem that appears to be true. In such a case, it should be called a great literature and not a historical event. It is also worth believing that Ved Vyas composed this book "*Jai*" or *Jai Samhita* in 10,000 verses. It is possible that this *Jai Samhita* was based on true events. But the 90,000 verses that were added later are definitely imagination, lies and have been added to make the incident entertaining. In this way, a book with 90 lies mixed with 10 truths may be a beautifully described literature but not a history.

Some scholars also believe that many characters of *Mahabharata* like Devaki's son Krishna and Shikhandi remained important even in later times. Apart from this, two sutra writers Shankhayana and Ashvalayana (800-600 BCE) were also well acquainted with the *Mahabharata* war. Shankhayana mentions the error committed by the Kurus which led to their defeat. Panini (c. 500 BCE) has also mentioned the people related to the *Mahabharata* war, Vasudeva, Bhima, Arjuna, Bhishma, Yudhishthira, Kunti and Kurus. Kautilya (c. 400 BCE) has mentioned the destruction of Duryodhana due to his unauthorized occupation of the kingdom of Pandavas. Panjajali (c. 200 BC) also mentions Bhima, Nakul etc. In the Puranas written between 514-414 BCE, the *Mahabharata* war has been described as a dividing line between Dwapara and Kaliyuga.

Overall, it can be concluded that a king named Kuru laid the foundation of a kingdom in Haryana. Over time, political differences led to family discord which ended in a terrible war. But this incident was neither widespread as has been mentioned. Later writers made it bigger according to their understanding and imagination. The names, places and characters in this story belong to the same era in which the writers wrote their work. But overall, the events of *Mahabharata* may not be historically significant, but they hold a prominent place in the cultural and religious fields. This kind of epic which is so literarily intense that scholars from all over the world analyze its authenticity is not found in the entire world. Therefore, this epic is the best in the whole world in literary, cultural and religious fields.

In nutshell, the Aryans arrived in India in 1500 BCE and also came to Haryana near the Saraswati and Drishadvati rivers and settled here. It was here that many religious texts were composed. It was here that kingship started based on tribal system. Due to political differences, family discord arose and which ended in the form of a terrible war *Mahabharata*. A sage named Ved Vyas penned it down and named it "*Jayasamhita*" of 10,000 verses. Later, litterateurs added more verses to it and named it "*Bharata*" of 24,000 verses. With time, writers continued adding verses to it and named it "*Mahabharata*" which now has a total of 1,10,000 verses. It also has been seen the discussion on its historicity which is quite logical. In this way, the land of Haryana was the land of Aryans where most of the events took place and most of the books were composed.

4

Rise of Republics

Yaudheya, Qulinda and Agra

At the time of the *Mahabbharata* war, there were some republican states in the Haryana border areas, among which Yaudheya, Agra and Qulinda were prominent. At the same time, many states were being established in *Janapadas* and *Mahajanapadas* in the Ganga and Yamuna valleys. The heirs of the Pandavas could not maintain their power for long and due to wars with each other, they began to merge in other *Janapadas* or *Mahajanapadas.* Magadha emerged as the largest *Mahajanapada,* later into state and finally as an empire. In Haryana and border areas, Yaudheya, Agra and Qulinda republics were at their peak and developed their respective areas. There was peace and prosperity in the republics and more especially during the time of Maharaja Agrasen trade and commerce fully flourished.

Republican System

It is well known that in the *Rigvedic* period there was a tribal system which was completely republican. Later on when the kings became powerful and the territory of the kingdom grew bigger, the republican system remained only in name and the post of the king became hereditary. Then *Janapadas, Mahajanapadas,* kingdoms and big empires were established. The Magadh empire was more powerful among these. Later Bimbisara, Dhanananda and Emperor Ashoka ruled the Magadha empire. But despite the *Mahajanapadas* and empires, the republican system still existed in the border areas and some areas of Haryana, among which the names of three republican states Yaudheya, Agra and Qulinda are prominent. When Alexander attacked India, he had to fight with many republican states. Probably Chandragupta Maurya was initially the head of the republican state of Taxila, who was ruling with the help of his well-wisher Chanakya and had also met Alexander. After the end of Mauryan rule, the local powers again established republican states.

It is worth noting that this republican system was different from the Aryan period or Vedic republican system. In this period, the position of the king was hereditary but he used to rule with the help of the parliament. The Maharaja was very powerful and he was the chief commander and the chief Shatrapa. He used to take all the decisions with the help of the assembly or parliament. The word "Gana" was inscribed on the coins of some rulers like the Yaudheyas, which shows the strength of the republican system of that period. In this system, one or more representatives from each village and city were made members of the parliament. The king used to formulate policies with the advice of these members. The opinion of the parliament was valuable on every subject. But there is no evidence whether the parliament could depose the king or not.

For ease of administration, these republics were divided into many units. These units were administrative centres as well as commercial centres. But due to lack of sources, no information is available about the governance of these units. The governance of villages and cities was run by panchayats and its members were elected by the public.

Republic of Yaudheya

From the word Yaudheya it is known that this word is similar to war (Yudh) and warrior (Yodha). Surely there must have been a race in Haryana which must have been very brave and warrior and must have taken part in many wars. Because of their love for war and being a warrior, they were called Yaudheya. With the passage of time their qualities became their identity. It is not known for sure when this happened, but definitely after the arrival of the Aryans, one of their own war loving species came into existence. Their oldest evidence is found in the *Mahabharata* period. In this world famous war, these brave men (Yaudheya) fought against Pandavas on behalf of the Kauravas. But after their defeat, they made a treaty with Yudhishthir and married their leader's daughter to Yudhishthir, from whom a son named Yaudheya was born. Evidence of all these things is found in *Mahabharata*, Panini's *Ashtadhyayi*, many Puranas and *History of Haryana* of modern historian K.C. Yadav.

After the *Mahabharata* war, the kingdom of the Pandavas could not last long and after its disintegration, many regional powers started becoming independent. Yudhishthira's son Yaudheya also established a separate republic in his name, which is called the Yaudheya Republic. Later, this republic was the largest republic in Haryana. Coins of this republic have been found from many parts of Haryana and Western Uttar Pradesh. A lot of coins related to this republic have been found from areas like Sonipat, Hansi, Kharkhoda, Jind, Sirsa, Hisar, Panipat, Gurgaon, Karnal etc. K.C. Yadav has quoted the excerpt from Sahni's book "*The Technique of Casting Coins in Ancient India*", as follows: "Among all the ancient materials found so far in the whole world for making coins, the material obtained from Rohtak is the best, most valuable and important. Thousands of clay moulds for minting coins have been found here.... The material obtained from Rohtak is older than the Roman moulds. And the moulds from Rohtak are better and more satisfactory than the Roman moulds."

The capital of the Yaudheya republic, which was fully mentioned in the fifth century BCE, was Prakritanaka (Naurangabad-Bamla). Rohtak and Sirsa must have been the major cities or economic capitals of that time. The boundaries of that state kept increasing and decreasing from time to time. Still, on the basis of coins, it can be estimated that the boundary of the Yaudheya state was from Alwar to Kangra and Abohar to Saharanpur. Other major cities of this republic were Khokharkot (Rohtak), Sujet (Ludhiana), Fazilka (Punjab), Saharanpur (Uttar Pradesh), Kangra (Himachal Pradesh) and Alwar (Rajasthan).

The power of the Yaudheyas suffered a setback with the arrival of the Shakas and Kushanas. Yaudheyas defended themselve from the Shakas and made themselve powerful but were at last defeated in the war by the Kushanas. That is why for some time coins of Kushanas were found in Yaudheya kingdom. But since the coins of the last Kushana rulers were not found in the Yaudheya kingdom, it can be assumed that the Yaudheyas had driven them out of their kingdom when the Kushan kingdom became weak.

The Yaudheyas had achieved many victories as evidenced by the inscriptions on their coins. Some inscriptions like "*Yaudheyanam Bahadhanyake*", "*Yaudheyon Ganastha Jai*", "*Yaudheyana Jayamantra Dharanam*", "*Yaudheya Bhagwat Swamin Brahmin Devasya*" etc. prove the greatness of Yaudheyas victory in war and military ability. The Yaudheyas had to face only a few defeats in the kingdom in hundreds of years. The first conquerors were the Kushans. Later, Rudradaman of Gujarat has also talked about defeating the Yaudheyas in his inscription in 150 CE. But both these defeats would have been momentary and would not have had any impact on the entire state. During the Gupta period, they were defeated by Samudragupta (335-375 CE) and the Yaudheya state merged with the Gupta state and Yaudheya ceased to exist.

Agra Republic

The knowledge of Agra Republic came to be known from 9 copper coins obtained by Rogers from Barwala. In 1938-39, H.L. Srivastava excavated Agroha where he found copper coins kept in an earthen vessel. A mint has also been obtained from Agroha. Apart from coins, mention of Agra is also found in ancient Indian literature. The oldest mention of Agra Republic is found in Panini's "*Ashtadhyayi*", a book of 500 BCE. This *Gana* (republic) is also mentioned in Vaidyayana's "*Shrota Sutra*" and Patanjali's "*Mahabhashya*". The *Mahabharata* mentions Agra *Gana* along with other republics. This *Gana* is mentioned in abundance in many Buddhist texts also.

At the time of Alexander's invasion of India, Agra Gana was a powerful group and Alexander had a war with this group. Alexander's historian Aggalsoi writes that at the time of the war with Alexander, there were 4000 infantry and 3000 horsemen in Agra Gana's army. They fought bravely against Alexander's army and caused loss of life and property.

Agreya, Agra etc. have been used for the people of Agra Republic in their coins. In the Buddhist text "*Mahamaturi*", Agras were written in Prakrit language as "Agodak". At some places the words "Agratya" and "Agach" have also been used which means people living in Agra region. It seems that the name of this area was Agra on the basis of Agra Gana. But later, due to the formation of a district, it was called "Agratya Janapada" and "Agach Janapada" was inscribed on the coins in Prakrit language.

The main city or capital of Agra Gana was Agrodaka where coins of this group were minted. Historians identify it with modern Agroha village. Earlier, this village was a contemporary of Yaudheya Republic, a huge city spread over 141 acres and there must have been very cordial relations between the two, that is why both the republics survived together for a long time.

Apart from the mention of Agra in some coin inscriptions and some literary sources, no source tells the history of the Republic of Agra. Later people have linked some imaginary stories and descriptions of imaginary kings to the Agra Republic. But history does not accept it on the basis of events and sequences. Some historians try to complete the incomplete history of the Agras on the basis of their research, like—Silakram has written in his book, "*Archaeology of Rohtak and Hisar District*" that after the end of the rule of Pushyamitra Shunga, the rise of Agra and Yaudheya republics took place.

Agra and Agartya people were completely settled in various areas of Haryana like Agroha, Banavali and Naurangabad. Copper coins have been found in these areas which were related to the Agras. S.C. Ray Chaudhuri has written in his book, "*Political History of Ancient India*" that Agroha was a vast city at the time of Alexander's invasion, which was known by many names like Agrodaka, Agodaka, Aggalpura, Agara and Aggalassoi.

On the basis of "*Haryana Heritage*", "*Hisar District Gazetteer*", it has been written that it is also possible that these parts may have supported Chandragupta Maurya in the war against the Greeks and they may have been included in the Maurya Empire. Ashoka's pillars of Hisar and Fatehabad are proof of this theory. H.L. Srivastava has written in his book, "*Excavation at Agroha*" that after the fall of Maurya and Shunga dynasty, along with the Yaudheyas, the Agras also freed themselves and started ruling in Hisar, Barwala and Bhiwani by making Agroha the capital. It is written in the "*Journal of Numismatic Society of India*" that a seal has been found from Agroha in which the title of the king is written as "Maharaja Mahakshatrapa Mahasenapati". Dr. Satyaketu Vidyalankar writes that Agroha existed 100 years before the establishment of the Kushana dynasty.

Maharaja Agrasen

It has already been said that many legends and fictions have been added to the history of the Agra Republic which have no connection with actual history. But due to sectional and social beliefs, it is very important to narrate it. One of the characters of these legends is Maharaja Agrasen. According to folk tales, Agrasen was born in the Dwapar Era in 5185 BCE in the house of Suryavanshi king Ballabh of Pratap Nagar. He was married to Madhavi, daughter of King Nagraj. Agrasen worshipped Lord Shiva intensely in Kashi. Ultimately Lord Shiva appeared and advised him to worship Mahalakshmi. When Agrasen worshipped Mahalakshmi, Mahalakshmi appeared and advised Agrasen to do business like a Vaishya. Mahalakshmi Devi also advised Agrasen to establish a separate kingdom and promote Vaishya tendencies.

Hence Agrasen started searching for a new kingdom with his wife Madhavi. At one place he saw that lion and wolf cubs were playing together. Agrasen considered the same place suitable for himself and established there a kingdom and named it Agroha. This time is considered to be 51 years before *Mahabharata*. With the grace of Goddess Mahalakshmi, agriculture and trade flourished in this state. Agrasen divided his kingdom among 18 sons and established 18 *gotras* in the names of their teachers.

Agrasen followed non-violence completely in his kingdom. The 18 gotras established by Agrasen were Garg, Mangal, Kuchal, Goyan, Goyal, Kansal, Singhal, Jindal, Thingal, Eran, Dharan, Madhukul, Vindal, Mittal, Tayal, Bhedhal and Nagal. Later, this kingdom could not withstand the attack of Huns, Kushans and other foreign tribes and these people spread to other parts of the country and started trading. They are still identified by their *gotras*.

Qulinda Republic

Qulinda was also an important republic among the republics that emerged after the fall of the Maurya Empire. We come to know about the existence of this group from the coins of Qulindas. Qulinda coins have been found from Narayangarh, Sadaura, Chhoti Karori, Badi Karori, Madanpur and Karnal of Haryana. These coins are proof that only a small area of Haryana, i.e. some upper part of Ambala district came under this republic. Apart from coins, this republic is also mentioned in some ancient Indian literature. This republic is mentioned in Panini's "*Ashtadhyayi*", some Puranas and Varahamihir's "*Brihatsamhita*". Greek scholar Ptolemy has also mentioned this republic.

Qulinda Gana fought against the Krishans along with the Yaudheyas. Later, Qulinda merged with the Yaudheya Gana. According to Dr. Altekar's opinion, the word "*Dwi*" inscribed on the coins of the Yaudheya Gana indicates the union of these two *Ganas*.

It can be concluded that from the time of *Mahabharata* war to the first century CE, many political powers emerged in North India and especially in Haryana region. Among these, Yaudheya, Agra and Qulinda republics were prominent. The coins found from excavations at various places in Haryana and their names appearing in many religious texts and scriptures highlight their kingdom expansion, power and importance. But still their information is limited and is full of legends. More research is needed in this regard. Their history can be fully revealed through the interest of historians, mutual debate, review of coins and research. Such republics which existed for many centuries, fought wars and set treaties, did trade and development, must have certainly been historically very important.

5

Pushyabhuti Dynasty

After the fall of the Gupta Empire, the chaos spread throughout North India and the entire region was again divided into small states. At that time, Haryana state was called Srikanth district, which was established in ancient times by a ruler named Srikanth of Naga dynasty. An influential chieftain named Pushyabhuti established his kingdom in this Srikanth district and made Thanesar his capital. There were many kings who ruled this kingdom in the Pushyabhuti dynasty. Nothing much is known about the early kings Naravardhana, Rajyavardhana and Adityavardhana from 500-580. Perhaps their states were very small and based on tribal structure. These three rulers were subordinate and could not even issue their own coins.

Prabhakaravardhana (580-605)

After the death of Adityavardhana, Prabhakarvardhana became the ruler of Thanesar. He was the first independent ruler of his dynasty. He had assumed many titles like Maharajadhiraj, Param Bhattarak etc. In his figurative language, Banabhatta has described him as a lion for the deer in the form of Huns, fever for the kingdom of Sindhu country, the one who takes away the sleep of Gurjars, a great personality for the king of Gandhara in the form of Sagandhiraj, who destroys the agility of fever and is like an axe for the creeper in the form of Lakshmi of the kingdom of Malwa. But there is no clear evidence that Prabhakarvardhana defeated them.

Prabhakarvardhana got his daughter Rajshri married to King Grihavarmana of the Maukhari dynasty of Kannauj. This made the rulers of Malwa, who were enemies of Kannauj, also his enemies. Prabhakarvardhana attacked Malwa and defeated its ruler. In 604, Prabhakarvardhana sent his son Rajyavardhana to defeat the Huns. But when Rajyavardhana returned after subduing the Huns, his father had died and his mother Yashomati had committed *sati*.

Rajyavardhana II (605-606)

After the death of Prabhakarvardhana in 605, Rajyavardhana became the ruler of Thanesar. But as soon as he ascended the throne, he got the news that the ruler of Malwa, Devgupta, had conquered Kannauj and killed his brother-in-law Grihavarmana and captured his sister Rajshri. Hearing this news, Rajyavardhana attacked Malwa and defeated Devgupta. But Devgupta's friend Shashank, the ruler of Gaur, tricked Rajyavardhana into marrying his daughter and killed him while having dinner. The enemies again captured Kannauj. In this way, Rajyavardhana's rule came to an end within a short time.

Harshvardhana (606-647)

Harshvardhana ascended the throne of Thanesar at the age of 16 after the death of his brother Rajyavardhana. Harsha's throne was full of challenges because his father had died, mother had committed *sati*, brother had died and sister was in the prison of the enemies. But he remained distracted. He formed a powerful army and started his conquest campaign.

Military Campaign

As soon as Harshvardhana took over the power of Thanesar, he started many military campaigns. Some of the important victories among them are given below:

Conquest of Kannauj

First of all, Harshvardhana attacked Kannauj because the ruler of Malwa, Devgupta, had established his power over there with the help of Shashank and had taken Harsha's sister Rajshri captive. In this war, Devgupta, the ruler of Malwa and Shashank, the ruler of Gaur, fled the field and Harsha easily captured Kannauj. But his sister Rajshri had escaped from the prison and went towards the forests and was about to commit *sati* when Harsha saved her. Harsha started ruling Kannauj with the advice of his sister. But after the death of Rajshri in 641, he annexed Kannauj to his kingdom and made it his second capital.

Conquest of Gaud or Bengal

The ruler of Gaud or Bengal was Shashank who along with the ruler of Malwa, Devgupta, killed Harsha's brother Rajyavardhana. Shashank hated Buddhism and destroyed many Buddhist monasteries. He also got the Bodhi tree cut and tortured the Buddhists a lot. Harsha launched a war campaign against such a fierce enemy and for this Harsha also made a treaty with the ruler of Kamrup, Bhaskarvarmana. Both the armies defeated Shashank. Shashank fled from the battlefield but continued to harass Harsha throughout his life. Harsha could completely control Gaud only after the death of Shashank in 637. Including the kingdom of Magadha, seventeen other small states also came under the control of Harsha. In this way, all the states between Gaud and Kannauj came under the control of Harsha.

Conquest of Orissa and Mithila

During Harsha's Gaur campaign, Shashank was defeated and fled to Orissa. Therefore, Harsha launched a campaign against Orissa also. Harsha's invincible armies also conquered both Orissa and Mithila. According to Chinese traveller Hiuen Tsang, Harsha had to fight for six years to achieve these victories.

Western Area Campaign

After conquering Gaud, Mithila and Orissa, Harshvardhana turned his attention towards the western region. Harsha's second biggest enemy Devgupta was still ruling Malwa. Harsha attacked Malwa and killed Devgupta. According to the Chinese traveller Hiuen Tsang, Devgupta died on the battlefield itself. Harsha annexed Malwa to his kingdom. Apart from this, Harsha captured fifteen other kingdoms. Prominent among them were Matipur, Mathura, Jalandhar, Brahmapur, Kullu, Sirhind etc. According to Hiuen Tsang, by 612, Harsha had captured the area from Pundvardhan in Bengal to the river Vyas in the west.

Victory of Vallabhi

Harsha attacked Gujarat or Vallabhi in 629. Harsha defeated its ruler Dhruvasena and took over Vallabhi. Defeated Dhruvasena took refuge with Dadda II, the ruler of Kutch. Dadda made Harsha and Dhruvasena friends and Dhruvasena accepted Harsha's supremacy. Harshvardhana also got his daughter married to Dhruvasena II. In this way, Harsha conquered an economically and politically important state like Vallabhi in a friendly manner. Apart from Vallabhi, Harsha also subjugated the feudal lords of Kutch, Anandpur and Surat.

Subjugation of Kamarupa

Harsha had attacked Shashank in collaboration with Bhaskarvarmana, the ruler of Kamrup or Assam. Hence, the friendship between the two grew so much that Bhaskarvarmana himself accepted Harsha's suzerainty. Bhaskarvarmana was also present in Harshvardhana's Kannauj conference like other subordinate kings and presented many elephants to Harsha as gifts.

War with Pulakeshin II

After completely conquering North India, Harshvardhana fought against a great ruler like Pulakeshin II of the Chalukya dynasty to conquer the vast kingdom south of the Narmada river. Hiuen Tsang writes that Harsha had prepared a huge army from his five divisions and set out to take on his southern rival. In 634-35, a fierce battle took place on the banks of river Narmada in which Harsha was defeated for the first and last time. Pulakeshin II assumed the title of Parameshwara after the victory. This war was so devastating that even Harsha became distraught. According to an inscription, "the heart of Harsha, at whose lotus feet the army of feudal lords with infinite wisdom had bowed down, was disturbed after seeing the gruesome scene of people and elephants killed in the war." After Harsha's defeat, the Narmada river became the boundary between the two states.

Conquest of Sindh and Kashmir

It is believed that Harsha conquered the Sindh state. Banabhatta writes that Harsha also conquered the snowy and inaccessible regions. Radha Kumud Mukherjee has called these regions Kashmir or Nepal. But most historians like Majumdar and Tripathi do not agree with Harsha's conquest of Sindh state and Kashmir or Nepal.

Administration

Harsha governed his vast empire on the basis of ancient traditions. The form of Harsha's rule was feudal which was people-friendly and based on public welfare. According to R.K. Choudhary, the feudal system established in the Gupta era was completed by Harsha. Both the central and provincial systems of Harshvardhana were racist. The needs of the public and the security of the country were taken care of.

King

In Harsha's central administration, the king was the highest authority. Harsha had assumed titles like Maharajadhiraja, Parameshwara, Parambhattaraka, Sarvabhoomi, Sakalottara, Pathnatha, Shiladitya etc. which were indicative of unlimited power. He was the biggest administrator, the biggest commander and the biggest judge. Despite his powers being autocratic, he was very kind, generous and charitable. He used to give donations to monks, Brahmins and the poor with open hands. In the Prayag conference of 643, he donated everything he had, even the clothes on his body and covered his body by asking clothes from his sister Rajshri.

According to K.C. Yadav, he built *dharamshalas* for refugees, patients and the poor, and rest houses, monasteries, *stupas* etc. for travellers. He himself used to travel to different parts of the state to know the condition of the people. Banabhatta has compared Harsha with Bhishma, Drona, Karna, Arjun, Yudhishthir, Shiva, Indra and Varuna. Hiuen Tsang writes that the day was very short for Harsha. He had divided the day into three parts. A part was spent in administrative work. And the remaining two parts in religious activities. He was very hard-working and while working for the welfare of his subjects, he would even forget to sleep, eat and drink.

Council of Ministers

Harshvardhana had formed a council of ministers to run his kingdom smoothly. The main qualification of his ministers was that they were good soldiers and proficient in their field. Banabhatta has mentioned the names of some ministers in *Harshcharita*. Harsha's maternal uncle's son Bhandi was his prime minister; Singhnad was his commander; Avasti was the war and foreign minister; Chandragupta was the head of the elephant army and Kuntaka was the head of the cavalry. Some such ministries were as follows:

- Prime Minister—Chief adviser to the King.
- Mahasandhi Vigrahadhikrit—Minister of War and Peace.
- Mahabaladhikrit—Army Minister or Army Chief.
- Cuttack—Chief of Elephant Army.
- Brihadeshwar—Hero of Cavalry Army.
- Mahapratihar—Palace Security Minister.

Regional System

Harshvardhana divided his vast empire into many units for the convenience of administration. The largest unit was called "Bhukti" which was like modern provinces. Bhukti was divided into "Vis" which were similar to modern districts. *Vis* were divided into "Pathak" which were similar to modern tehsils. The smallest unit was called "Grama". All these units were administered by the following officials:

Uparika: Administrator of the Province or Bhukti
Vishpati: Administrator of Vish or District
Pathapati: Pathak or Chief Officer of Tehsil
Sarvadhik: Inspector of all Departments
Prastpal: One who keeps the government papers safe
Karanik: Writer
Gramik: Head of the village

Income and Expenditure

The main source of income of the state was land tax which was 1/6th of the total produce of the farmer. As per the mention in Harsha's copper plates, tax was collected in three ways—(1) Bhag Vidhi—taken from the farmers in the form of grains. (2) Hiranya Vidhi—collected in cash. (3) Bali Vidhi—The farmer voluntarily paid tax to the king in the form of gifts. There is no doubt that this tax method must have been implemented in Harshvardhana's kingdom at different places according to the capacity of the people. Apart from this, the state also got a lot of income from customs duty, sales tax, fines imposed on criminals, business tax, forest tax etc. The officer who collected tax was called "Bhaugik".

According to Hiuen Tsang, Harsha used to divide the entire income into four parts for expenditure. One part was spent for government work, the second part for the salaries of employees, the third part for welfare works and the fourth part was spent in giving donations. According to Romila Thapar, soldiers were given cash and other officials were given land as salary.

Judicial System

With the aim of providing proper justice to the subjects, Harshvardhana had established many courts in different parts of the empire. At that time the courts were called "Dharmasthan" or "Dharmasan" and the judges were called "Dharmadhyaksha". Those who interpreted the law in the courts were called "Pramatri". Feudal lords also had the right to set up their own courts in the areas under their control. Village cases were decided by Panchayats.

During the period of Harsha, punishments were harsher than during the Gupta period. For serious crimes, there was death penalty and exile, for treason there was life imprisonment and for disobeying social rules, hands, feet, ears, nose etc. were cut off. Fines were imposed to punish ordinary crimes. To know the truth, there was a system of tests of fire, water, poison and *tula* (balance). Despite such a harsh penal system, incidents of theft continued to occur in some areas. According to Chinese traveller Hiuen Tsang, he himself was robbed by thieves twice.

Military Management

Harshvardhana had formed a large army which had 60,000 elephants, one lakh cavalry and even more infantry. According to Hiuen Tsang, Harsha's army was also divided into four parts—Foot, cavalry, chariot and elephant army. There is also a description of the camel army in Banabhatta's *Harshacharita*. For the cavalry, good breed of horses were imported from Iran and Afghanistan, which were very suitable for quick action. Elephant forces were used to attack forts.

Religion, Literature and Education

Religion, education and literature got a great boost during the reign of Harsha. Harsha himself was a very religious and capable writer. According to R.C. Majumdar, "Harsha proved himself to be a unique ruler in the arts of war and peace alike. He could wield the pen as skilfully as he could wield the sword."

Religion

Harsha himself was a religious person. Initially he used to worship Shiva and Surya but later he got inspired by a Buddhist monk named Divakaramitra and his sister Rajshri and joined Buddhism. First he became a follower of Hinayana sect and later of Mahayana sect. He banned animal slaughter, organized an annual meeting of Buddhist monks, built a large number of Buddhist Viharas and Stupas and propagated Buddhism by sending Buddhist preachers across the country.

Harshvardhana, besides being a follower of Buddhism, was tolerant and generous towards other religions. In the Prayag conference, he worshipped Buddha on the first day, Surya on the second day and Shiva on the third day. He never discriminated while giving appointments and donations. In the Kannauj meeting of Harshvardhana, 3000 Mahayana and Hinayana Buddhist monks and Bhaskarvarman, apart from 19 rulers, 3000 Brahmins and Jains, 1000 scholars of Nalanda University and thousands of common people participated. This meeting continued for 23 days and was presided over by Hiuen Tsang.

Literature

Harshvardhana himself was a high-class litterateur and had patronized many other litterateurs. Harsha himself composed three plays "*Ratnavali*", "*Nagananda*" and "*Priyadarshika*". These three texts were written in Sanskrit language. Harsha's court poet Banabhatta composed *Harshacharita* and *Kadambari*. Apart from this, Mayur, Matang, Diwakarmitra, Bhartrihari and Jaysen were the court scholars of Harsha. He had composed books named "*Suryashatak*", "*Ratnakoot Sutra*", "*Sarvadarshan Sangrah*" and "*Vakyadeep*".

Education

Harshvardhana paid a lot of attention to education during his reign. He made proper arrangements for education in monasteries and temples. Primary education was given in temples and for higher education one had to go to monasteries which were famous for different subjects. The monastery of Taxila was famous for medical science and the monastery of Dharmashila for religious education.

At that time, the internationally renowned Nalanda University was the most prominent. It had 10,000 students and 1,500 teachers. Hiuen Tsang also studied there for five years. Harsha donated 200 villages for the expenses of this university.

Hiuen Tsang's Account

Hiuen Tsang was a Chinese traveller who visited India between 630 and 644. He came at the age of 30 to study Buddhism. First, he reached Kashmir, then from there he visited Kapilavastu, Sarnath, Gaya, Kushinagar etc. and reached Nalanda. He studied deeply for five years at Nalanda University. Hearing about Hiuen Tsang's fame, Harsha called him to Kannauj where he stayed for eight years. He returned to his homeland in 644 where he died in 647. Hiuen Tsang has described his fifteen-year Indian experience in his book "*Si-Yu-Ki*" (Account of the Western World).

About the King

Hieun Tsang had been in contact with Harsha for eight years and was, therefore, greatly impressed by his character. Hieun Tsang writes that the king used to be so busy in the welfare of his subjects and the affairs of the kingdom that he would forget to eat and drink. The king was a great philanthropist and gave freely to the poor, Brahmins and Buddhist monks. In the meeting of Prayag in 643, the king had donated everything he owned, even his jewellery and clothes. The king had religious tolerance. He had provided food to 500 Brahmins in the meeting of Prayag.

About the Politics

During Harsha's reign, the rule was people-friendly. In the words of Hieun Tsang, "The day was very short for him, he had divided it into three parts. He used to spend one part of it in government related works and the remaining two parts in religious works. He did not feel tired while working and while doing good work, he used to forget everything like sleeping, eating and drinking." Hieun Tsang writes that at that time the main source of government income was land tax. He used to take 1/6th of the income of the farmers as tax. All the people were happy. The penal laws were strict, yet there used to be petty thefts and he himself had been robbed twice.

Hiuen Tsang writes that the king had a large army which included one lakh horsemen, sixty thousand elephants and fifty thousand infantry. He writes about Kannauj that this city was spread over an area of eight kilometres long and two kilometres wide. There were more than 100 Viharas in this city in which more than a thousand monks lived. There were also more than 200 Hindu temples in this city.

About Social Life

Hieun Tsang has written about the social life of Harsha's period that at that time the caste system and untouchability were prevalent. Brahmins used to do religious work, Kshatriyas used to rule, Vaishyas used to do business and Shudras used to do farming. Chandalas used to do lowly jobs, who used to live outside the cities. While entering the cities, they used to come playing sticks in their hands so that people stay away from their shadow and touch. Marriages were not inter-caste. Polygamy was more prevalent. Child marriage was not prevalent but widows were not allowed to remarry.

Hiuen Tsang writes that the main food items of the people of that time were wheat, rice, milk, curd, *ghee*, butter, vegetables and fruits. Consumption of meat and garlic, onion etc. was less. People consumed wine made from grapes and sugarcane. Hiuen Tsang writes that at that time stitched clothes were rarely worn. Men had to wrap a sheet around their waist and women wore long dresses. There was no *Parda Pratha* at that time. People were more fond of jewellery.

About Religious Life

Hieun Tsang writes that at that time Hindu religion was prevalent and Brahmins were respected. That is why Hieun Tsang called India the country of Brahmins. Most of the people worshipped Shiva,

Vishnu and Surya. *Yagya* was prevalent and idol worship was done in temples. Hieun Tsang writes that Buddhism was divided into 18 branches in which Hinayana and Mahayana were prominent. All of them had separate principles, religious texts and monasteries. Due to these differences, this religion was heading towards decline. Religious places like Bodh Gaya and Kapilavastu had become deserted. Due to the efforts of Harsha, the Mahayana branch had become quite popular.

Nalanda University

Hieun Tsang writes that Nalanda University was the most famous training centre of that time. Many students from Lanka, Tibet, China, Mongolia, Korea and South-East Asia used to come here to study. There were more than 10,000 students and 1,500 teachers. Sheelbhadra was the Vice Chancellor of this university. Apart from Buddhist literature, Vedic literature, mathematics, astrology, logic, jurisprudence, grammar, medical science etc. were taught in the Nalanda University. It's library was very huge.

In this unit we studied that the rise of Harshvardhana and expansion of the kingdom shows the rise of importance of Ganga-Yamuna Doab. There is no doubt that it has gained a lot of fame from the descriptions of Banabhatta and Hiuen Tsang. Harsha's rival Chalukyas of the South, giving him the title of "Sakalontarpathnath" further strengthens the importance of Harsha. Apart from this, the importance of Kannauj in the politics of the later Gupta period cannot be denied. Harsha established control over an influential agricultural region like Kannauj which was important in the growth of the city. It can be said about Harshvardhana that he was the last Indian-origin emperor of North India, the last preacher of Buddhism and a successful and efficient ruler.

6

Pratihara, Tomar and Chauhan

After the death of Harshvardhana, his vast empire disintegrated. Haryana was sometimes under the rule of King Yashovarman of Kannauj and sometimes under the Pala ruler Dharmapala. Tomars also ruled Haryana. Gurjara-Pratihara became the rulers of this state in 805. Initially, the Tomars had accepted the subordination of the Pratiharas. But in the first half of the tenth century, the Tomars became independent and ruled the state of Haryana including Delhi. In the second half of the twelfth century, the Chauhanas ruled Delhi and Haryana. In this way, due to lack of political stability in Haryana and absence of a powerful ruler, it could not progress in social and economic development. But because of being ruled by three powers, it is historically very important.

Rule of Pratiharas in Haryana

Haryana had accepted the suzerainty of the rulers of the Pala dynasty, Dharmapala. But in 805 CE, the ruler of the Pratihara dynasty, Nagabhatta II, defeated King Dharmapala and annexed the Haryana region to his kingdom.

Nagabhatta II (805-833)

Nagabhatta II was the ruler of Gurjara-Pratihara dynasty. Although there is a lot of difference of opinion among scholars regarding the origin of Pratiharas. Some people like Colonel Tod says that Pratiharas were foreigners and invaded and settled in India and some believe them to be of pure Indian or Agnikula origin of Abu. One of their branches ruled from Ujjain and Nagabhatta II of the same Ujjaini branch had subdued Haryana and made the Pratihara dynasty powerful.

From the Gwalior Prashasti we come to know that the kings of Andhra, Vidarbha, Sindh and Kalinga had surrendered to Nagabhatta just as flies surrender to Deepshikha. Probably they had befriended Nagabhatta due to fear of Rashtrakuta king Govind III. But before this confederacy could attack, Govind attacked Northern India and defeated Nagabhatta. Govind III went ahead and forced kings like Chakrayudha and Dharmapala to surrender. After that Rashtrakuta king Govind III returned to his kingdom.

As soon as Govind III went back, Nagabhatta attacked King Chakrayudha of Kannauj and annexed his kingdom and made Kannauj his capital. Nagabhatta also assumed the titles of Param Bhattarak, Maharajadhiraj, Parameshwar. *Skandapuran* shows that the region of Brahmavarta (Hariyana) was under Nagabhatta.

Hearing the news of Chakrayudha's defeat, Pala king Dharampal of Bengal attacked Nagabhatta but was defeated. We get evidence of this incident from the inscriptions of Gwalior, Jodhpur and Chapsu. In this way, Nagabhatta gained control over Bengal also. Many writings also reveal that the Chauhanas (Chahamanas) of Shakambhari had also accepted the subordination of Nagabhatta II. In this way, after hoisting the flag of victory all over North India, in his last days in 833, Nagabhatta II sacrificed his life by taking water *samadhi* in the Ganga.

Rambhadra (833-836)

After Nagabhatta II, his son Rambhadra ascended the throne. He was an incompetent ruler and during his time many parts of the Pratihara kingdom became independent. Among those who became independent were Kalinjar and Gujarat. According to "*Nagabhatta*

Charita", Rambhadra's son Mihirbhoja had taken over the throne.

Mihirbhoja (836-885)

Mihirbhoja, also known as Bhoj I, was the most powerful king of the Pratihara dynasty. His title is also found in the Gwalior inscription. Hence, he is also known as Varahamihir. He had his title "Adivarah" engraved on his coins. The Varah and Dhasur inscriptions show that Mihirbhoja had once again taken control of Kalinjar Mandal and Gujarat. Mihirbhoja's Pehwa inscription shows that a trade centre like Pehwa in Northern India was also under Bhoja's rule. Kalhana's "*Rajtarangini*" shows that Bhoja had also taken control of Punjab after defeating the Thakkiya dynasty. Even Kathiawar's Balavarma, who had liberated Prithvi from the Huns, was Bhoja's vassal. Bhoja also had control over Saurashtra. Devgarh and Gwalior inscriptions show that Mihirbhoja also had control over Northern Uttar Pradesh and Madhya Pradesh.

It is believed that Mihirbhoja defeated the Rashtrakutas of Ujjain, but the Bamughra inscription shows that Dhruva II, the feudatory ruler of Gujarat under the Rashtrakutas, defeated Mihirbhoja. After some time, Mihirbhoja fought the Rashtrakutas again but there was no result because both sides talk of their respective victories.

Mihirbhoja had also defeated the Pala ruler Devpala, but it is known from the inscriptions that Mihirbhoja was defeated. In this case, Gwalior Prashasti claims that Rajlakshmi, who was Devpala's wife, left him and went to Mihirbhoja. But the inscription states that Devpala had shattered the pride of Gurjarnath. It is believed that Mihirbhoja was victorious in the second war. In this way, Mihirbhoja's kingdom extended from the Himalayas in the north to Bundelkhand in the south and from Uttar Pradesh in the east to Gujarat and Kathiawar in the west. In his last days, Mihirbhoja abdicated the throne for the purpose of pilgrimage, handing over the responsibility of the kingdom to his son Mahendrapal I.

Mahendrapala (885-910)

After Mahendrapala ascended the throne of Kannauj, he fought a war with king Narayan Pala of the Pala dynasty in which Mahendrapala was victorious. As a result, Bengal and Bihar also became part of his kingdom. But Mahendrapala was not a brave and diplomatic man like his father and many of his kingdoms became independent during his lifetime. After his death, the Tomars also became independent and started ruling a large part of Haryana. In the inscription of Mahendrapala's time obtained from Pehwa, Mahendrapala is praised in the fifth verse but the genealogy of the Tomars is given in the remaining two verses.

Tomar Dynasty

Tomars have been addressed in history by different names such as Tomar, Tavar, Tunvar, Tovar, Tor, Tung, Tumur etc. They consider themselves to be the descendants of Kshatriyas.

Rise of the Tomar Dynasty

Initially the Tomars were under the rulers of the Pratihara dynasty. The Pehwa inscription mentions the Tomars ruling around Kurukshetra or Thanesar as feudatories under the Pratiharas. This inscription shows that the founder of Tomar dynasty in Haryana was Jaula or Jaul. Among his successors, Anangpal I (736-754) established his influence towards the Yamuna river and established a city named "Dhillika" in place of Indraprastha, which later became famous as Delhi. But even during the time of Anangpal, Tomars were feudatories of Pratiharas.

After Anangpal, Vasudeva (754-773), Gangadeva (773-794), Prithvipal (794-814), Jayadeva (814-834), Narpal (834-849), Udayaraja (849-875), Vijayaraja (875-879), Vichchharaja (879-919) etc. led the Tomar dynasty. All of them were feudatories of the Pratiharas. During the time of Pratihara ruler Mahipala (912-944), the Tomars liberated themselves and started ruling Dhillika and surrounding areas independently. Among the successors of

Vichchharaja or Jejjuka or Pipaladeva, Raghupala (919-940), Vilhanpala (940-961), Gopala (961-977) were not independent because their coins are not found. Only Vichchharaja or Peepalraj are mentioned to have become independent. Harshanath's inscription of 1030 also shows that the Tomars were defeated in the battle of Pipla. Hence, Tomar once again became a subordinate ruler.

Growth and Decline of Tomar Dynasty

As already mentioned, Vichchharaja or Pipladev was the first independent ruler of the Tomar dynasty, but its independence could not last long. Chauhan ruler Chandan of Sakambhari defeated Tomar ruler Pipaldev. Pipladev's successors Vilhanpal and Gopal also remained under the Chauhans. But there is evidence of Gopal's successor Sulakshanpal (997-1005) becoming independent again. The reign of Sulakshanpal's successor Jaipal (1005-1021) was disappointing due to repeated attacks by Mahmud Ghaznavi and he also had to lose independence. During the reign of Tomar ruler Kumarpal Dev (1021-1051), Maudud, grandson of Mahmud Ghaznavi, attacked his kingdom. Kumarpal formed a group of Indian rulers and fought against Maudud in Thanesar in 1043 and was victorious. In this way Tomar ruler Kumarpal once again became independent and got coins minted in his name.

The most famous ruler of Tomar dynasty was Anangpala II (1051-1081). He built many buildings, *prasad*, forts, temples, schools etc. in Delhi (Dhillika) to which he had established on the site of Indraprastha. It is believed that the same ruler had brought the iron gate of Mehrauli to Delhi and got it installed in 1052. Surajkund outside Delhi was also built by Anangpala II. But his son Tejpala (1081-1105) was a very incompetent ruler. Tejpala was defeated by Ibrahim, the ruler of Ghazni and accepted submission. Around 1139, Chauhan ruler Arunraja attacked the Tomars and defeated them and drove them across the Yamuna. But Tomar still remained a headache for the Chauhans. Chauhan ruler Vigraharaja IV, i.e. Visaldeva (1150-1164) again defeated the Tomars and captured Delhi and Hansi and established an umbrella rule of the Chauhanas. Prithviraja III (1171-1192) was the most prominent and powerful ruler of the Chauhanas in Delhi. By this time, the feudalism of the Tomars had also ended.

Rise and Development of Chauhanas

The Chauhan dynasty was founded by Guvak in Sambhar. Among his successors, Singhraja established an independent state in Jaipur in 944, and assumed the title of Maharajdhiraja. In the eleventh century, the great ruler of this dynasty was Ajaydeva who established the city of Ajaymeru (Ajmer) and made it his capital. Seeing the weak condition of the Tomars in 1139, a Chauhan ruler named Arunraja, who attacked Delhi and Haryana, drove the Tomars across the Yamuna. Chauhan Prashasti in Ajmer Museum shows that Arunraja's armies polluted the waters of Yamuna and the women of Haryana shed tears. After this, Vigraharaja IV, i.e. Visaldeva completely crushed the Tomar power and again captured the forts of Delhi and Hansi. It is known from the Bijolia inscription that Vigrahraja IV or Visaldeva had snatched "Dhillika" or Delhi from the Tomar dynasty. And in this way the rule of Chauhans was established over entire Delhi and Haryana.

In 1160, Prithviraj II (1160-1172), who was the nephew of Vigraharaja, became the ruler of Chauhan kingdom. He suppressed the rebellion of Vigraharaja's son Nagarjuna and protected his kingdom from the attack of the Turks by fortifying Hansi. Prithviraj III (1172-1192), known as Rai Pithora or Prithviraj Chauhan, was the last and most powerful ruler of the Chauhanas. Even during this time, Nagarjuna, who was the son of Vigraharaja, captured Gurgaon and the surrounding areas. But Prithviraj Chauhan defeated him and another rebel Deva Bhatta and ended them completely. It is believed that he also suppressed the rebellion of Bhadanak ruler Sahanpala. Apart from this, he had defeated many rulers including Chalukya and Chandela. The most prominent battles of Prithviraj Chauhan were the battles of Tarain which were fought against the Turkish invader Mohammad Ghori.

Battle of Tarain

The wars between Mohammad Ghori and Prithviraj Chauhan are known as the First Battle of Tarain (1191) and the Second Battle of Tarain (1192). Mohammad Ghori, the ruler of Gaur and Ghazni, captured Punjab and moved towards Delhi. Gauri's army had ten thousand horsemen while Prithviraj's army had two lakh soldiers. In this first, battle of Tarain, Ghori was injured and defeated. According to Ishwari Prasad, never before had Muslims faced such a terrible defeat at the hands of Hindus. But in 1192, Mohammad Ghori again attacked the Chauhanas with one lakh twenty thousand horsemen. This is called the second battle of Tarain (1192). At this time, the number of Prithviraj's army was more than three lakhs. Prithviraj was defeated and killed in this war. According to Dr. V. Smith, "The second battle of Tarain laid the foundation of the Muslim empire in Northern India. The Turkish victory of later times was the result of this important battle."

This is the very important chapter in which the three major Rajput powers were discussed who were considered the last native rulers of North India. Gurjar-Pratihara dynasty which was probably the most powerful of all three powers. Dozens of rulers of the Tomar dynasty remained under the Pratiharas. In this way, the Tomars were the weakest among these three powers because they were also defeated by the Chauhanas many times. In the end, the Chauhanas became powerful but the Turks ended their power and established their kingdom in India. The defeat of Chauhanas by Turks laid the establishment of the Muslim power in North India and subsequently the whole of India. In this way, after Harshvardhan, there was a period of Ghori's invasion and instability and anarchy in North India. This was also the reason for the success of the Turks. The rulers of North India, who were always facing wars, could neither take care of the people nor did any development work and finally, they came to an end and another era began which is called the Middle Age or medieval period.

7

Ghaznavi, Ghori and Battle of Tarain

After the Hunas, Kushanas and Shakas, there was no invasion in India for about 500 years. In this long peaceful atmosphere, the local kings forgot that they could also be attacked from outside. Perhaps the thought arose in the minds of all those kings that no one could attack them from outside. Perhaps the thought arose in the minds of all those kings that they were very powerful and no one had the courage to compete with them. Perhaps because of this thought they became arrogant and became weak militarily and economically by fighting among themselves. Alberuni, in his book "*Tahqeek-e-Hind*", has described the feelings of Indian kings in this way, "Hindus believe that there is no other country like their country, there is no other nation like their nation, there is no other king like their king, there is no other religion like theirs.... If they go to other countries and see people of other nations, their views will change soon." This statement of Alberuni shows Indian power and moral hollowness. When foreign powers came to know about this condition of India, they attacked India and became victorious.

Ghaznavi Invasion

Ghaznavi attacks in India started from the beginning of the eleventh century. Mahmud Ghaznavi, who was a skilled warrior and commander, was the first Turkish invader to attack India. Later his successors also made some attacks but they were not as successful as Mahmud. However, the invaders were victorious in these attacks and started the rule of Muslims in India.

Objectives of Mahmud Ghaznavi's Invasion

After the death of Subuktagin, his son Mahmud (997-1029) ascended the throne of Ghazni at the age of twenty-five years. He received the *Khila't* (robe of honour) and, the title *Saifu-d-daula* (sword of the state) by his father, and *Yaminu-d-daula* (right hand of the state) and *Aminul Millat* (head of the nation) from the Khalifa of Baghdad Al Kadir Bi-llah. He was the first ruler who got the title of Sultan from Khalifa and before him all the rulers were simply called as Amir. He attacked India 17 times from 1000 to 1027. His attacks in India are still remain controversial and topic of research. The main controversy is about the objectives of his invasion to the scholars define in defferent ways according to their thoughts and provided facts. The objectives mentioned below are according to the analysis of the history scholars.

Religious Objective

The historiographers of this age have depicted the Muslim invasion as the holy war or war against infidels but ended their story with loot and plunder and collection of immense booty. They believe that Mahmud was a fanatic Muslim and wanted to spread Islam in India. Because whoever the people accepted Islam in India was not harmed. It was also the case that he used to loot temples and break idols. He had taken the title of "But Shikan" (*Idol Breaker*). But after Habib and Nizami's research on Mahmud, this perception has started changing. If he wanted to spread Islam, he would not have resorted to war and would not have returned after looting the treasures. He started attacking temples much later when he got immense wealth from the temples of Nagarkot.

No doubt the invaders have boosted the army's morale with the religious fervour or passion of holy war as it was the trend of the

Arabs and the Middle East but their main motto was the collection of the money. The territorial expansion and religious motifs were secondary or mere pretext to solve the money collection process. Ibn al-Athir in his *Kamil ut Tawarikh* writes that in the invasion of Sultan Mahmud in 1004-05 against Bhatia or Bahera region beyond Multan. His victory impressed the locals and many of them embraced Islam. Utbi has stated no forcible conversion in his account. Utbi says that Mahmud appointed a person there to teach those who had embraced Islam and lead them in the right way.

State Expansion

Some scholars are of the opinion that Mahmud's Ghazni state was small and he wanted to expand it by conquering India. This opinion is also not accepted by most historians. They argue that if Mahmud's aim was state expansion, he would have taken control over the conquered states and appointed his governors over them. But except Punjab, he did not include any part of India in his state.

Economic Objectives

India remained free from invasion and flourished for almost 500 years. Due to the hard work and business of the people here, there was immense wealth and reserves of gold and silver. The people here were very religious, so they donated most of the money to temples or kept it safe there. Stories of the immense wealth of the people here were heard even in foreign countries. Hence Mahmud Ghaznavi started attacking here. He would loot the treasure and return.

Sultan Mahmud first time invaded India in 1001, at Purshaur (Peshawar) under the ruler Jaipal with his 15,000 cavalry. He badly defeated Jaipal and his army. Al Utbi in *Tarikh-i-Yamini* narrates, "The necklace was taken off the neck of Jaipal—composed of large pearls and shining gems and rubies set in gold, of which value was two hundred thousand dinars; and twice that value was obtained from the necks of those of his relatives who were taken prisoners, or slain.... God also bestowed upon his friends such an amount of booty as was beyond all bounds and all calculation, including five hundred thousand slaves, beautiful men and women." Jaipal committed suicide due to shame, leaving the throne to his son Andpal.

Abu Rihan Al Utbi especially mentions the Sultan Mahmud's campaign of Bhimnagar (Farishta mentions it as Nagarkot and some as Kot Kangra) in 1008-09. Its fort was very strong, situated on the promontory of a lofty hill, amid impassable waters. The kings of Hind, the chiefs of that country, and rich devotees used to amass their treasures and precious jewels, and send them time after time to be presented to the large idol that they might receive a reward for their good deeds and draw near to their God. Utbi mentions that the Sultan advanced near to this crow's fruit, and this accumulation of years, which had attained such an amount that the backs of camels would not carry it, nor vessels contain it, nor writers had recorded it, nor the imagination of an arithmetician conceive it. Sultan easily overpowered the enemy and looted all the treasures accumulated in the temple. Utbi says that God bestowed on him as plunder the products of mines and seas, the ornaments of heads and breasts, to his heart's content. The treasures were laden on the backs of as many camels as they could procure, and the officers carried away the rest. The stamped coin amounted to seventy thousand royal dirhams, and the gold and silver ingots amounted to seven hundred thousand four hundred *Mans* in weight, besides wearing apparel and fine cloths of town. After this, his target were only the temples from where he got immense treasures of gold and silver. Habib and Nizami have said that Mahmud was greedy for wealth, and in the greed of wealth, he used to attack India again and again. Havell has even said that "If Mahmud had expected to get immense wealth by looting Baghdad, then he would have looted the holy city of the Caliph with the same cruelty as he had looted the holy temple Somnath."

Ghaznavi Invasion of Haryana

Mahmud Ghaznavi himself and three other successors, Masood,

Maudud and Ibrahim attacked Haryana region in their respective times and were victorious. The invasions in Haryana region are as follows.

Mahmud's Attack on Narayangarh

Mahmud Ghaznavi set out to attack Thanesar in 1009. On the way, Anandapala, the ruler of Punjab, sent a letter to Mahmud in which it was written, "I am your servant and your tax payer..... If the Sultan happily abandons this attack, I am ready to give the wealth equal amount of Kurukshetra." But this had no effect on Mahmud and he moved ahead, but on the way, Ajaypala, the Tomar ruler of Haryana and Delhi, fought bravely with Mahmud's forces at the place of Narayangarh. Mahmud was victorious in this war and went back. This was Mahmud's eighth attack on India.

Mahmud's Thanesar Campaign

In 1013, Mahmud set out to attack Thanesar. This was Mahmud's tenth attack on India and second attack on Haryana. There was a possibility of immense wealth in the temples of Thanesar and since Thanesar was a holy place, there was also a possibility of strong opposition from all the Hindus. According to K.C. Yadav, Tomar ruler Ajaypala again appealed to the people to stand against Mahmud but failed. Mahmud attacked Thanesar and emerged victorious and plundered the town as much as he could. He also destroyed the historical statue of Chakraswami. In the words of J.L. Mehta, "Like a storm, Mahmud had achieved his goal and with the same speed with which he had come, he had gone out of the reach of the armies of the Hindu rulers, moving towards Ghazni." This was no less than a road trip full of extreme barbarity.

Masood's Attack on Hansi, Thanesar and Sonipat

Mahmud Ghaznavi's son Masood (1030-1041) also attacked Hansi in 1037. According to Baihaki's "*Tarikh-e-Subuktagin*", Masood had said that "I have to take the fort of Hansi .... I will not undertake any other campaign until I get the fort of Hansi." In this war, the ruler Kumarpala Dev was defeated. After that Masood also attacked Sonipat and Thanesar and in this way Masood got control over the whole of Haryana.

Modud's Thanesar Campaign

After the death of Masood, Haryana went out of his hands, so his son Modud (1041-1050) attacked Thanesar in 1043. The Tomars fought bravely and for the first time after a fierce battle, the Indians won. In this war, Kumarpala Dev was able to avenge his first defeat.

Ibrahim's Victory in Haryana

After the death of Modud, his successor Ibrahim (1059-1099) again attacked Haryana. He conquered Jalandhar, Sirhind, Ropar, Buria (Ambala) etc. At that time Tomar king Tejpala was a very incompetent ruler and he accepted Ibraham's submission without fighting. In this way, the whole of Haryana again went to Ghaznavi state.

Invasion of Muhammad Ghori

After the invasion of Mahmud Ghaznavi and his successors, Chauhanas became very powerful and established their single rule over the whole of Haryana. During the reign of Chauhan king Prithviraj III, the Chauhan kingdom was at the peak of power and development. During the reign of this great ruler, the Turks once again started attacking Indian territories. This time the task was carried out by Shahabuddin Mohammad Ghori, the Governor of Ghazni state. He attacked Haryana several times from 1175-1206. This time his aim was not to loot wealth but to establish a state. At this time, the ruler of Ghazni dynasty Khusro Malik was ruling Punjab from Lahore. Mohammad Ghori captured Peshawar in 1179 and Shyalkot in 1185. In 1186, Mohammad Ghori attacked Khusro Malik's capital Lahore with the help of Chakradeva, the ruler of Kashmir. Using force and deceit, Ghori captured Malik and captured Punjab. In 1190, Ghori also captured Sirhind in Punjab.

First Battle of Tarain

After taking control of Punjab and Sirhind, Mohammad Ghori wanted to take control of Delhi and Haryana. To complete this task, Ghori marched towards Delhi in 1191 with 10,000 capable cavalry. Delhi's Chauhan ruler Prithviraj III also prepared a huge army. Prithviraj's brother and governor of Hansi Govindrai also gathered a large army from Haryana. In this way, Prithviraj's total army had one lakh horsemen, same number of infantry and twenty thousand elephants. But modern historians give less number of Prithviraj's army. Anyway, both the armies gathered in the field of Tarain (Tarawadi), 14 miles away from Thanesar. There was a fierce battle between the two and the Chauhan army uprooted the feet of the Turk army. Govindrai attacked Ghori directly and injured him. He was about to fall from the horse when a Khilji chieftain saved him and took him out of the battle.

According to Farishta, "Muizzuddin's right and left lines were broken and there were not many soldiers left in the middle line. At this time, an officer of the Sultan requested that the Amir Afghan and Khilji army of both the right and left sides were not in the battlefield. In such a situation, it would be better if the Sultan immediately turns his reins towards Lahore. The Sultan was unhappy with this advice and drew his sword for the fight. Meanwhile, Khanderao (Govindrai) saw the Sultan and he turned the elephant towards him. The Sultan attacked Khanderao with a spear, due to which his reins broke. But Rai showed great courage and patience and hit the Sultan on the face in such a way that he almost fell off the horse. At the same time, a Khilji infantryman saw the Sultan in a difficult situation and jumped and sat on his horse. He took care of the Sultan and took the horse out.

Minhaj-us-Siraj explains the first battle of Tarain or Taraori (according to him Narain) in 1191. He mentions that Rai Kolah Pithora (Prithviraj Chauhan) came up against the fort, and the Sultan returned and faced him at Tarain. All the Rais of Hindustan were with the Rai Kolah. The battle was formed and the Sultan, seizing a lance, made a rush upon the elephant which carried

Govind Rai (Pithora's brother) of Delhi. The latter advanced to meet him in front of the battle, and then the Sultan drove his lance into the mouth of the Rai and knocked two of the accursed wretch's teeth down his throat. The Rai, on the other hand, returned the blow and inflicted a severe wound on the arm of his adversary. The Sultan reined back his horse and turned aside, and the pain of the wound was so insufferable that he could not support himself on horseback. The Musalman army gave way and could not be controlled. The Sultan was just falling when a sharp and brave young Khilji recognized him, jumped upon the horse behind him, and clasping him round the bosom, spurred on the horse and bore him from the midst of the fight. The Turkish army was defeated and fled from the field. The Rajput army chased Ghori's army for seventy kilometres. According to Ishwari Prasad, "Never before had the Muslims had to face such a terrible defeat at the hands of the Hindus."

The defeat of Tarain had a deep impact on Ghori. He punished the careless chieftains and equipped the army in a new way. In the words of Mohammad Ghori himself, "Ever since I was defeated by the ruler of Hind, I stopped going to my wife. I never changed the clothes I was wearing. I did not see the faces of those Khilji, Khurasani and Ghori nobles whose carelessness caused me to face defeat. This time (instead of trusting these nobles) I will move towards Hind with faith in Allah."

Second Battle of Tarain

Mohammad Ghori wanted to take revenge for his defeat of first battle of Tarain. So, in the very next year in 1192 Mohammad Ghori intended to attack again. He divided his army into many groups with a well-organized strategy and came to the battlefield in Tarain. This time his army was one lakh twenty thousand. Prithviraj Chauhan had also made good preparations. Except for King Jaichand of Kannauj, all the kings of the rest of North India were with in alliance of Prithviraj. In this way, the total army of Prithviraj was more than three lakh. According to Farishta, "With the help of 150 Rajput chieftains, Prithviraj entered the battlefield to fight Mohammad Ghori with a huge army of three lakh horsemen, thirty thousand elephants and many infantry soldiers."

In 1192, a fierce battle took place between the two in the field of Tarain. Prithviraj's advance party was led by Govindrai. Bhola was handling the left side and Badamshah Rawal was handling the right side. Prithviraj was so far behind in the middle that the arrows could not reach him. From Mohammad Ghori's side, Kharbak was leading the advance party, Ullah was on the right side and Mohammad Ghori himself was in the middle surrounded by horsemen. For the first three hours of the war, the Turk army was fighting from Delhi and engaging the Rajputs. Suddenly, Ghori started retreating. The Rajput army started chasing the Turks, considering itself victorious. At the same time, 1200 specially trained Turk soldiers attacked the Rajputs. There was a stampede in the Rajput army and a large number of Rajput soldiers were killed. Prithviraj also fled from the field and was caught.

"*Tabakat-e-Nasiri*", says that "Pithora got down from the elephant in the last phase and ran away on a horse." He was captured from Surasuti (Sirsa) and killed. According to Hasan Nizami, he was arrested and taken to Ajmer where he ruled like a subordinate king. Because on the other side of some coins of Prithviraj, "Shri Mohammadsam" is written which indicates his subjugation. Later Prithviraj was killed and his son was made the ruler of Ajmer who accepted the subordination of Ghori. Govindrai's successor also accepted the subordination of Mohammad Ghori in Haryana.

Hasan Nizami explains the second battle of Tarain in 1192, by hiding the defeat of Mohammad Ghori in the first battle in 1191. The text shows that Rai Pithora, the ruler of Ajmer was unjust towards his Muslim subjects. On hearing the news Mohammad Ghori sent the ambassador to Ajmer for fair dealing with the Muslims and the ambassador also invited him for the true path. On unsatisfactory reports of the ambassador, Mohammad Ghori marched towards Ajmer and defeated Rai Pithora in the battle of Tarain. Mohammad Ghori pardoned the life of Rai Pithora and marched to Ajmer where he put the Rai to death on certain breach of trust. Hasan Nizami describes the reason of the death of Rai Pithora, "Ancient hatred against the Musalmans was deeply rooted and concealed in the bottom of his heart, appears to have been detected in some intrigue, which is only very obscurely indicated, so that orders were issued for his death." Mohammad Ghori conferred the government of Ajmer to the son of Rai Pithora.

After the second battle of Tarain, the existence of small Rajput states ended and a well-organized Turkish rule was established in India. According to A.L. Srivastava, "The second battle of Tarain is an epoch-making event in Indian history. This battle proved to be decisive and the victory of Mohammad Ghori was confirmed in it. "In the words of J.L. Mehta, "The fall of Prithviraj Chauhan proved to be very disastrous for the Rajputs." V.A. Smith has written that "The second battle of Tarain laid the foundation of the Muslim empire in North India. In due course of time, the victory of the Turks was the result of this important battle."

Protest against Turks in Haryana

After the battle of Tarain, the Turks took control of almost entire Haryana and Delhi. Big kings either became extinct or became assistants to the Turkish rule as feudal lords. But the public did not accept this decision and there was opposition to the Turkish rule in many places.

Opposition of Jats

Jats and Rajputs dominated the Hansi-Hisar region and in 1192 they gave a tough challenge to the Turks on the border of Bangar. Ultimately, the Jats were defeated. According to Hasan Nizami, "When the venerable month of Ramzan (September 1192) of 588 Hijri arrived, the devil entered the minds of the cursed Jats and they raised their hands to fight against the (Turk) commander."

Sirsa Residents' Protest

Like the Jats of Hansi-Hisar, the people of Sirsa also took up arms against the Turkish chieftains and were ultimately defeated. Such incidents happened in Rohtak and many other places but the Turks were victorious everywhere.

Ahirwal's Opposition

Ahirwal, which is called the area around Rewari, rose against the Turks. Tejpala, the administrator of Rewari, not only fought the Turks but also defeated them and killed the Turkish commander Ibrahim. The chief commander Qutbuddin Aibak sent a huge army against Tejpala. This time the Ahirs were defeated and hundreds of warriors including Tejpala were killed.

Opposition of Mewatis

Sardar Hemraj of Mewat gathered all the Mewatis and fought the Turkish army. In this fierce battle, the Turk commander Wajihuddin died and his army suffered a crushing defeat. Chief commander Qutbuddin Aibak sent a large army to take revenge. Hundreds of Mewatis including Hemraj were killed in this battle. After this victory, the Turks established their supremacy over the Mewat region.

Reasons for the Success of Turks against Rajputs

Despite their world-renowned bravery, the Indian Rajputs were repeatedly defeated by the Turks who were far smaller in number than them and lost their power for ever. The following could be the reasons for this defeat of the Rajputs and the success of the Turks.

Carelessness of Rajputs

After the Huns, there was no foreign invasion in India for about 500 years. The result of tranquility was that both the kings and the army here became militarily weak and careless. They forgot the old invasions and never thought that there could be a foreign invasion in the future. Whatever wars they fought were mutual wars which did not require much power and strength. Overall, there was a life of peace and tranquility in India where people were busy in agriculture and trade. According to K.C. Yadav, in such a situation, Mahmud Ghaznavi and Mohammad Ghori attacked us while we were asleep.

Ideals and Pride of Rajputs

After the victory of some clans in the mutual wars of Rajputs, a feeling of pride also developed in them. They started thinking that there is no one more warrior or powerful than them. In such a situation, they did not sharpen themselves by doing military exercises. Apart from that, one ideal of Rajputs was that they did not resort to deceit in war. They were true to their words.

Social Decline of Rajputs

Rajputs were divided into big social organizations or castes and fought with each other over small matters. They never united and paid attention towards the political unity of India. On the contrary, there was absolutely no caste system among Muslims. They fought unitedly and emerged victorious.

Religious Fervour Among Turks

The Turks had a religious zeal. They believed that if they died in the war, they would attain heaven. That is why they fought the war without caring about their lives. Mohammad Ghori himself had said that after the first defeat, he would fight the war trusting in Allah. The Rajputs did not have such feelings and neither did they have so much faith in God.

Climate of India

Due to the hot and humid climate of India, the land here was fertile. Therefore, the people of India did not have to work hard for their livelihood. As a result people became lazy and useless. Whereas the climate of the Turks' territory was dry and cold and the lands were rocky and mountainous. Therefore, they had to work hard for livelihood. Therefore, they were more hardworking and brave. Turks had the courage to struggle for several days without eating or drinking anything.

It may be concluded that India remained free from foreign wars for about 500 years. Agriculture and trade flourished, and reserves of gold and silver were accumulated. But militarily the state and the army became ineffective. Apart from the quarrels among the native kings, they did not have to face any foreign power. In this period of slackness, after a peaceful period of about 500 years, the Turkish invaders caught the Indians sleeping. They were victorious because they had unity. They had the passion to die in the name of God. Apart from this, they were more brave and warriors. After these Turkish invasions, power went into the hands of the Turks and a new era, the Middle Age, began which later ended with the arrival of the British.

8

Balban and His Invasions in Haryana

Balban's attack and his retributions are more famous in Mewat region of Haryana. Mewat is the land of an ancient tribe Meos, which has been loosely defined in various times of history. Its source of attraction is its cultural and traditional peculiarity and complexity. The scholars all over the world were surprised to know about its rich history through bards and Mirasis. The Arab and Persian chroniclers gave much importance to this area. Perhaps Meos, the inhabitants of this area, has no parallel in the Indian History, regarding their fight for independence as well as for their retribution by the rulers. The history witnesses that the renowned Rana Sanga fled from the battlefield while his partner Hasan Khan Mewati was gallantly martyred on the spot while fighting Babur in the battle of Khanwa.

Among the rulers and amirs of Delhi only a few tried to subjugate the people of the turbulent area of Mewat in the suburb of Delhi. Balban (Ulugh Khan) was one of them, who created havoc by mass level murder and destruction in Mewat area, covering the many hundred miles in Haryana and Rajasthan. He routed the Mewatis, both as a ruler and Amir and various invasions invaded the area and subjugated them permanently. The above reference does not mean that the Mewati turbulence was new to the Balban, but it was Balban, who tried to crush them permanently for the first time in the history of present Mewat. Balban made it a policy matter to completely control the area and eliminate the area from the marauders and set up peace, law and order in that country.

It has been frequently narrated in this book that Mewati got the turbulence from inheritance, but the cool Indian atmosphere affected them as to the other immigrants like Aryans, Huns, Kushans, and Muslims. The fresh turbulence of Mewatis was due to the taxation system of the government. The alkaline soil and barren land of Mewat made the Mewatis' life very tough, and subsequently, it made them brave and warring in comparison to other communities of India. They frequently faced the natural disaster like famine, drought, and flood, which compelled them to base their livelihood on loot and plunder. They also rose in open rebellion whenever they were unable to pay the heavy taxes imposed by the government.

It is to be noted that the Meos of Mewat were not robbers as repeatedly yelled by the contemporary chroniclers but a band of irregular, freelance and unpaid armies which were, due to some circumstantial reasons, always in revolt against the Delhi rulers. They even slain many of the Delhi commanders who tried to attack the area. They even not spared Balban, a man of horror, and carried off a large number of his camels, without which the army could hardly have taken the field. By the rulers of Delhi, they were treated with the most merciless cruelty. The Meos were hunted down like beasts, and massacred in thousands. In the series of persecution and suppression of the Meos, Balban invaded the Mewat area in 1256, 1260 and in 1266 when he ascended to the throne.

Balban's Attack in 1256

As narrated by the various historians of different ages about the rebellious nature of the Mewati people, they were always being plundered and tortured by Delhi authorities. For the first time, their rebellion was checked during 1256, when Balban (Ulugh Khan) was in command of Mewat with his headquarters at Rewari. At that time, one of the Delhi rebel leader Kutlugh Khwaja sought refuge in Mewat, where the local Mewati chief Ransi Ran Pal was ruling the area. Ransi Ran Pal, the local ruler by giving him protection openly invited the troubles and curse of Delhi. According to some local traditions, it was Ant Pal who ruled Mewat with his capital at Ajangarh which he founded around 1240. Mewat was first time invaded in his rule in 1256, by Ulugh Khan, minister of Sultan Nasiruddin Mahmud Shah. Ulugh Khan invaded Mewat country for the first time and after a pitches battle forced the rebels to fly. After this episode, the name of Ransi Ran Pal never been heard in any historical text. According to the local traditions and genealogy of the ruling dynasties of the area, it seems more probable that Ransi Ran Pal was actually Ant Pal, who ruled Mewat with his capital at Ajangarh to which his father Bandh Pal founded around 1216, with the assistance of a *Darvesh* Shah Alakh.

Balban's Attack in 1260

From the invasion of Balban on the Mewati leader Ransi Ran Pal (Ant Pal of Ajangarh) in 1256, the enmities between two were increased day by day. The Mewatis again organized with much vigour and valour under Malkha or Mangal who became local head of the Mewati territory with its capital at Indore. The Meos wanted to chastise the Balban in order to revenge their previous failure. They were waiting for the pretext to attack on the Ulugh Khan. They find a chance in 1260, when Ulugh Khan was in the way to Rewari. The Meos carried off a large number of Balban's camels from his army. It was the signal of their open rebellion against Balban. Ulugh Khan once more invaded the Mewat area to subdue the turbulent Mewatis. It is said that the people of Mewat were considered by Ulugh Khan as knaves, Hindus, thieves, and highway robbers and in order to subdue them, he once again invaded on Mewat in 1260.

Ulugh Khan marched towards Mewat on 9 March, 1260, with 10,000 horsemen in armour, a large army of brave and warlike soldiers. He captured the Santur or Satur (Indore), the capital of

Mewat. About 12,000 Mewati ladies, gents, and children were put to death. For twenty days, the work of slaughter and pillage continued and the ferocity of the soldiery was stimulated by the reward of one silver *tanka* was offered for every head, and two for every prisoner brought in alive. The contemporary sources also mention that Ulugh Khan and his army also plundered another stronghold of Mewat named Salmur (Alwar) to which they never penetrated before. On 29 March, 1260, the army returned to the capital with 250 chieftains of the Meo tribe, who had stolen the camels and other leading men of the tribe, to the number of 250, 142 horses, and 21,00,000 silver *tankas*. Ishwari Prashad says that Balban carried 60 bags of cotton each containing 35,000 *tankas*. Two days later the prisoners along with the ruler Malkha were publicly massacred with great cruelty near Hauz Rani in front of the Badaun Gate. Some were thrown under the feet of elephants; others were cut in halves with knives. Persian sources have described their punishments as, "the rebels were flayed from head to foot and at the hand of their skinners, and they quaffed, in the goblet of their own heads, the sherbet of death." Even the Mohammadan historians themselves admit that such an example of retribution was made that no one had ever heard a tale so terrible.

Balban's Attack in 1266

When Ulugh Khan ascended the throne of Delhi in 1265 with the title of Balban, the Mewat area, adjoining the Delhi territory, was ruled by Kaku Rana. Not much is known about Kaku Rana and no Persian or British historian has mentioned his activities. He only finds the place in the oral history of Mewat told by the bards or *Mirasis* and other traditional stories. Maulvi Abdus Shakoor in his *Tarikh Meo Kshatriya* has mentioned a court scene of Kaku Rana. However, Swaleh Khan Athar in his *Tarikh Meo Mehar* refutes any relation between Balban and Kaku Rana. He is even doubtful of their being as contemporary.

By all observations, it can be concluded that Kaku Rana was a chief of Mewat, whose position was not very important as he worked in a democratic style by aids and advice of the village headmen and common people. In order to fight the royal forces of Delhi, he made his stronghold at Garhdhamna, a place in the outskirts of Mehroli. He also might have controlled the some parts of Mewat area from Indore, which was once the stronghold of Malkha. It was perhaps the strategy of the Meos, to set up their military base at Garhdhamna to fight against Balban.

Abdus Shakoor mentions that in this campaign, the Balut Meo leader Kaku Rana invited the chiefs of Bayana and Bairath and all the chaudharies of Mewat with all their forces. All the presenters of the court suggested him to give the Balban tough resistance as usual. It was the fiercest attack of Balban and surprisingly, the Meos also fought with full of their strength. One lakh of the royal army was slain by the Mewatis, and the most probability the same numbers of Mewati were also put to the sword. From that time, the city was delivered from the attacks of the Mewatis. It is also notable that during this time, Yadubanshi Adhan Pal was the ruler of Kultajpur near Tijara. His association with Kaku Rana, in the battle of 1266, might be possible. After this battle, Adhan Pal had taken refuge in Sarehtha.

According to Ziauddin Barani in his *Tarikh-e-Firoz Shahi*, the daring of the Mewatis in the neighbourhood of Delhi was carried to such an extent that the western gates of the city were shut at afternoon prayer. Meos plundered the travellers on the roads, entered the city by night, and robbed the inhabitants in their houses, and even by day robbed and stripped water-carriers and women drawing water from the large reservoirs *Sar-e-Hauz* just within the city walls, so that it became necessary to shut the gates on the western side of the city immediately after the hour of afternoon prayer. No one dared to go out of the city in that direction after that hour, whether he travelled as a pilgrim or with the display of a sovereign. These daring acts of the Mewatis caused a great ferment in Delhi. Barani further says that the Sultan felt the repression of the Mewatis and for a whole year he was occupied in overthrowing them and in scouring the jungles.

Sultan built a fort at Gopalgarh, and many Police posts were established and placed in command of Afghans. They were assigned the land for maintenance, and the army was supplied with hatchets. They also cleared away the woods around Delhi. The tract thus cleared was considerable and became well cultivated. Balban gave the town and areas to the distinguished chiefs with the direction to lay waste and destroy the villages of the marauders, to slay the men, to make prisoners of the women and children, to clear away the jungle, and to suppress all lawless proceedings. The noblemen set about the work with strong forces, and they soon put down the daring of the rebels.

The last operation of Balban seems to have been so effectual that there is little mention of Mewat for a hundred years, during which the chiefs of Mewat appear to have maintained satisfactory relations with the authorities at Delhi. This type of cruel treatment was common throughout the period of Delhi Sultanate, and it became the proverb as the proper way of treating Mewatis. According to Cunningham, the Meos as Hindus often successfully resisted the arms of the Mohammadan kings of Delhi until the time of Feroz Tughlaq, when they were converted into Islam. However, in spite of their change of religion, the Muslim Meos were just as turbulent as their Hindu ancestors, and they remained virtually independent of the time of Timur's invasion until the conquest of Northern India by Babur.

During Mughal rule, the Meos were also turbulent and Emperor employed Raja of Khandela (Chandela) named Girdhar, to suppress their leader Avith. At that period, according to James Tod, the empire was in a most disordered state, and the mountainous region, called Mewat, was inhabited by daring and ferocious bandits, called Meos, who pillaged in gangs even to the gates of the capital. The task of taking, dead or alive, the leader of this bandit, was assigned to the chief of Chandela, who performed it with signal gallantry and success. Aware that, by the display of superior force, his enemy would remain in his lurking places. Girdhar put himself on terms of equality with his foe, and Avith a small but select band hunted the Mewati leader down, and in the end slew him in single combat.

The same harsh treatment was continued down to the time of Marathas who had possessed the whole area of Mewat. Under M. Perron's rule, it was a common custom to immure the Mewatis alive between four walls. However, afterwards, the British government in 1806-07, tried its level best to maintain their relation with the Mewatis more humane. According to the *East India Gazetteer* of Mr. Walter Hamilton mentions that this system of terror wholly failed, for, notwithstanding the impending tortures that threatened them, the Mewati outrages continued to increase, and the peaceful parts of the country were kept in a state of unceasing alarm and anxiety. In 1807, a correspondence was opened with some of the chiefs by Mr. Seton, then resident at Delhi, and some measures of a mild, conciliatory nature adopted towards the Mewatis.

The old marauding and martial act of the Mewatis is totally absent during the course of time. Now they are quite religious and hard working. However, their nature and behaviour is still arrogant and abusing as the following proverbs for the Mewatis regarding their nature and behaviour still suits them:

1. *Pahle Laat, Pichhe Baat,*
   (First beat, then treat)
2. *Dekhi Teri Mewat,*
   Pahle Gaali Pichhe Baat

(See what a place is your Mewat, where abuse must precede the talk.)

9

Battles of Panipat

Lodi, Hemu and Marathas

Haryana region, which is situated between Delhi and Lahore, has been a battlefield throughout the medieval period due to its important geographical position. Whoever tried to capture Delhi had to fight in Haryana region. This chapter will cover the two world famous battles fought in Panipat in Haryana. It will also cover Humayun's escape and the economic and administrative efforts of Sher Shah Suri. In this way we will see that Delhi and Haryana are historically more important than almost any other region in India.

Babur's Invasion

At the time of Babur's invasion in 1526, India was ruled by Ibrahim Lodi. He was a very arrogant and impractical ruler. His big chieftains were angry with him. The Sultan started punishing the even the high level chieftains who disobeyed him. According to A.L. Srivastava, "Although Ibrahim Lodi was not completely devoid of ability and intelligence; he had to face a tragic failure. He was a brave and fearless warrior and a successful commander. He was honest and hardworking."

Zahiruddin Babur, the ruler of Fargana (Andijan), established his power in Kabul after losing his kingdom of Andijan and

Samarkand. He liked Kabul a lot, but still he wanted to establish power in India. The political situation in India and the opposition and dissatisfaction of the chieftains towards the Sultan inspired Babur to attack India. It is believed that Indian Rajput ruler Rana Sanga and Lodi chief Daulat Khan Lodi invited Babur to attack India.

First Battle of Panipat (1526)

At the time of the fall of the Delhi Sultans, the attack of Mongol ruler Amir Timur was quite destructive but he went back seeing the seriousness of the situation. After that, there was peace in Delhi Sultanate for about 350 years. Babur, who was a descendant of Amir Timur, attacked India in 1526, but like Amir Timur, he did not go back but also established the Mughal state in India itself.

Reasons for the First Battle of Panipat

The first battle of Panipat took place in the fields of Panipat in 1526 between Babur and Ibrahim Lodi. There were the following reasons for this battle.

Political Situation of India

At the time of Babur's invasion, the political condition of India was not good. The whole of India was divided into two parts, North and South, with different political conditions and cultures. Delhi Sultanate was the biggest state in North India. Apart from this, there were other small states like Bengal, Gujarat, Malwa and Mewar. The biggest state in the South was Vijayanagar and another Khandesh was a small state. All these states were enemies of each other. Babur writes in his autobiography "*Tuzuk-e-Babri*" that "When I invaded India, there were seven major states there: Five Muslim and two Hindu. Apart from these states, there were other small states which were not so popular but still had great importance in the politics of India. The five main states of India were Delhi, Bengal, Gujarat, Malwa and Khandesh, while among the Hindu states, King Sangram Singh of Mewar and Krishnadevaraya of Vijayanagar were quite powerful."

Babur's Ambition

Babur writes in his autobiography "*Tuzuk-e-Babri*" that, "From the capture of Kabul to the victory of Panipat (1526), I never gave up the idea of conquering India." After the failure of Samarkand, Babur put all his energy into conquering India. Babur was also inspired by the victory of his ancestor Amir Timur and he considered it his right to take over India.

Role of Ibrahim Lodi

Ibrahim Lodi was a capable, intelligent, fearless warrior and successful commander. Also, like Balban, he was strictly disciplined and arrogant. He imposed strict discipline and court etiquette on his nobles and chiefs. The Sardars or chieftains were very sad due to these strictness which created an atmosphere of conspiracy. Punjab's administrators Daulat Khan Lodi, Alam Khan Lodi and Mewar's ruler Rana Sangram Singh (Rana Sanga) even invited Babur, the ruler of Afghanistan, to attack India. He also promised military help to Babur against Ibrahim Lodi.

Babur's Failure in Central Asia

Babur became the ruler of Fargana in 1494 after the death of his father Umar Sheikh Mirza. He also captured Samarkand, the kingdom of his ancestor Amir Timur, but due to adverse circumstances, both the kingdoms were lost from his hands. Then Babur established his kingdom in Afghanistan (Kabul) in 1504. After success in the battle of Panipat, he became the ruler of India in 1526. Babur himself writes, "Because I had the desire to conquer and establish a vast empire, I was not one to sit quietly after being disappointed by one or two defeats." Babur tried his luck on the country of India. The vastness and wealth of India was attracting him. Babur himself writes, "The main quality of India is that it is a vast country and gold and silver are found in large quantities here."

Babur's Military Abilities

Babur was a capable soldier and commander. He was related to Amir Timur through his father Omar Sheikh Mirza and to Genghis Khan through his mother Qutlugh Nigar Khanum. He was so brave that he became famous not only by his name Zaheeruddin but by the nickname Babur (Babbar Lion). Due to his military ability, his small army of thousands was superior to the enemy's army of lakhs. Babur was the first general who fought with gunpowder and artillery in India.

Victory of Punjab

Punjab Governor Daulat Khan Lodi had a hand in inviting Babur to attack India. But to capture India, it was necessary for Babur to first conquer Punjab. There were differences of opinion between Babur and Daulat Khan on this matter and Babur made five attacks on Punjab from 1519 to 1525 and finally, he captured Punjab. This boosted his morale. On the other hand, king of Mewar Rana Sanga had also assured Babur of all possible help in attacking Delhi.

Events of the First Battle of Panipat

On 17 November, 1525, Babur, aged forty-two, launched his fifth and final invasion of India, marching from Kabul at the head of an army of 8,000 men, composed of subordinate Timurid princes and their retainers, Pashtun allies from South-Eastern Afghanistan and artillery and matchlock contingents advised by Turkish officers from Anatolia. On the way he was joined by Humayn from Badakhshan and Khwaja Kilan from Ghazni. When he crossed the Indus on 16 December, the entire army amounted to 12,000 men including non-combatant camp followers.

As Babur advanced towards Sialkot and forced Daulat Khan, who had girded himself with two swords as a challenge against the invader, to capitulate. Daulat Khan's son Ghazi Khan fled but his another son Dilawar Khan joined Babur. Alam Khan Lodi also joined Babur in a forlorn condition. By 12th April, 1526, Babur reached Panipat, sixty-five kilometres North-West of Delhi, and secured his defences. Sultan Ibrahim Lodi also advanced from Delhi with a big army to meet the invader and also encamped at Panipat with his huge army.

For eight days from 12 April to 19 April, the two armies stood face to face. Two advance parties of the Afghans fell upon the Mughal army, the first under Hamid Khan, which came into contact with Babur's right wing, was completely routed by Humayun, the second under Datid Khan and Hatim Khan was similarly routed. The Mughals also possessed the relatively new technology of matchlock and cannon firepower, which Ibrahim lacked. Most importantly, Babur deployed the same flanking cavalry tactics that Uzbek cavalries had used to defeat him decades earlier in his struggles over Samarkand.

Babur in his Memoir says,

> "....I put my foot in the stirrup of resolution, set my hand on the rein of trust in God, and moved forward against Sultan Ibrahim, son of Sultan Sikandar, son of Buhlul Lodi Afghan, in possession of whose throne at that time were the Delhi capital and the dominions of Hindustan, whose standing-army was called a lakh (1,00,000), whose elephants and whose Begs' elephants were about 1000."

Babur says,

> "....Seven hundred carts were brought in. The order given to Ustad Ali Quli was that these carts should be joined together in Ottoman fashion, but using ropes of raw hide instead of chains, and that between every two carts 5 or 6 mantelets should be fixed, behind which the matchlockmen were to stand to fire. Panipat is there with its crowded houses and suburbs. It would be on one side of us; our other sides must be protected by carts and mantelets behind which our foot and matchlockmen would stand."

Babur further says,

> "On our right was the town of Panipat with its suburbs; in front of us were the carts and mantelets we had prepared; on our left and elsewhere were ditch and branch. At distances of an arrow's flights sally-places were left for from 100 to 200 horsemen."

On the 21st April, 1526, on Friday the Sultan's army advanced to the attack and the famous first battle of Panipat was started. By mid-day, the decisive battle of Panipat had left Sultan Ibrahim's vast army disappeared, and he himself lay dead on the field with 15,000 of his men. Babur won the battle by coolness under fire, his use of artillery, and effective Turkish wheeling tactics on a divided, dispirited enemy.

Babur himself says,

> "When the incitement to battle had come, the Sun was spear-high; till mid-day fighting had been in full force; noon passed, the foe was crushed in defeat, our friends rejoicing and gay. By God's mercy and kindness, this difficult affair was made easy for us! In one half-day, that armed mass was laid upon the earth. Five or six thousand men were killed in one place close to Ibrahim. Our estimate of the other dead, lying all over the field, was 15,000 to 16,000, but it came to be known, later in Agra from the statements of Hindustanis, that 40,000 or 50,000 may have died in that battle. Hisar's Faujdar Hameed Khan was killed along with his forces. The second ally, Nahar Khan, son of Hasan Khan Mewati, was taken prisoner and his army was destroyed in the war. Babur moved forward and established his authority over Delhi and Agra and laid the foundation of the Mughal era."

Opposition of Mughal Rule in Haryana

After capturing Panipat and Delhi, Babur divided the won territories of Haryana into four parts, Mewat Government, Sirhind Government, Delhi Government and Hisar Government. Babur was mostly engrossed in wars and hence could not concentrate fully on administration. Hence, rebellions took place at many places. First of all 3000 Afghans of Hisar Firoza revolted. To suppress this rebellion, on 21st November, 1526, Babur sent an army under the leadership of Amir Timur Sultan and Abul Fatah. Many Afghans were killed and the rest fled to save their lives.

The second number was from Mewat. Sardar Hasan Khan Mewati had sent an army under the leadership of his son Nahar Khan in the battle of Panipat. Along with Ibrahim Lodi, Nahar Khan was also defeated and taken prisoner. Babur's nobles advised Babur that if Nahar was left alive, Hasan Khan would join Babur. But this did not happen. As soon as Nahar Khan became independent, Hasan Khan joined Rana Sanga. Together they gave a tough fight to Babur in the field of Khanwa.

Ahmad Yadgar's "*Tarikh-e-Salatin-e-Afghana*", a Rajput named Mohan Mandar in Kaithal raised a flag against the Mughals and attacked the estate of the Qazi of Samana and killed his son. Babur sent Ali Quli with an army of three thousand to attack the village of Mohan Mandar. But the Mughal army could not stand against the villagers and were defeated. Then Babur sent 6000 army under the leadership of Tarsem Bahadur and Naurang Beg. They killed many Mandars and captured a thousand Mandars. The pillar was constructed from the heads of those who died. Mohan Mandar was buried waist deep and killed by an arrow attack.

Haryana under Humayun and Sher Shah

Haryana developed a lot under the rule of Humayun and Sher Shah. Sher Shah made a lot of improvements in the administration during his time.

Reign of Humayun

After Babur's death on 26th December, 1530, his son Humayun ascended the throne. He gave the Mewat Sarkar in Haryana to Mirza Hindal and handed over Hisar and Sirhind to Mirza Kamran. Apart from this, Kamran had the Sarkars of Punjab, Kabul and Kandahar. When Humayun was busy fighting the Afghans under Sher Khan, Mirza Hindal rebelled. Kamran also did the same. Humayun defeated them but instead of punishing them, he forgave them. Sher Khan defeated Humayun in the battles of Chausa (1539) and Bilgram (1540) and captured Haryana and the entire Mughal state.

Haryana under Sher Shah

Sher Shah had a connection with Haryana by birth. His grandfather Ibrahim came to India from Afghanistan during the time of Bahlol Lodi. He got the chieftainship of 40 soldiers from Jamal Khan, the landlord of Hisar, and also got some villages of Narnaul pargana for his livelihood. Ibrahim made great progress with the help of his son Hasan Khan. Hasan Khan took up a job with Umar Khan, a courtier of Bahlol Lodi, and got Shahabad pargana as jagir. After Ibrahim's death, his jagir of Narnaul was transferred to his son Hasan Khan. It was here that Sher Shah was born as a boy named Farid in 1486.

After becoming the ruler, Sher Shah divided Haryana into four Sarkars—Delhi, Mewat, Hisar, and Sirhind. The administration of each Sarkar was in the hands of two officers, the chief shiqdar and the chief munsif. The chief shiqdar was mainly a military officer whose job was to maintain the army and run the administration of his government. He also used to decide criminal cases. The chief munsif was a judge whose job was to decide civil cases.

Sher Shah had divided each Sarkar into Parganas whose officers were shikdar and munsif. Their work was similar to that of the officers of the Sarkar. Apart from these, there were also officers named kanungo and khazanchi. The smallest unit of governance was the village which was managed by mukaddam and patwari. panchayat also had an important function in the village. Apart from these, there was also a Chowkidar in every village.

Sher Shah died on 17 May, 1545 when a landmine exploded. His successors turned out to be incompetent, so Humayun once again captured Delhi in 1555. But on 26 January, 1556, Humayun died after falling from the stairs of his library and his son Akbar ascended the throne.

Life and Achievements of Hemchandra

Hemchandra *alias* Hemu was born at a place called Qutubpur in Rewari district. His father's name was Purandas and he belonged to the Dhusar caste, which is also a sub-caste of Baniyas. At an early age, Hemu took up a job with the Sur rulers and progressed to the post of minister like "Shahna-e-Bazar". After that he was made the head of the Intelligence Department and later "Daroga-e-Dak Chowki". According to Abul Fazal, "Being adept at cunningness, Hemu proved himself to be a very capable person in the eyes of Islam Shah through his business acumen." Islam Shah used to take Hemu's advice in important matters of the state.

After the death of Islam Shah, Hemu became the prime minister of the Sultanate during the time of Adil Shah. Hemu appointed qualified persons by removing incompetent persons. According to Abul Fazal, the nominal king was Adil Shah but in reality the one who ran the state was Hemu. While being the prime minister, he had also taken command of the army in his hands. According to Badayuni, Hemu used to invite soldiers to his place for dinner many times and used to console them a lot. In this way, all the Afghans were happy with him. But taking advantage of Adil Shah's incompetence, many Afghan chieftains declared themselves independent. Taj Khan Kirani claimed South Bihar, Mohammad Khan Sur claimed Bengal, Bazbahadur claimed Malwa and Ibrahim Sur and Ahmad Khan Sur claimed the Afghan state. According to Niyamatullah, the author of "*Mazkhan*", "Every province and village was in the flames of rebellion." In such bad days, Hemu fought 22 battles and destroyed all the enemies.

When Humayun died on 26 January, 1556, Adil Shah who was in Bihar sent Hemu to attack Delhi. Hemu marched towards Delhi with 7000 horsemen, 20 elephants and Afghan chieftains. He captured Agra by driving away the governor of Agra, Sikandar Khan Uzbek. After this, he attacked Delhi. Allahdad Khan and Rai Hussain Dalwani were supporting Hemu. The command of the Mughal army was in the hands of Tardi Beg. The two armies fought in Delhi (Daulatabad) on 7 October, 1556. Tardi Beg was supported by Afzal Khan, Ashraf Khan, Mir Mohammad Sherwani, Haider, Muhammad Khan, Isqadar Khan and Abdul Uzbek. The Mughal army was defeated in this battle and Tardi Beg fled. After being victorious in the war, Hemu changed his mind and decided to become independent. He distributed all the wealth of Agra and Delhi among the Afghan soldiers and turned them over to his side. He ascended the throne on 7 October, 1556 and assumed the title of Vikramaditya. As soon as Hemu became the ruler, he appointed his governors in distant regions and imposed his direct control on Delhi and its surrounding areas, especially Haryana.

Second Battle of Panipat (1556)

The land of Haryana has always been blood-stained. From the *Mahabharata* war to the wars of Tarain, Panipat, Karnal etc., all were fought in Haryana. The people in Haryana were also very brave and used to take part in several wars. In 1556, once again a fierce battle took place in Panipat, this time it was between Akbar and Hemchandra.

Accession of Akbar

Humayun was able to rule Delhi again for less than a year when he died after falling from the stairs while coming down from the library. At that time Akbar was on a war campaign in Punjab. Akbar's guardian Bairam Khan built a brick platform in Kalanaur on 14 February, 1556 and coronated Akbar. At this time Akbar was only 13 years old and he was surrounded by enemies from all sides. The most dangerous of his enemies was Hemu. Hemu first captured

Agra and then Delhi and declared himself emperor of Hindustan. Delhi's Mughal commander Tardi Beg had fled from Delhi.

When the news of the defeat of the Mughal army at the hands of Hemu in Delhi reached Akbar, he was engaged with Sikandar Shah in Jalandhar, Punjab. As soon as Akbar received the news, he left his uncle Khwaja Khizar Khan to fight Sikandar Khan and himself marched towards Delhi. On the way, the defeated chieftains of Delhi including Tardi Beg met Akbar at Sirhind. Bairam Khan was very angry with his cowardice. He murdered Tardi Beg right there. The Mughal army advanced and Hemu and Akbar fought in the field of Panipat in which Akbar was victorious.

Reasons for the Second Battle of Panipat

The plains of Panipat were writing the story of Mughal supremacy for the second time. This ground proved to be a boon for the Mughals for the second time also. The reasons for this war were as follows:

Enmity between Mughals and Afghans

There was an old enmity between the Mughals and the Afghans because Babur had captured the power of Delhi by defeating Ibrahim Lodi. Sher Shah took revenge by defeating Humayun in Chausa and Bilgram and snatching power from the Mughals. Similarly, there was a tussle going on between the Mughals and Afghans regarding the power of Delhi. Humayun then defeated the Afghans in the battles of Machhiwara and Sirhind and captured Delhi. But after the death of Humayun, Afghan Sultan Adil Shah once again captured Delhi through his prime minister Hemu. But this time Hemu became the king of Delhi and the second battle of Panipat took place between the Mughals and Hemu. After the defeat of Hemu and the Afghans in this war, Afghan power ended for ever.

Political Void in Delhi

The date of death of Humayun, 26 January, 1556, was hidden

for some time because his son Akbar was engaged in a war in Punjab while pursuing Sikandar Sur. When Akbar got the news of his father's death, his coronation took place in Kalanaur on 14 February, 1556. At this time Akbar was 13 years old. This was a time of political vacuum in Delhi. At this time there were three contenders for Delhi. First was Akbar, second was Afghan and third was Afghan prime minister Hemu. Meanwhile, taking advantage of the opportunity, Hemu captured Delhi and Agra and assumed the title of Vikramaditya.

Mughals' March from Sirhind to Delhi

On 15 April, 1556, an order was given to march from Jalandhar towards Delhi and a war meeting was held in Sirhind. Tardi Beg, who had fled from Delhi, was given death sentence and the morale of the soldiers was boosted for victory. Akbar moved towards Delhi with 20,000 army. His commander was Bairam Khan.

Role of Hemu

Although the Mughal-Afghan conflict had been going on for decades, Hemu brought it to an end. He fought a total of 22 battles for the Afghans and emerged victorious. After that, the dream of becoming the emperor of India took over his mind and heart. And finally, he declared himself the emperor in Delhi. He formed a large army to protect his kingdom and himself and came to the field of Panipat to defeat the Mughals.

Events of the Second Battle of Panipat

Once again two armies gathered at the Panipat field where a fierce battle had taken place 30 years ago. Hemu's army had 1,00,000 horsemen, 1,000 elephants, 51 big and 500 light cannons. According to Abul Fazal, Hemu's army was 50,000 and Akbar's army was 20,000. Akbar had set up his camp in Thanesar and Hemu in Panipat. In such a situation, Akbar sent an army of 10,000 horsemen under the leadership of Ali Quli Khan to Panipat to assess Hemu's strength. Hemu also sent his artillery a little ahead under the leadership of Mubarak Khan and Bahadur Khan. Ali Quli Khan attacked them as soon as he saw them. Hemu's artillery was not very powerful, so the Mughals captured Hemu's artillery. The loss of artillery from Hemu's hands weakened Hemu's army considerably. Bairam Khan boosted the morale of his victorious soldiers and made them swear not to retreat from the battlefield.

Hemu divided his army into three parts from the Panipat battlefield. He himself was in command of the central part. He had 30,000 Afghan and Rajput horsemen and 500 elephants with him. Saadi Khan was in command of the right side. The battle started from Hemu's side. The central part of the Mughal army moved forward under the leadership of Bairam Khan and Mughal general Ali Quli Khan attacked Hemu from behind. Hemu's chieftains Saadi Khan Kukkad and Bhagwan Das were killed. An arrow hit Hemu's eye and went out tearing the pupil. Hemu fainted. When he regained consciousness, he took out the arrow from his eye, due to which the pupil came out and Hemu once again fainted. Hemu's *mahout* took Hemu towards the forests but Ali Quli Khan caught him and killed him. The victorious Mughal army left for Delhi and the rule of the Mughal dynasty was established again under Akbar.

Hemu's Fall

During the Afghan ruler Adil Shah (1553-55), Humayun again turned to Delhi. Humayun, with the advice of his adviser Bairam Khan, defeated Adil Shah's brother Sikandar Sur in Punjab and took control of Punjab, Delhi and Agra. After the Afghan defeat, Hemu went to Bengal along with Adil Shah. When Hemu received the news of Humayun's death in January 1556, he marched towards Delhi *via* Etawah, Kalpi with a large army. Defeating the Mughal chieftains on the way, he increased his army and reached Agra and defeated Sikandar Khan Uzbek and drove him away. Then Delhi Governor Tardi Beg was also defeated in Tughlakabad and fled to Sirhind. After all these victories, Hemu himself became the emperor of Delhi.

On 5 November, 1556, a battle took place between Hemu and Akbar's army in the plains of Panipat. Hemu was defeated in this battle and was killed. Although Hemu was a brave soldier and commander, he had the courage to fight, but his military acumen was much less than that of Bairam Khan. Hemu lost as his army was large because the artillery had already slipped out of his hands. When the strong cannons of the Mughals fired shells on Hemu's army, Hemu's elephants started running away after crushing their own soldiers. Overall, all the circumstances were against Hemu and Hemu had never commanded such a large army before. An arrow suddenly entering Hemu's eye also became the reason for his defeat and downfall. Hemu was killed in this battle and most of his chieftains and soldiers were killed.

After Akbar's victory, he regained the lost kingdom. Enemies were selectively avenged and thousands of Afghans were wiped out. A military contingent was also sent to Hemu's ancestral village Rewari. His 80 year-old father was killed. All the relatives along with the entire treasure were brought to Delhi and after a few years they were freed.

Here it could be seen that the Mughals and Afghans struggled for decades for the power of Delhi. Ultimately, the Mughals won and their rule lasted for many centuries. A general named Hemu also became the ruler for some time due to circumstances, but when the same favourable circumstances which made him successful became unfavourable, he fell. The ammunition and cannons were used extensively in India and these cannons proved that whoever had more of them would be victorious. However, the foundation of a new dynasty, the Mughal dynasty, was laid in whose hands the future of India was.

10

Raja Hasan Khan Mewati, the Hero of Haryana

Raja Hasan Khan (c. 1517-1527), popularly known as Raja Hasan Khan Mewati, was virtually ruling Mewat area in Haryana and Rajasthan from his capital at Alwar during the lifetime of his father Alawal Khan before 1527. It is said that around 1517, Hasan Khan was started to rule the Mewat region in the lifetime of his father Alawal Khan. During that time the ruler Alawal Khan was too old to take important decisions of his government. The date of his accession is not sure, and it is also not sure that his coronation took place or not, but it is the fact that Hasan Khan was ruling the area of Mewat from the time of Ibrahim Khan Lodi as his father Alawal Khan was too old in age. Hasan Khan's formal coronation after his father's death could not have taken place as his father was found dead in his camp in the battlefield of Khanwa and thereafter Hasan Khan was also killed in the battlefield in fighting with Babur. Being the brother-in-law of the ruling monarch Ibrahim Lodi, Hasan Khan had full power and position at the Delhi Court.

Although, Ibrahim Lodi was infamous in his nobility and kinsmen but Hasan Khan always favoured him at the times of distress. Henry Frederick Malcolm writes that by a course of cruelty, misgovernment, arrogant behaviour, ill-treatment, and oppression,

Ibrahim Lodi alienated the affections of his people from his family and at length drove his nobles to open rebellion who formed secret conspiracies against him. All the provinces like Bengal, Jaunpur, Malwa, Gujarat, and other outlying provinces become independent. The Eastern districts of Awadh and Bihar took up arms against him. Daulat Khan Lodi, the governor of the Punjab and Alam Khan, uncle of Ibrahim, revolted against the ruling Sultan and invited Babur to relieve India of the tyrant. Rana Sangram also made overtures to Babur and asked him to intervene.

Babur advanced towards Panipat with the strong military of 12,000 against 1,00,000 forces of his enemy Ibrahim Lodi. The two forces met at Panipat in April 1526. In this fateful battle of Panipat, Hasan Khan along with his father Alawal Khan, favoured the imperial army and send a force under his son Nahar Khan in the battlefield. Hasan Khan was the nominal feudatory of Delhi Sultanate and enjoyed full independent power to rule his own country of Mewat. Babur became victorious and Ibrahim was slain during the battle. Nahar Khan, the son of Hasan Khan was also kept in Mughal captivity.

After the battle of Panipat, Babur realized the importance of Hasan Khan and started negotiations with him by alluring Nahar Khan, who was in his captivity. Some quotes of Babur need to be mentioned to fully understand about Hasan Khan. Babur says in his Memoir as follows:

> "The country of Mewat lies not far from Delhi, and yields revenue of three or four crores. Hassan Khan Mewati had received the government of that country from his ancestors, who had governed it, in uninterrupted succession, for nearly two hundred years. They had yielded an imperfect kind of submission to the Sultans of Delhi. The Sultans of Hind, whether from the extent of their territories, from want of opportunity, or from obstacles opposed by the mountainous nature of the country, had never subdued Mewat. They had never been able to reduce

> it to order, and were content to receive such a degree of obedience as was tendered to them."

In India, Babur wanted to win Hasan Khan in his favour but he made an alliance with Rana Sanga, the prime opponent of Babur. Babur again says about Hasan Khan,

> "After my conquest of Hind, following the example of former Sultans, I also had shown Hasan Khan distinguished marks of favour. Yet this ungrateful man, whose affections lay all on the side of the Pagans, this infidel, regardless of my favours and without any sense of the kindness and distinction with which he had been treated, was the grand promoter and leader of all the commotions and rebellions that ensued, as has been related."

In order to get the favour of Hasan Khan, Babur set free to Nahar Khan, the son of Hasan Khan, who was his prisoner from the time of Battle of Panipat. According to Babur,

> "...Nahar Khan, Hassan Khan's son. I again received him into favour, and bestowed on him a *Pargana* of several lakhs for his support.... I bestowed on Sultan (Chin Timur Sultan) the city of Tijara, which was the capital of Mewat, granting him at the same time a settled provision of fifty lakhs. To Tardi Khan, ... I gave an appointment of fifteen lakhs, with the charge of the fort of Alwar."

By the statements of Babur, it becomes clear that he wanted Hasan Khan to become a feudatory chief of some parts of Mewat area and mere an assistant in matters of Mewat administration and subjugation of other Indian *rajas*. Babur was fully aware of the political importance of Mewat and wanted to hold it through his governors. Hence, he divided the country of Mewat into three regions, Alwar and Tijara to his own men and remaining Mewat for Nahar Khan. However, Hasan Khan instead of felling in the allurement of his coreligionist, preferred to join the alliance to drive out the invader. Rushbrooke Williams mentions as, "Sangram Singh and Hasan Khan Mewati, an unholy alliance whose only bond of union was a common desire to expel Babur from India."

Rushbrook has quoted from Babur that after the battle of Panipat, the Indian rulers became independent of Delhi and started a campaign against Babur. Kasim Sambhali set himself up in Sambhal, Nizam Khan in Bayana, Hasan Khan Mewati in Mewat, Mohammad Zaitun in Dholpur, Tatar Khan Sarang-Khani in Gwalior, Husain Khan Lohani in Rabiri, Kutub Khan in Etawa, Alam Khan in Kalpi, according to Babur, were the promoters of all the agitations and disturbances, which surrounded him. Among all the above-mentioned people Babur considered Hasan Khan most dangerous one. Babur himself called Raja Hassan Khan Mewati as an infidel, the prime mover, and agitator in all these confusions and insurrections. Babur called Rana Sanga as one-eyed *Dajjal.*

Babur received the information that Hasan Khan and Rana Sanga were in open rebellion and had collected a large force in Mewat. Following the information about the rebellion, Babur ordered for the enlistment of new troops, and Ibrahim's treasures were distributed among the army. Elliot & Dowson have cited Ahmad Yadgar's quotation, of his *Tarikh-e-Salatin-e-Afghana* that, Hasan Khan was a man of royal descent from several generations, and his family had possessed regal power from the time of Firoz Shah Tughlaq. Rana Sanga, who was at that time a powerful chief sent a message to Hasan Khan saying, "The Mughals have entered Hindustan, have slain Sultan Ibrahim, and taken possession of the country. It is evident that they will, likewise, send an army against both of us, if you will side with me, we will be allies, and not suffer them to take possession."

Rana Sanga showed himself to Hasan Khan as the caretaker and well-wisher of Hindustan but in a real sense he was a big opportunist which is being proven by Babur's own words. Babur says in his Memoir about Rana Sanga,

> "Although Rana Sanga, the pagan, when I was in Kabul, had sent me an ambassador with professions of attachment, and had arranged with me, that, if I would march from that quarter into the vicinity of Delhi, he would march from the other side upon Agra; yet, when I defeated Ibrahim, and took Delhi and Agra, the pagan, during all my operations, did not make a single movement."

Defeating the allied force under Rana Sanga was an anxious moment for Babur. His men were quaking in anticipation of the struggle with their unknown foes. Babur himself says,

> "At length, observing the universal discouragement of my troops, and their total want of spirit, I formed my plan. I called an assembly of all the Amirs and officers, and addressed them:
> 'Noblemen and soldiers! Every man that comes into the world is subject to dissolution. When we are passed away and gone, God only survives unchangeable. Whoever comes to the feast of life must, before it is over, drink from the cup of death. He who arrives at the inn of mortality must one day inevitably take his departure from that house of sorrow—the world. How much better is it to die with honour than to live with infamy!'"

By quoting the couplet from Firdausi's *Shahnama*:

> "With fame, even if I die, I am contented;
> Let fame be mine, since my body is Death's"

He continued,

> "The Most High God has been propitious to us, and has now placed us in such a crisis, that if we fall in the field, we die the death of martyrs; if we survive, we rise victorious, the avengers of the cause of God. Let us,

> then, with one accord, swear on God's holy word, that none of us will even think of turning his face from this warfare, nor desert from the battle and slaughter that ensues, till his soul is separated from his body."

At that memorable speech, he swore for renunciation of wine, broke his drinking cups, poured out the stores of liquor on the ground, and promulgated his total-abstinence manifesto to the army. It was a time for solemn vows of reformation, and in common with many of his followers the Emperor adopted the usual token of a pledge, by letting his beard grow. The count of forces of Babur was not known, but Rana Sanga along with his two lakh men had a very large following. The chiefs of Bhilsa, Sihuddin had 30,000 horse; Hasan Khan of Mewat had 12,000 horses; Rawal Udai Singh of Dongarpur with 10,000 horses; Medini Rai of Chanderi with 10,000 horses; Barmal Idri with 4,000 horses; Nirpat Hada with 7,000 horses; Sitter of Kuchh with 6,000 horses; Dharm Deo—4,000 horses; Narsing Deo 4,000 horses, and Mahmud Lodi, brother of the late Sultan Ibrahim, another claimant for the throne, had collected a body of 10,000 mercenaries to support his pretensions.

In this battle which was fought at Kanwaha in 1527, Babur again became victorious by leaving behind thousands of dead. Raja Hasan Khan Mewati and other associated were among the slain. Rana Sanga retreated over the hills of Mewat, having announced his fixed determination never to re-enter Chittor but with victory. Had his life been spared to his country, he might have redeemed the pledge; but the year following his defeat was the last of his existence, and he died at Baswa, on the frontier of Mewat, not without suspicion of poison. Babur says in his Memoir about the slain in the battlefield,

> "Many were slain, and fell in the battle, and some giving up their lives for lost, turned to the desert of ruin, and became the food of crows and kites and hillocks were formed of the slain, and towers raised of their heads. Hassan Khan Mewati was enrolled in the

band of the dead by a matchlock shot."

Elliot & Dowson mention, as quoted in the translation of *Tarikh-e-Salatin-e-Afghana* of Ahmad Yadgar, a slight different story:

> "Mirza Hindal and Mohammad Mehdi Khwaja, the king's son-in-law were sent with an immense army, which was shortly afterwards followed by Babur himself. When Hasan Khan was informed of the approach of the victorious army, he sent to tell Rana Sanga of it. Upon this, the Rana left his home, and assembled an army of Hindus with the intention of making war. He marched and joined Hasan Khan, and prepared for action in the plains near Firozpur Jhirka. Rana Sanga placed Hasan Khan on the right, and took up his own post on the left. As he was secretly displeased with Hasan Khan, he determined to ensnare and ruin him. He, therefore, privately sent a Vakil to Mirza Hindal and Khwaja Mehdi, to say that he was the slave and obedient servant of the King, and that he consented to the reading of the *Khutba* and the coining of money in His Majesty's name; that Hasan Khan had compelled him to go to war, but that he would not fight the royal troops, but retire early; and that they should make arrangements so that Hasan might be either captured or slain, as in the event of his death, they would obtain the country of Mewat."

Ahmad Yadgar further narrates:

> "When the battle began, and both parties were slaughtering each other. Mehdi Khwaja attacked Hasan Khan, who was unable to contend with him, and after a short enforcement took to flight, and his soldiers were scattered all over the country. Lad Khan, a slave of Hasan Khan, having displeased him, joined his

> brothers, and by their advice behaved with infidelity towards his benefactor. When Hasan Khan had been forsaken by all his friends and followers, and no one remained with him, he arrived at a well, and said to his servant, 'If you have anything to eat, bring it.' He brought some cakes and roast meat, and placed them before him. He had eaten only a few morsels, when a noble of Shah Babur arrived. Hasan Khan arose in a state of confusion, with the intention of mounting, when his servant drew his sword on him, wounded him, and threw him into the well; after which, he seized his horse, and fled. After his flight, Hindu Beg pursued and plundered his army, none of whom attempted to resist. The troops of the vanquisher of the Universe obtained immense booty in horses, camels etc., and gained a great victory."

Nahar Khan carried away his father Hasan Khan Mewati's dead body to Tijara and buried him in the complex of the mosque built by Hasan Khan in his lifetime. Nahar Khan constructed a dome over the grave. Nahar Khan also established his rule over the area of Tijara.

Raja Hasan Khan Mewati was a brave and loyal subordinate of Ibrahim Lodi. His fight with the Babur in Panipat was not because of any political motives but sided with Lodis to prove his loyalty to his suzerain. Another reason for supporting the Lodis was that Hasan Khan was the real cousin of Ibrahim Lodi. However, unfortunately, he was defeated along with his master. He passed the restless day and night on the repeated call of his inner sense for the revenge as the defeat has blotted on his political career. He found it a fair chance to take the revenge when Rana Sanga appealed to him to join against the Babur. He had not only given his military support to Rana but also played a leading role to manage the confederacy. However, perhaps due to the treachery he was unable to achieve the goal. He was not the power hungry but a master of his own will. He did what his inner sense allowed.

A local poet has very beautifully written about Hasan Khan in the following couplets:

> "*Dhaulo Anda Titar Ko, Aur Daulo Hi Chaubaro Re,*
> *Kood Pado Langda Ko Poto, Nau Sau Gai Sanbhalo Re,*
> *Lakho To Mero Lakh Taka Ko, Dahi Doodh So Palo Re,*
> *Doodh Dahi Ko Bhooko Na Hai, Pani Ko Lapsayo Re,*
> *Agam Dekho Pichham Dekho, Kahin Na Paani Payo Re,*
> *Lal Das Ki Kothi Chal Rahi, Jaaye Jar Jhukayo Re*"

[His (Hasan Khan's) palace was white in colour and looked like a white egg of Partridge. Hasan Khan, the grandson of lame (Zakaria Khan) jumped into the war (against Babur), was the owner of nine hundred cows (a proverb for the richest man). His annual income was one lakh *tanka* from his kingdom, and he was grown up eating with curd and milk. However, he was thirsty for water (divine thirst) not of the curd and milk. He looked forward and backward (all around) but could not find the water (divine blessings). Eventually, he drank the divine water (blessed of benevolence) from a *Sufi* Saint Lal Das, who was very famous at that time.]

11

Revolt of Jats and Satnamis

There were many rebellions in India during the Mughal period. Some of these were for a short period of time and some lasted for a long time. Jats, Mewatis and Satnamis were prominent among these rebellions, which took place in Haryana during the reign of Mughal emperor Aurangzeb. It is very strange that during the period of Aurangzeb, India had to face the most rebellions despite being the most powerful empire. Jat and Satnami rebellions were among them which were held in Haryana.

Resistance of the Jats

The Jats are a hardy tribe, pre-eminently agricultural, and well known for their valour, indefatigable energy, martial spirit and untiring perseverance. The region mainly occupied by them may be roughly defined as the whole Pakistan and in India western Uttar Pradesh, Punjab, Haryana, Rajasthan and some areas of Madhya Pradesh. All of them do not belong to the same religious fraternity but prefer different religions, viz. Hinduism, Sikhism and Islam, and they take their tribal name as a proud heritage. The origin of the Jats, like that of the Rajputs, has been a subject of keen controversy. Some regard them as descendants of the nomadic Scythian hordes of Central Asia who invaded India through the north-western passes like the Sakas and the Hunas settled in India. Now the theory of Aryan origin is more acceptable as of the Meos and Rajputs. The Jats claim that they are descendants of the ancient Yadavas.

In 1669, the Jat peasants rose under their leader Gokla, the zamindar of Tilpat. Seizing the occasion of Aurangzeb being in the Deccan near to Bijapur, they proved that they cared neither for his power, his policy, nor his governors. They planned, and succeeded in, a very bold undertaking. The faujdar of Mathura Abdun Nabi, who opposed them, was slain in the action. The rebels then sacked the pargana of Sadabad, and disorder and confusion followed in the neighbouring district of Agra also. Gokla assembled twenty thousand men, met the Mughal army under Hasan Ali Khan, faujdar of Mathura, at a place twenty miles off from Tilpat. Gokla was defeated with the loss of 5,000 men and seven thousand Jats with Gokla and his family were made prisoner. Mughals also met a heavy loss of 4,000 men. Gokla was eventually slain at Agra.

But the spirit which Gokla had infused into his men did not die with him, and after several years, other capable leader Rajaram, son of Bhajja Singh, chief of Sinsini, took his place against the Mughals. Rajaram made Deeg the capital and later Bharatpur became the capital of Jats. He gave military training to the Jat peasants, equipped them with fire-arms, and gave them the semblance of an organized and regular army. They carried on plundering raids on this highway and the suburbs of Agra. The emperor's long stay in the Deccan and consequent military weakness in northern India had encouraged them to plunder the ill-guarded rich convoys passing through their region.

Under Rajaram, a great number of Jats assembled and marched to the mausoleum of Akbar at Sikandara. They began their pillage by breaking in the great gates of bronze which it had, robbing the valuable precious stones and plates of gold and silver, and destroying what they were not able to carry away. The Jat leader Rajaram even tried to ransack Akbar's tomb, which was foiled by Faujdar Mir Abul Fazl. A fierce fight followed and Raja Ram was driven back after losing about 400 of his men.

In 1688, Mahabat Khan, on his way from Gujarat to his new government of Lahor, was encamped at Sikandara, and, taking the field against the Jats, killed 400 of them. At this time Shaistah Khan, the Emperor's uncle, was appointed governor; but, before he took charge, the Jats renewed their attack on Sikandara, and plundered the tomb, taking the carpets, with the silver and gold vessels, and damaging most of the tombs and the mausoleum. However, Rajaram sacked the tomb of Akbar, and damaging the building, carried away carpets, lamps, precious stones, and gold and silver vessels etc.

Their actions grew more shocking that they even desecrated the Emperor Akbar's remains from his grave. Attacking the dead emperor's remains was an act of deep disrespect to the departed soul. Throwing relics, as has been written of earlier, reportedly into a fire was a clear sign of Hindu rebellion against Mughal. Highly perturbed at the atrocious deeds of the Jats, Aurangzeb sent his seventeen year's grandson Bedar Bakht to take charge of the military operations against them. In July 1688, a severe battle was fought between them and the Jat leader Rajaram was killed by a Mughal musketeer who was hiding in a tree. Bedar Bakht then besieged the fort of Sinsani in 1690. Meanwhile, Bishan Singh Kachhwaha, Raja of Amer (Jaipur), who had been appointed faujdar of Mathura with special duty of suppressing the Jats besieged the fort of Sogor on 21 May, 1691. Thus, fell the two important strongholds of the Jats, and their power was humbled for the time being but not crushed permanently.

After Rajaram, his successor Churaman (1688-1723) became the head of the Jats. After the death of Aurangzeb, Bahadur Shah I accepted the political position of Churaman. The entire Haryana between Rajasthan and Delhi was under Churaman. After Churaman, Badan Singh (1723-55) and then Surajmal (1755-63) became the Jat rulers.

Surajmal strengthened the Jat power from Bharatpur. He was a clever, fearless and powerful ruler. Because of his cleverness he is also called Socrates of Jats. His kingdom included Agra, Mathura,

Bharatpur, Dholpur, Mainpuri, Hathras, Aligarh, Etawah in Uttar Pradesh and Rohtak, Farrukhnagar, Mewat, Rewari, Gurgaon etc. in Haryana.

After the defeat of the Marathas in the third battle of Panipat, Surajmal's popularity increased significantly in North India. He gave the responsibility of Haryana to his son Jawahar Singh. At that time, Sawaliya dacoit in Mewat had the protection of Baloch Sardar Asadullah Khan of Tauru. Jawahar Singh wanted to arrest Sawaliya but the Sardar of Tauru was not allowing this to happen. Nawab Musabi Khan of Farrukhnagar was also with Nawab Asadullah Khan of Tauru in this work. Both of them defeated Jawahar Singh in the war. When Jawahar Singh attacked for the second time, Surajmal was also with him. This time Jats were victorious on 12 December, 1763. Surajmal deceitfully imprisoned Musabi Khan along with his family. This action of Surajmal angered his old friend Najeeb Khan.

Surajmal next attacked Najib Khan Ruhela. In this battle, Surajmal was killed on 25 December, 1764 and the Jats were defeated. But some Jat Sardars were still saving Jat power in Haryana. Najib attacked Buwana village of Sonipat in Haryana. About 2000 Jats were killed in this war. After this victory, Najib attacked Bhiwani (October 1765) in which thousands of people were killed. In this way, Ruhela Sardar Najib freed Haryana from Jat power.

After Najib's death in 1770, Mirza Najaf Khan took over the Mughal command. Najaf Khan recaptured Agra by defeating Jat Raja Nawal Singh (1771-1776), the successor of Jat Raja Jawahar Singh (1764-1771). Najaf Khan also defeated Naval's successor Ranjit Singh (1776-1805).

Causes of Jat Resistance

The following were the reasons for the Jats to oppose the Mughals and establish their own power:

(i) The condition of the farmers had worsened due to continuous famines and most of the Jats were farmers.

In such a situation of misery of the farmers during the reign of Aurangzeb, the cruel collection of taxes made the condition of the Jat farmers worse. All the Jats became anti-government. In such a situation, they started looting, especially the government treasury and the equipment of the army. This resistance of the farmers turned into a rebellion.

(ii) Aurangzeb spent almost half of his ruling years in waging war with the Muslim kings of the South India. In such a situation, arbitrary rule of the chieftains was going on in North India due to which the farmers became rebellious. They not only rebelled but also declared themselves chieftaincy by electing their leader. The absence of Aurangzeb emboldened these rebellious chieftains. But Aurangzeb did not give them much importance and did not return to Delhi from the South. In such a situation, the rebellious Jats tried to establish an independent state and were successful to a great extent. This would certainly never have been possible in the presence of Aurangzeb.

(iii) Initially, the Jats were having their confrontation with rajput king Jai Singh but as the rajputs under Jai Singh were favouring the Mughals, the Jats under Gokula began to target the Mughals.

(iv) Some historians connect the Jat rebellion with the religious policy of Aurangzeb. But this has nothing to do with reality and this theory has been deliberately created to increase Hindu-Muslim animosity. The whole matter was economic and the Jats had planned to establish a separate state on the basis of their bravery. The rebellion was started by Gokula and he had refused to pay taxes to Mathura's Faujdar Abdun Nabi. This non-payment of taxes led a war between the two and Abdun Nabi was killed. Later, Gokula also looted the royal treasury of Mathura. Abdun Nabi's successor Hasan Ali Khan took revenge from Gokula in 1669 and achieved victory by killing him.

Satnami Rebellion

In Haryana, during the reign of Aurangzeb, the farmers of Narnaul, who are called Satnamis, revolted. Like the Jats, this revolt was also over the collection of agricultural tax. The Satnami sect was a part of the Hindu sect. Satnami considered himself the descendant of the devotees of Ravidas, the famous saint of the *Bhakti* movement. This sect was founded in 1657 by a saint named Veerbhan in Narnaul, Haryana state. Despite being a Hindu, he worshipped the true God (Satnam) apart from Brahminist ideology and idol worship. The way of worshipping them was that while chanting Satnam, these people got absorbed in devotion and had direct contact with God. Most of the people of this sect were from the lower class of Hindu society which mainly included tanners, sweepers (*Bhangi*), carpenters, goldsmiths, farmers etc. Due to this there was no caste system. Like saints, they wore simple clothes and had their heads shaved. They did not consume meat and liquor.

The Satnamis were good warriors who used to give a befitting reply to the oppressors by staying organized. According to Saki Mustaid Khan, the author of "*Mashir-e-Alamgiri*", the Satnamis were a helpless group of goldsmiths, carpenters, sweepers, leather workers and other artisan and craftsmen castes. Their arrogant mind was completely dark. Rebellious arrogance had taken root in their minds and their heads had become very heavy on their shoulders. It is written in the early land revenue papers of the Mughal period that the Satnamis were very rebellious people.

Satnamis were mostly involved in agriculture and some business. They were honest, hardworking and remained united by maintaining mutual brotherhood. According to Mughal administrator Khafi Khan,

> "These people used to wear clothes like devotees but did agriculture and business. However, their business was on a small scale. In matters of religion, they had established the name of truth which was the meaning of Satnami. It was forbidden for them to earn money

> other than their sustenance. If someone exploited or oppressed them or imposed authority on them, they did not tolerate it. Most of them kept arms or weapons."

As they used to shave their head and face including eye-brows, they were popularly called Mundiyas or Mundas. According to their belief they used to take bath on every full moon in Pohkar Lake west of Ajmer which was their place of pilgrimage. They collect from all directions at that place of pilgrimage, adjoining the country of Kirat Singh, younger son of Raja Jai Singh. A formidable rising of the Satnamis took place in the districts of Narnaul and Mewat which were their native place. In 1672, a petty quarrel near Narnaul between a Satnami cultivator and a Mughul foot-soldier of the local revenue collector led to the outbreak.

There was a squabble between the two parties over a tax related matter and a fight broke out in which one Satanami was injured. In such a situation, many Satnamis gathered and beat a revenue collector to death. When the news reached the royal officer (Shikdar) of Narnaul, he sent a military contingent to settle the matter. The Satnamis defeated the soldiers and snatched away the arms. Some Satnamis gave a religious colour to this dispute that started over economic matters and gathered all the Satnamis under one flag who tied a shroud on their heads and jumped into the war.

In these circumstances on the occasion of full moon the Satnamis gather from all directions at a place of pilgrimage, the assembly amounted to some twenty-five thousand upon the bathing-day. After the bathing ceremonies were completed, an old sorceress told them that if they would follow her orders she would make them masters of the city of Delhi, the king not having more than ten thousand horsemen, because all his other troops had gone with Shah Alam on the expedition against Shivaji.

K.C. Yadav says that an old woman encouraged his courage and enthusiasm by saying that she would recite such a mantra that the enemy's weapons would not have any effect on the Satnamis fighting under her flag and even if any Satnamis were killed, his

80 Satnami will stand at the place. The morale of the Satnamis increased so much that when Faujdar Tahir Khan attacked, he was defeated by the Satnamis. They looted the entire Narnaul city, demolished mosques and took over the administration of the district by establishing their own government. According to Saki Mustaid Khan, the Satnamis believed that they were repeating the war of *Mahabharata*.

The Satnamis agreed to the proposal of the old sorceress and marched towards their homeland Narnaul with such vigour that when the news reached the court Aurangzeb was particularly disturbed in mind, and sent out against them his ten thousand horsemen. The Mundas fought with such vigour, upheld by the sorceries of the old woman, that they routed Aurangzeb's army. At this result he was more disturbed than ever. They had already arrived within fifteen leagues (45 miles) of Delhi, when he ordered out all the troops he had been able to raise. But Aurangzeb felt that these men would never have undertaken such a great attempt without the help of sorcery.

To suppress the Satnamis, Aurangzeb sent an army of ten thousand to Narnaul on March 15, 1672, along with experienced chieftains like Prince Mohammad Akbar, Razandan Khan, Hamid Khan, Sayyad Khan, Madiya Khan, Dabi Khan, Kamaluddin Perol Mewati, Shakdaryar Bakshi etc. There was a rumor in the Mughal army that the Satnamis defeated the Mughals with small weapons by relying on magic. Aurangzeb also wrote out himself several papers, and sent them to be hung on the heads of the elephants and horses, and on the standards, fatiguing himself greatly with the preparation of all those papers. As soon as the war started, 5000 Satnamis attacked the Mughal army like hawks. Almost all the Satnami people were killed in this war. The spells of Aurangzeb prevailed over those of the old woman, and the two thousand Mundas of this sect fell fighting on the field and many of them were killed during the pursuit including the old woman herself. The rebellion was thus crushed and the affected areas brought under control. The remaining Satnami migrated to other places. Satnamis still could be found in Bhandar village of Rajpur district of Madhya Pradesh.

Reasons of Satnamis Rebellion

The rebellion of the Satnamis during the reign of Aurangzeb was so terrible that it disturbed and shaken the machinery of the government. The reasons for this rebellion were as follows:

(i) In 1670, a countrywide famine broke the backs of all the farmers, labourers and traders. Almost all the people were affected by this famine. In such a situation, the Mughal government was placing more emphasis on tax collection rather than help. Collecting taxes from the starving people was not only a difficult task but also a risky one. There were frequent clashes between tax collecting employees and local people. A minor clash in a village of Karnal turned into a huge rebellion of Satnamis. The initial victory of the Satnamis in this rebellion greatly boosted their morale and it began to be believed that some other invisible power was helping the Satnamis.

(ii) Aurangzeb's officers' method of collecting taxes was very harsh and cruel. Farmers and other people suffering from famine were unable to pay taxes. In such a situation, forced tax collection was testing people's patience. When government employees did not get money even forcibly in the form of taxes, they used to insult the taxpayer. The Satnamis, who were ready to sacrifice their lives for their honour, took up arms and went out for rebellion and were successful in the beginning.

(iii) Aurangzeb's *Jaziya* tax was a heavy burden for the Hindu people during the famine. If people were unable to pay the land tax then how would they pay the *Jaziya* tax. Apart from this, this tax was to be paid only by Hindus and not by Muslims, it was promoting discrimination. The Satnamis took up arms against this and revolted.

(iv) Some authors also consider Aurangzeb's religious policy responsible for this rebellion. But most historians are not satisfied with this fact. The Satnamis neither completely believed in Hindu religion nor worshipped idols, nor did they believe in the caste system or Hindu scriptures. If Aurangzeb's policy was anti-Hindu then how was it anti-Satnami? No Hindu caste or sect even helped the Satnamis in their rebellion. The Satnamis themselves had given it a religious colour to unite everyone against the Mughals. They demolished many mosques in Narnaul city and district and started collecting taxes himself and established the Satnami government.

In this chapter it has been seen that during the Mughal rule, mainly during the reign of Aurangzeb, many powers like Jats, Sikhs, Marathas, Satnamis etc. emerged. It seems strange that these powers succeeded in the presence of a strict ruler like Aurangzeb, but it is true. The *Jaziya* tax, Aurangzeb's absence from North India for twenty-five years and the morale of the native powers were mainly responsible for this. In Haryana, the Jats and Satnamis, who were mainly farmers and artisans, raised the flag of rebellion. The Satnamis were defeated because till their rebellion, the Mughal emperor was present in North India, i.e. Delhi. But at the time of the Jats' rebellion, Aurangzeb was engaged in a war with Muslim kings in South India, so the Jat power did not end.

12

Provincial Administration, Irrigation and Revenue System under Mughals in Haryana

Mughal administration or governance was a mixture of Iranian, Arabic and Indian elements. According to Jadunath Sarkar, "It was an Indian version of the Iranian and Arabic system. The system of governance of the Abbasi Caliph of Iraq was the most favourite system of governance of the Mughals." But on establishing their rule in India, they also included those indigenous elements in their system of governance whose utility had been proved after long-term use. Apart from the governance system, the taxation system, irrigation system, justice and trade system were also implemented according to Indian interests. These system were so practical that even the British who ruled later did not make any significant changes in it.

Provincial Administration in Mughal Period Haryana

Mughal Emperor Akbar made few changes in the administrative system of Sher Shah Suri and divided his vast empire into a total of 15 provinces—Kabul, Delhi, Agra, Ajmer, Awadh, Lahore, Bihar, Allahabad, Ahmadnagar, Berar, Bidar, Malwa, Khandesh, Ahmadabad and Bengal. Akbar divided all the provinces into Sarkars and the Sarkars into Parganas. During the time of Akbar, a large part of Haryana region came under Delhi province and some part under Agra province. The chief officers of the province and their duties were as follows:

Subedar or Army Commander or Nazim: He was the head of the provincial administration and the commander of the provincial army. During the time of Akbar, he came to be known as Subedar or Nazim. His main tasks were to maintain peace in the province; to administer justice impartially; to encourage agriculture, industry and trade; to construct roads, wells, canals, hospitals etc. for the people of the province; supporting the revenue employees; suppressing small rebellions etc.

Diwan: Diwan was the official of the finance department in the provinces, who was appointed by the emperor himself. Diwan was actually a kind of restriction on the subedar who gave every information about the state to the emperor. Its functions were to keep accounts of the income and expenditure of the province; to make arrangements for the care of the provincial treasury; Determining land tax and making proper arrangements for collection; providing loans to farmers as per need; to decide civil cases; giving information about the condition of farmers to the central Diwan etc.

Bakshi: Like the central Mir Bakshi, there was also a provincial Bakshi. Its functions were to recruit provincial soldiers and maintain discipline among them; inspecting horses from time to time; strengthening military organization; taking part in campaigns with soldiers on the orders of the king etc. Many times he also worked as the head of the intelligence department.

Sadar or Qazi: The king used to appoint the Sadar on the advice of the central Sadar. He was the head of the charity and religious department and he was also the chief justice of the province. He used to decide all the cases except revenue related disputes. Sometimes, when there was more work, the Qazi and Sadar used to be separate.

Wakia Navis: Wakia Navis used to give information to the emperor about the events happening in the state and the work of the government employees in the province. Under him there were many spies and writers who always used to roam around the state.

Kotwal: In the provinces, the head of the cities was the Kotwal or police officer. His main tasks were to establish peace in the city; to manage the cleanliness of the city; to keep a watch on mischievous elements; managing the cemetery and cremation ground and taking care of the foreigners coming to the city.

Administration of Sarkars

Akbar had divided his province into several Sarkars. The Sarkars into which he had divided the Haryana region were as follows:

(i) **Rewari Sarkar:** Rewari had great political importance. It had parganas like Pataudi, Bawal, Rewari, Gohana, Rativas, Sohna, Bhoda etc.

(ii) **Delhi Sarkar:** It included the parganas of Jharsa, Panipat, Jhajjar, Palwal, Beri, Gannaur, Karnal, Modausi etc. of Haryana.

(iii) **Agra Sarkar:** It included the parganas of Pahari, Hodal, Jhirka, Umri, Kotla, Nanehra, Tijara, Nagina, Indri and Nuh from Haryana region.

(iv) **Narnaul Sarkar:** Narnaul Sarkar included the parganas of Narhedi, Kanhauri, Kanode, Barha, Khadana, Baroda, Khandevala etc.

(v) **Hisar Sarkar:** Hisar Sarkar was very big. It included parganas like Sirsa, Asakhera, Dhatrat, Agroha, Hisar, Bhogiwal, Jamalpur, Aharoni, Jind, Punian, Sheoran, Bhadangi, Sidhmukh, Barwala, Bhiwani, Bhattu, Shanjada-Dehat, Birwa, Fatehabad etc.

(vi) **Sirhind Sarkar:** It included the parganas of Thanesar, Ambala, Dogal, Sultanpur, Baraur, Khizrabad, Pundri, Mustafabad, Shahbad, Kaithal etc.

Mughal Emperor Akbar had appointed the following officers for the management of the government:

(i) **Faujdar:** Faujdar was the military and executive officer of the Sarkar. He maintained peace and order in the Sarkar. A small military contingent was also under his authority. He helped the Amil in collecting land tax.

(ii) **Amalguzar or Amil:** He was the head of the government's finance department. His main functions were—to take care of the comforts of the farmers; to investigate legal cases and the registers of the Patwaris; to inform the higher officials about the condition of agriculture and the prices of the markets; to improve barren land; to classify fertile land on the basis of land produce or fertility power etc.

(iii) **Bitikachi:** Apart from being an assistant to Amalgujar, Bitikachi was also his opponent. He used to prepare records related to land produce and give receipts to the farmers for paying the taxes. It also determined the boundaries of the village.

(iv) **Khazandar or Potdar:** Every Sarkar had a Khazandar or treasurer who kept the money collected from the farmers safe. One key of the treasury was with the Khazandar and one key was with the Amalguzar.

Administration of Pargana

Akbar had divided the Sarkars of his states into Parganas. Officers and employees were appointed for each Pargana. The major parganas of the Sarkars in Haryana were—Fatehabad, Jhajjar, Palwal, Tausham, Panipat, Dujana, Beri, Barwala, Safidon, Karnal, Pataudi, Sonipat, Indri, Gohana, Hodal, Thanesar, Ambala, Kaithal etc. There were the following administrative officers in the Pargana:

(i) **Shikdar:** Shikdar was the chief executive officer of the pargana. His functions were to maintain peace in the pargana; suppress rebellion; punish thieves; decide ordinary criminal cases; obey the orders of higher officials; help the Amil in collecting land tax etc.

(ii) **Amil:** He was the head of the revenue department of the pargana. He had direct relations with the farmers. He used to assess and collect revenue. He used to investigate the records related to land measurement. He also decided civil cases.

(iii) **Kanungo, Potdar and Karkun:** Kanungo was the head of Patwaris in Pargana. There was more than one Kanungo in a Pargana. He kept records related to the land of the Pargana. Potdar was the treasurer of the Pargana. His main function was to collect land revenue from the farmers and deposit it in the treasury. There were also some Karkuns in the Pargana who kept agricultural records in Persian language. During the reign of Akbar, an officer named Bitikachi worked in place of Karkun.

City Administration

The biggest official for the administration of the cities was the Kotwal who was appointed by the centre. He had a small military contingent with which he controlled the city. The main functions of the Kotwal were to protect the lives and wealth of the city dwellers; to suppress riots and rebellion; to arrange for the stay of foreigners; to look after the weights and measures; to control the markets; to put a stop on alcoholism, prostitution, gambling etc. A Chowkidar was appointed to assist the Kotwal, who used to guard the locality day and night.

Management of Villages

The village was the smallest unit of the state. The village was administered by the Gram Panchayat. An intelligent person was made the head or chief of the village. The main functions of the Panchayat were to resolve people's disputes; maintain peace in the village; look after religious places; pay attention to cleanliness and education; prepare for festivals and games etc. There were Chowkidars, Mukadams and Patwaris to help the Gram Panchayat. The Chowkidar used to guard the village.

Judicial System

The biggest decisions were made in the court of the emperor. Only the emperor could give the death sentence. To run the judicial administration in the provinces, there were the following three types of courts in the time of Akbar.

- (i) **Court of Subedar and Qazi:** Haryana region came under Delhi and Agra province and Subedar of each province used to administer justice in their respective provinces in Haryana. Qazi often used to hear criminal cases.
- (ii) **Court of Faujdar and Amalguzar:** In Sarkars, Faujdar used to hear cases while civil cases were heard by Amil or Amalguzar. They also sometimes took the help of Qazi at the time of justice.
- (iii) **Court of Shikdar and Amil:** In every Pargana there was a court of Shikdar and Amil. Criminal cases were heard by Shikdar and civil cases were heard by Amil.
- (iv) **Panchayat:** The smallest unit was the village, in which most of the small matters were settled by the Panchayat.

Irrigation System in Mughal Period in Haryana

The main source of income of the Mughal state was agriculture. During this period, about 90 per cent of the population earned their living through agriculture. The farmer used to harvest two crops in a year—*Kharif* and *Rabi*. In "*Ain-e-Akbari*", Abul Fazal has mentioned 16 crops for *Rabi* season and 25 crops for *Kharif* season. Where there was more rainfall, there was abundance of sugarcane, cotton, wheat etc. But in dry areas, *jowar*, millet, *moong*, *moth*, gram, barley etc. were found in abundance. There were good sources of irrigation.

Agriculture

Each region of Haryana was famous for its different crops. Contemporary texts give details of which crops were grown in which region. Ibn Battuta has praised the rice of Sirsa in his book

"*Al-Rehla*" and has written that "The rice here is very good. Its yield is also good. Rice is sent from here to Delhi." Timur has mentioned the good sugarcane crop in Sirsa in his autobiography. Sharfuddin has mentioned the good quality of wheat in Panipat in "*Zafarnama*". According to Bal Kisan Brahmin, cotton was grown in abundance in Sirsa. Abul Fazal's "*Ain-e-Akbari*" mentions good crops in this region, but he has mentioned sugarcane crop in particular. Delight, who came during Jahangir's time, has also mentioned advanced agriculture here.

Motmad Khan in his "*Iqbal Nama-e-Jahangir*" has mentioned the best variety of mangoes in the northern region. Mentioning the good production of indigo in Gurgaon and Faridabad districts, it has been described that 1000 bales of indigo were produced here every year. According to Bernier also, indigo was produced in large quantities in Haryana region. It refers to the production of rice and sugarcane in Palwal. It is also mentioned that millet crop is plentiful in these regions. George Thomas, in his memoirs, mentions the crops of wheat, barley, gram, *jowar*, millet, *moong* etc. in Hisar, Hansi and Bhiwani areas.

Means of Irrigation

Farmers generally depended on rainfall for irrigation. Apart from rainfall, artificial methods were also used for irrigation. Wells and ponds were the main means of irrigation, through which irrigation was done especially for *Rabi* crops. Many methods were used to extract water from the well, among which *Dhekli*, *Chadas*, Pershian wheel or *Sakhiya* were the prominent ones. Due to the high price of Persian wheel, not every farmer was able to use it. *Dhekli* was the best means of irrigation for common farmers. The Mughal administration used to help the farmers in digging wells. George Thomas has said that due to the water level being very low here, there were only one or two wells in a village from which the entire village benefited. In Karnal and Panipat, where the water level was high, *Rahat* was used in the well. Apart from wells, irrigation was also done from ponds but due to limited water, these could be used only for a short period of time.

Canals

Before the Mughal period, Firoz Tughlaq had dug the biggest canal like the Western Yamuna Canal which started from Tajewala from Yamuna and reached Hisar, and irrigated thousands of acres of land. The second canal started from Sutlej river and reached Jhajjar. The third canal was Firozabad Canal which started from near the hills of Sirmaur and reached Hansi and Hisar. The fourth canal started from Ghaggar and reached from below the fort of Sirsa to Harni Kheda, Firozabad. The fifth canal was brought from Yamuna to Harni Kheda, Firozabad.

No ruler paid much attention to these canals during Akbar's or Mughal period. Yes, Akbar did get these canals repaired but not properly. Because it is known from Waris's "*Badshahnama*" and Inayat's "*Shahjahannama*" that by the time of Shahjahan's rule these canals had become completely bad. Shahjahan got these canals repaired during his period. He also got another canal dug from the western Yamuna canal near Safidon which went up to Shahjahanabad, Delhi. This canal was named "Nahr-e-Bahisht". Due to Shahjahan's attention to the canals, agriculture had progressed a lot during his time. After Aurangzeb, all the canals were ruined during the time of anarchy.

Land Revenue System in Mughal Period Haryana

Haryana was a leading region in the field of agriculture. When wooden plows were used in most places, farmers of Haryana used iron plows in their ploughs. Due to abundance of livestock here, cowdung manure was used more and the crops were also very good. Therefore, the government used to get good land tax from this region.

Zabti System

During Babur's time, land tax was taken from farmers on almost half of their produce. Due to this heavy taxation, the public was not happy at that time. After that Sher Shah reduced the tax rate to one-third and provided a lot of relief to the farmers. Akbar also made a lot of efforts to improve the condition of farmers and land. Akbar arranged for the Zabti system to determine land tax in Haryana.

Akbar started the Zabti system with the help of his Diwan Muzaffar Khan and Todarmal. The purpose of implementing this system was to fix the state's share in the revenue on a solid basis; to make such arrangements for paying the state's share in cash and kind that neither the state nor the farmers suffer any loss; to make such arrangements for the prices of the goods that the state gets a definite estimate of its annual income.

In this Zabti system during reign of Akbar, the cultivable land of every farmer, village, pargana was measured. Akbar used a 41 finger yard for measurement while Sher Shah used a 32 finger yard. In place of the rope chain, a new model *Zarib* (chain) called *Tanab* was used. This chain was made of bamboo and had iron strips on both its ends. There was no danger of the chain shrinking or breaking. At that time, a *Bigha* was 3600 square yards. After measuring the land, the land was classified into four parts.

- **(i) Polaj:** The high quality land which could be cultivated all the year round was called Polaj.
- **(ii) Parauti:** The land which was left fallow for a few months in a year to gain fertility power was called Parauti.
- **(iii) Chhachhar:** This land was left uncultivated for three to four consecutive years.
- **(iv) Banjar:** Banjar was the barren land and it was the lowest type of land. This land was left fallow for five years or more.

"*Ain-e-Akbari*" shows that on the basis of fertility, the Polaj and Parauti land were divided into three parts—good, medium and inferior. The government's share was decided on the basis of the average yield of these three varieties. Land tax was collected only on sown land. 1/3rd of the produce of Polaj and Paroti land was taken as land tax. Chhachhar land was divided into 1/15 shares in the first year, 1/5 in the second and third years, 4/15 in the fourth year and 1/3 in the fifth year. Similarly, land tax started from 1/20th of the barren land and reached 1/3rd of the produce in the fifth year. During the Mughal period, taxes were preferred to be taken in cash.

Emperor Aurangzeb started collecting *Zakat* from Muslims and *Jaziya* from Hindus. Later it was abolished but the subsequent weak rulers increased the tax to 2/5th. But during these days no one paid the tax because there was an atmosphere of anarchy in the entire kingdom. Revolts of farmers and native kings had also increased.

Akbar used to reduce or waive taxes in times of natural disasters. During the time of Akbar, two letters *Kabuliyat* and *Patta* were implemented. The governments used to get the farmer's signature on the confession letter and keep it with them. The lease deed was given to the farmer. Land revenue was collected twice a year in the months of *Ashadh* and Autumn.

Industrial Development

Domestic and handicraft industries were quite developed in medieval Haryana. At that time, in every village, goldsmiths, potters, weavers, blacksmiths, tarkhans etc. used to make many things, like jewellery, earthen pots, clothes, agricultural implements etc. These people used to get a part of the crop from their lords instead of taking cash in exchange for these things. The artisans of the cities were given cash in exchange for goods. During the Mughal period, the cities of Haryana were very famous for the specialized production of various goods.

At that time, agricultural equipment, jewellery, sheets, carpets, shoes, clothes etc. were made in the cities. In Panipat, carpets and woollen blankets were made. Clay utensils were made in Jhajjar and metal utensils in Rewari. In the cities, artisans were paid cash wages. Some artisans and labourers also worked in the royal factories. According to "*Ain-e-Akbari*", at that time, a carpenter was paid 3-4 daams per day, a mason 5-7 daams per day, an ordinary labourer 2 daams per day and a skilled labourer 4 daams per day.

According to many historians, the prices of goods at that time were very low, yet there was a huge difference in the standard of living of the rich and the poor. According to K.M. Ashraf, the food expenses of one person were around 20 Jital per year.

Business Development

Compared to other regions, Haryana had less internal and external trade, yet due to the efforts of the Mughal government, many avenues for trade development were open. A network of roads was laid across the entire region. There were two main routes for domestic trade—the first route went from Delhi to Lahore *via* Sonipat, Panipat, Karnal, Pipli, Ambala. The second route went to Lahore *via* Sonipat, Panipat, Kaithal, Sirsa etc. Goods were sent abroad from Lahore. There was a proper arrangement of inns and water wells on both these routes. The Sher Shah Suri route built by Sher Shah was used a lot for business purpose. Due to the construction of a bridge over the Markanda river during the Mughal period, trade increased a lot. A lot of trade also took place from the route going to Multan from Delhi *via* Dadri, Bhiwani, Hansi, Hisar etc.

There were many roads in Haryana for regional trade, on which there were markets of Narnaul, Rewari, Sirsa etc. At that time trade was done by local traders and foreign traders. From here, rice, gram, indigo, *naushadar*, sugarcane, *ghee* etc. were exported and paddy, salt and clothes were imported. Animals were also traded in this region. Pelsart has specifically mentioned the trade of *Naushadar* of Kurukshetra and indigo of Mewat. In Mewat, indigo was sold at Rs. 20 per maund, which was Rs. 10 cheaper than the Bayana indigo.

Thus, it may be concluded that a smooth governance system was implemented in most of the areas of the country including entire Haryana during the Mughal period. The main essence of this system was that farmers, labourers and all the people could get justice and other comforts. Irrigation arrangements, tax exemption during famine and government assistance in times of distress were provided to farmers. The land revenue was also so much that every farmer could easily pay it. The Mughal administration also paid attention towards trade and industry and for this there was good arrangement of roads and security. Inns, wells and Kos minarets were built for travellers and traders' assistance.

13

Bhakti and Sufi Movements in Haryana

After the continuous Muslim invasions on India, animosity and hostility between Hindus and Muslims increased. Although the newly established Muslim rulers tried to increase unity and brotherhood between the two communities but this effort was largely unsuccessful. As a result of hostility between two sects both religions were began to moving towards fanaticism. In such a situation, in the medieval period, the saints of both the religions began to propagate the love and brotherhood as the base of all religions. Hindu saints took the help of *Bhakti* and named it *Bhakti* movement and Muslim *Sufi* saints named it *Sufi* movement. These movements based on love and brotherhood became quite popular more particularly among the common people. Haryana was also affected by these movements because there were abundance of *Bhakti* and *Sufi* saints in this region.

Bhakti Movement

In the medieval period, the saints of the *Bhakti* movement moved away from rigidity, orthodoxy and complex custom of Hindu religion and moved forward with a different ideology of love and devotion. This novel method of teaching and preaching the religion gave a feeling of happiness and peace to the devotees, and they became engrossed in meditation while singing hymns. It was believed that these *Bhakti* saints had direct contact with God.

Introduction of Bhakti Movement

In Hindu religion, four fruits of human life are considered very important—*Dharma, Artha, Kama*, and *Moksha*. Similarly, in this religion, emphasis has been laid on three means—the path of knowledge, the path of devotion and the path of action. In the medieval period in India, some reforms were made by moving away from the complex customs of Hindu religion. By this reformed ideology, promotion of love and devotion, the Hindu religion became so easy to adopt in personal life. *Bhakti Marg* not only made it simple but also made it very popular. Earlier, Hindu religion had become distorted due to the rituals, external ostentation and complexities prevalent in the society.

Ramanuja took the initiative to start this new wave of *Bhakti* movement in the South. The credit for bringing it from South India to North India goes to Ramanand. Many other saints also played very important role in the development of this movement, among whom Kabir, Nanak, Chaitanya, Ramdas, Eknath, Tukaram, Namdev etc. were prominent. In *Bhakti* ideology, devotees used to serve God truly. In this ideology, when a man gives up everything and completely engages in the service of God, then he is called a true devotee of God.

According to some historians like Tarachand and Nizami, the mutual social and cultural contact and ideological exchange between Hindus and Muslims gave birth to a feeling of sympathy, cooperation and harmony between the two, which led to the beginning of the *Bhakti* movement. K.M. Panikkar is of the opinion that Hindus, fed up with the atrocities and autocratic rule of the Muslims, sought refuge in God. But the generally accepted opinion about the emergence of *Bhakti* movement is that the saints of the *Bhakti* movement believed that God is one, so they started worshipping one God, opposed polytheism, idol worship and raised their voice against casteism. R.G. Bhandarkar believes that the basis of the *Bhakti* movement is the teachings of *Shrimad Bhagvad Gita*.

The *Bhakti* movement was greatly influenced by the ideas of Islam. Yusuf Husain has written that the *Bhakti* movement can be divided into two periods. The first period was from the *Bhagvad Gita* to the thirteenth century common era. The second period was from the thirteenth to the sixteenth century common era, when Islam spread in India. During this period, Islam and Hinduism were influenced by each other's ideas. It is worth mentioning here that the spiritual saints opposed both orthodox Hinduism and orthodox Islam. Due to the close contact between *Sufi* and *Bhakti* ideologies, there must have been an exchange of ideas and opinions between the two.

Features of *Bhakti* Movement

Bhakti ideology was of two types, *Sagun* and *Nirgun*. In *Sagun* worship, God was worshipped through incarnation, idol worship, *Bhajan-Kirtan* etc. *Sagun* saints included Ramanand, Meera, Chaitanya, Ramanuja etc. In *Nirgun* worship, emphasis was laid on personal *sadhana* and penance. Saints like Kabir, Namdev, Nanak etc. were included in this ideology. The main features of the *Bhakti* movement are as follows:

(i) **Emphasis on Religious Simplicity:** The saints of the *Bhakti* movement laid emphasis on religious simplicity. They opposed casteism, customs, rituals, ostentation, superstition, dominance of priests etc. Due to these characteristics, people from the untouchable class of Hindu religion started joining the *Bhakti* movement in large numbers and made this movement very popular. Saints like Nanak and Kabir even opposed idol worship. According to them, religious sacrifice, worship and fasting are all ostentation. To attain God, man's heart must be pure. He should adopt qualities like honesty, non-violence, kindness etc.

(ii) **Feeling of Communism:** The followers of the *Bhakti* movement tried to establish coordination between the people of Hindu and Muslim religions. Guru Nanak was also greatly influenced by the teachings of Islam. To establish coordination, the saints of *Bhakti* and *Sufi* ideologies opened the path of devotion for all religions and castes. They considered all the untouchables, rich and poor, high and low etc. to be equal. Kabir made people of both the communities his disciples. Giving up politics, Vallabhacharya tried for Hindu-Muslim unity. For this noble work, he took the help of religion and culture.

(iii) **Emphasis on Love:** In this ideology, emphasis was given on love by abandoning ego. Love and dedication are the power by which one can conquer the vices like anger, greed, attachment, illusion and ego. Man can attain God's grace and *Guru Bhakti* through dedication. For devotion to God, man must have the feeling of love and devotion in his mind.

(iv) **Monotheism:** People of *Bhakti Marg* believed in one God. According to them, the people of different religions call the same God by different names. Those who sincerely serve and worship God are called devotees of God. Devotees of *Saguna Marg* considered Ram and Krishna as their deities and worshipped them, while *Nirguna* worshippers believed that God does not reside in idols but in the heart of man.

(v) **Social Reforms:** During medieval period, the society was divided into many classes and castes. There was mutual hostility, untouchability and discrimination among them. Despite belonging to the same religion and society, they were far away from each other. In such a situation, *Bhakti* ideology tried to bring everyone on one path and tried to bind them together by eradicating social evils. They also preached Hindu-Muslim unity. Opposed the evils prevalent in the society like *Sati*, slavery, female child infanticide etc. Many efforts were also made to improve the condition of women in the society.

(vi) **Glorification of Guru:** The saints of the *Bhakti* school glorified the importance of the *Guru* or teacher. According to them, in the darkness of human life, *Guru* is like a lamp which brings the light of knowledge and shows the right path. Guru Nanak said, "Guru is the boat of devotion and the ladder to reach the divine home." *Guru* awakens the sleeping soul of human being. Saint Kabir has said, "*Guru Govind dou khade kake lagu paay, Balihari Guru aapne Govind diyo batay*" (When both the *Guru* and Govind are standing in front of me, I will bow down to the *Guru* first, as he showed me the way to Govind). The dedication of the *Guru* has been accepted in the *Bhakti* movement.

Spread of *Bhakti* Movement

In the medieval period, when the wave of *Bhakti* movement was sweeping across India, Haryana too was not left untouched by it. Here too there were many saints who spread *Nirguna Bhakti* and composed many books and poems in Hindi or *Khadi Boli*.

(i) **Nath Panthis:** The *Bhakti* movement in Haryana started with the Nath Panthis. Prathudak (Pehwa) and Rohtak were its main centres. It was founded by Chauranginath in Arthal Bohar (Rohtak district) in the thirteenth century. He created literary works named "*Vayutri Bhuvan Upadesh*" and "*Pranesaghali*". There is a glimpse of pure devotion and philosophy in these creations. After Chauranginath, the other monk of Nath sect was Mastnath. His work area was Rohtak only. His speeches are written in typical Hindi.

(ii) **Surdas:** Surdas (1497-1554) was born in a village named Sihi in Faridabad district. Surdas was blind by birth but he is counted among the greatest poets of the world. Surdas was not only a poet but also a saint of *Bhakti* ideology. Surdas's ideas influenced crores of people not only of Haryana but also of North India. Among his many books, "*Sursagar*", "*Sahitya Ratna*" and "*Sursaravali*" are the main ones. "*Sursagar*" describes the childhood of Krishna's life. Surdas had taken his ideas from "*Bhagwat Purana*". "*Sursagar*" is an original text, it depicts immense devotion and love towards Krishna. These books are in Braj language.

(iii) Veerbhan: Veerbhan, a contemporary of Dadu Dayal, was born in 1543 in a village named Vijesar near Narnaul. He founded the sect of Satnamis. Veerbhan believed in one God whom he named Satnam or Truth. Veerbhan opposed the caste system, idol worship and other ostentation. He laid emphasis on pure life and practice of *yoga*. Veerbhan's followers did not consume meat and alcohol. His book of speeches is called "*Granth Saheb*" and it has a lot of influence of Dadu sect.

(iv) Garibdas: The famous saint Garibdas was born in 1717 in a Jat family in a village named Chhudani in Jhajjar district. He was influenced by the *Nirguna* treatise of the *Bhakti* movement. He composed about 25,000 verses, and these verses are known as the book "*Miravarbodh*". "*Bijak*" and "*Ratnasagar*" are his two other famous compositions. He founded a sect, which is called Garibdasi. Garibdas believed in one God and brotherhood of man. He did not discriminate between rich and poor, high and low etc. He attacked the mutual bitterness between religions and advocated unity among sects. He saw similarity in many facts of Hinduism and Islam, hence his followers included both Hindus and Muslims. According to Garibdas, *Maya* is the enemy of man and only the name of God can save him from it. According to him, devotion is achieved by knowledge, by killing the ego, by having faith in the *Guru* and by loving God.

(v) Nischaldas: Nischaldas was born in a Jat family in 1791 in Kugad village of Hansi tehsil. He was a follower of Dadu Panth, a great poet and saint. He wrote books like "*Vichar Sagar*", "*Kritprabhakar*", "*Muktiprakash*" etc. in Sanskrit language. Raja Ram Singh of Bundi was also among his followers. Swami Vivekananda was also influenced by his writings.

Importance and Impact of *Bhakti* Movement

The saints of the *Bhakti* period set such a goal before the people that an ordinary people could follow it without any difficulty. By following the *Bhakti* ideology, the people need not to depend on Brahmins. Their religious teachings attracted the common people a lot because it was simple and straightforward and there was no room for exploitation by Brahmins. These saints preached equality, friendship, brotherhood etc. They especially created a new awakening among the people of the lower class and tried to give them a higher position in the society. These saints also preached to remove Hindu-Muslim discrimination. They told that both are children of the same God, so they should live together.

K. Damodaran has written that the *Bhakti* movement in India expanded in many forms and had many fundamental principles. Unity of people despite differences in religions, equality of all before God, opposition to caste system, emphasis on devotion, opposition to idol worship, opposition to pilgrimages and opposition to physical torture, opposition to religious ostentation etc. were the fundamental principles of *Bhakti* movement. A.L. Srivastava has written that the *Bhakti* movement spread in all directions of India and its influence remained for many centuries. This movement was a movement of common people and it had two goals, the first goal was to reform Hindu religion, so that it could avoid the propagation of Islam. The second goal was to create a compromise between Hindus and Muslims and create a feeling of mutual love among them. Regional literature also progressed greatly due to the *Bhakti* movement.

Dr. Yusuf Hussain is of the opinion that the *Bhakti* movement brought Hindu and Muslim civilizations in contact and brought about a change in the outlook of both. This movement provided an opportunity for the devotees of Hindus and Muslims to meet at one place. They tried to create a society in which there is equality and justice and people of all religions can make spiritual and moral progress.

Rise and Development of *Sufi* Movement

There are many opinions among scholars regarding the origin of Sufism or the word *Sufi*. Some believe that this word originated from the word "*Safa*" which means pure. According to one view, the word *Sufi* originated from the word "*Suf*" which means woollen or blanket. The saints or *Darveshes* who used to preach their religion carrying woollen blankets were called *Sufis*. Some scholars also believe that the word *Sufi* originated from the Greek word "*Sophia*" which means knowledge. There is evidence that the word *Sufi* was used since the ninth century common era. *Sufis* did not have enmity towards any religion, caste or sect.

Sufis originated from the principle of "*Wahdat-ul Wajood*" in Islam which means that God, the owner of the whole world, is one. According to this belief, union with God occurs only when the feelings of man come in contact with God and he adopts the path of retirement. The principle of "*Wahdat-ul Wajood*" was first given by *Sufi* saint Sheikh Muhiuddin and Ibn al-Arabi which was also accepted by the *Sufis* of India. To meet God, *Sufis* used to forget all the things of the world. They were neither concerned with political power nor with other worldly things. The aim of *Sufis* was to meet God and serve man.

As for the origin of the Sufism or *Sufi* ideological origin and development there are also many opinions among scholars. In Yusuf Hussain's view, *Sufis* were born in Islam and had no influence on outside ideas and customs. A.L. Srivastava says that Sufism was greatly influenced by Hindu ideas and customs. *Sufis* took the ideas of non-violence and non-fighting from Hindus, Buddhists and Jainas.

Dr. Tarachand is of the opinion that Sufism was not a simple thing. It was like a river in which many small rivers joined at many places. The fundamental source of *Sufis* was the Holy *Quran* and the life of Hazrat Mohammad (pbuh). Prof. K.A. Nizami is of the opinion that the Chishti order of *Sufis* adopted many customs and traditions of Hindus. Bowing before the Sheikh, giving water to the guests, shaving the head and asking for utensils and cups were also taken from Hindus and Buddhists.

Teachings of the *Sufi* Movement

The main principles or teachings of Sufism are as follows:

(i) According to Sufism, God is present in every particle of the universe and He is one (*Wahdat-ul Wajood*). That God is the director of all humanity above the differences of caste and religion. In Sufism, love is considered to be the true form of God.

(ii) According to *Sufi* saints, the soul is a part of God. It has five external and five internal elements. There are two main qualities in the soul—*Nafs* and *Rooh*. *Nafs* is the source of all vices, while *Rooh* is the place where God resides. There is always a conflict between these two.

(iii) According to the *Sufi* saints, God melted *Haqikat-ul Mohammadiya* and made the constellations Sun, Moon, Venus, Mars, Jupiter, Saturn and transformed *Noor-ul Mohammadiya* into fire, air, water and earth.

(iv) The *Sufi* saints believed that man is the manifestation of all the attributes of God. A perfect human is only one who has achieved the complete realization of unity with God. From Adam to Prophet Mohammed, Auliya, all come in the category of perfect human.

(v) *Sufi* saints emphasized the importance of *Guru*. According to the saints, only the *Guru* shows the path of love to the seeker, and without a *Guru* no one can find God.

(vi) The late *Sufis* emphasized the importance of music in attaining God. In Nizamuddin Auliya's opinion, music is a unique medium to encounter divine love and harmony.

Sufi Saint Preacher

The centre of *Sufis*' work is called *Khanqah*. People from far and wide used to come here for spiritual advancement. In many *Khanqahs*, arrangements were also made for fooding and lodging of travellers and followers. *Sufis* were so respected and revered that after their death, their graves were considered holy places and many people even worshipped them. This Sufism had many parts which were called *Silsila*. According to Abul Fazal, there were a total of thirteen *Silsilas* in India. But three *Silsilas*—"*Chishtia Silsila*", "*Suhrawardi Silsila*" and "*Qadriya Silsila*" were more prominent.

The development and propagation of Sufism in Haryana took place during the pre-medieval period, i.e. the Sultanate period. The Chishti order was first established whose founder was Khwaja Moinuddin Chishti. Its main centres were Ajmer in Rajasthan and Hansi in Haryana. The names of some *Sufi* saints are as follows:

(i) **Baba Fariduddin Ganjeshkar:** Baba Farid was a disciple of the prominent *Sufi* saint Qutbuddin Bakhtiyar Kaki. They came in Haryana and settled in Hansi. Due to his religious works the Chishti order became very popular in Haryana. He built many *Khankahs* and had great prestige in India. He believed that a *Darvesh* should stay away from the emperor, money and royal positions. He opened his doors to the lower classes and the destitute. He gave the light of truth and faith to countless misguided and downtrodden people. His messages were very popular and sacred to both Hindus and Muslims. In his messages, there was a strong feeling of tying both the religions together by abandoning rituals and ostentation. He gave up hatred, violence and animosity and taught the lessons of sympathy and mutual love. His personality was very impressive, humble, generous and soft-spoken. He did not refute any religion in his entire speech.

(ii) **Shaikh Jamaluddin:** Shaikh Jamaluddin was also a *Sufi* of Hansi. Earlier he was a clerk of Hansi. Later he left his job and became a disciple of Shaikh Farid. He was a very educated and knowledgeable person. He wrote two books named "*Diwan*" in Persian and "*Ulhamat*" in Arabic. These books throw important light on contemporary religious thoughts and institutions.

(iii) Shaikh Nooruddin: Shaikh Nooruddin was also a *Sufi* of Hansi. He was a contemporary of Sultan Firozshah Tughlaq. In Haryana he greatly expanded the Chishti order and remained very popular among the public.

(iv) Shaikh Sharfuddin: Shaikh Sharfuddin was a famous *Sufi* saint of Panipat who was also known by the name of Bu Ali Shah Qalandar. Khwaja Shamsuddin was his friend and lived in Panipat.

Apart from Hansi and Panipat, *Sufi* movement also flourished in other cities of Haryana like Narnaul, Kaithal, Jhajjar, Hisar, Mewat etc. Among these *Sufi* saints, Sheikh Qutbuddin Mannawat, Tajuddin Sheerwar, Sheikh Mohammad, Syed Mujibuddin, Syed Mugisuddin, Syed Alauddin, Maulana Jamaluddin Kaithal, Malik Tajuddin Zafar, Malik Jamaluddin, Malik Jamal, Syed Ali Jhajjar and Gola Mir Hisar were prominent. The accounts of Abul Fazal and Badayuni show that Sufism had spread to many parts of Haryana during the time of the Mughals. Thanesar and Panipat became new centres of Sufism.

(v) Hazrat Jalaluddin: Hazrat Jalaluddin was a famous *Sufi* saint of Thanesar. According to Badayuni, he was a disciple of Shaikh Abdul Quddus of Gangoh. He was proficient in his external and internal knowledge. He devoted his entire life to devotion to God and propagation of religion. Emperor Akbar also came to Thanesar to see him once with Bairam Khan and another time with Abul Fazal.

(vi) Shaikh Chehli: Sheikh Chehli was also a *Sufi* saint of Thanesar. He was the spiritual *guru* of Dara Shikoh.

(vii) Shaikh Amanullah: Shaikh Amanullah was a Mughal era saint of Panipat. People of all religions, Hindus and Muslims respected him. He also wrote many books.

(viii) Shaikh Nizamuddin: He was a *Sufi* saint of the Mughal period in Narnaul. He was one of those few *Sufis* who had chosen a life of monasticism by their own will. He had given up worldly desires. According to Badayuni, he used intoxicants to complete religious rituals.

(ix) Shaikh Junaid Gurbati: Shaikh Gurbati was a preacher of Sufism from Hisar. Shaikh Gurbati sang devotional songs at a gathering of *Darveshes* called by Shah Hussain of Khwarizm.

(x) Khwaja Sayyed Shaikh Musa: Khwaja Sayyed Shaikh Musa was the son of Maulana Sayyed Badruddin Ishaq who was the disciple of Baba Fariduddin Ganjishakar of Pak Patan. Sayyed Shaikh Musa was very renowned Islamic scholar of his time. By nature, he was very humorous, brave, and kind hearted. He was an excellent Arabic and Persian poet and also a very good musician. He was also a great archer, wrestler, and swimmer. In the field of medicine, he was also very experienced.

In 1325, Mohammad Tughlaq ascended the throne of Delhi in the same year his teacher Khwaja Nizamuddin Aulia left the world for ever. In the next year in 1326, Mohammad Tughlaq started transferring his capital to Daulatabad; he forced the aristocracy comprising the sayyads, shaikhs, ulema and mystics to leave the city of Delhi. In this very frustrating situation Sayyad Shaikh Musa also left Delhi and moved to southward passing through Mewat area. It is said that near Palla village in Mewat, the turban of the Saint was caught by spiky and thorny bushes of Arawali hills. Perhaps Sayyed Shaikh Musa considered it a heavenly order and decided to stay in the same village Palla. At that time, Palla was a village of the Hindu Gujar community. He started Islamic preaching in the area. Slowly and gradually he became very popular in Mewat and its people. Not only, the Mewati people but the people from the far-flung areas like Delhi and Rajputana started visiting his *Khankah*. By preaching Islam in the rest of his days he left the world in 1332.

(xi) **Sayyed Akbar Ali Shah Chokha:** He was born in 1530 in Khurasan. Shah Chokha migrated to Ajodhan, where he coincidently met a *Sufi* Saint Nizamuddin Narnauli. Shah Chokha became his disciple and settled himself at Narnaul. Shah Chokha along with Nizamuddin Narnauli annually visited Sayyed Qutub Shah of Delhi through the route of Dhauj, Khori Shah Chokha, Firozpur Jhirka, Tijara, Kot Qasim and Rewari. After some years in 1564, with the permission of his teacher Nizamuddin Narnauli he settled on the top of the hills of the village Khori Shah Chokha. He started Islamic preaching in the area. Slowly and gradually he became very popular in Mewat and its people. Not only, the Mewati people but the people from the far-flung areas like Delhi and Rajputana started visiting his *Khankah*. In 1591 Shah Chokha died in the same village.

Other *Sufi* saints of Haryana during the Mughal era include Sheikh Abdul Kabir, Shaikh Nizamuddin, Shaikh Salim Chishti, Kabir-ul Auliya, Nizamuddin Hussain, Mullashah, Mohammad Shah Dujan, Mulla Naseeruddin Tarkhan, Abdul Shakur Silma, Sheikh Abdul Quddus, Ghulam Qadir Jilani etc. were prominent, who taught the lessons of love and goodwill through *Sufi* sects in Haryana.

Contribution of Sufism in Society

Sufi saints spread love and goodwill in the society, which bound Hindus and Muslims in the thread of unity. The medieval period was an era when Muslim rulers invaded India and established their rule. The people of India had an unknown fear of Muslims, due to which a lot of distances had increased between the two communities. Sufism ended those distances and taught the lesson of mutual brotherhood and unity. These saints were symbols of simplicity and both Hindus and Muslims were equally influenced by them. They accepted poverty by their own will and lived among the common people. With these ideology, the Hindu people here came to know the truth of Islam and abandoned the illusion that they had been nurturing in their minds for centuries.

Sufi saints were mostly married, yet they did not leave the life of simplicity. This largely affected and attracted the married people family members. *Sufi* saints had liberal thoughts and fanaticism had no place among them. They believed in love for God and service to mankind. They believed in *Advaitvad* of *Bhakti* ideology. They considered service to man as a higher task than devotion. They considered serving the poor and the poor as his ultimate duty. When *Sufi* saints presented Islam in India with such a liberal ideology, every section of the society accepted it and recognized it as a religion of love.

Influence of Hinduism on Sufism

If we look at the Vedic tradition, Hinduism was a very complex religion which a common man could not follow easily. The *Bhakti* movement presented Hinduism as a religion for the common man. They told that this religion can be followed without the rituals of Hinduism and without caste and creed, just by devotion to God. When Islam came to India, it also incorporated some religious elements in itself:

- **(i) Influence of Yoga and Pranayama:** *Yoga* and *Pranayama* practised by Hindu *Yogis* and devotees had a deep influence on Sufism. The influence of *Yoga* can also be seen in the verses of Sheikh Wahiduddin Nagauri.
- **(ii) Influence of the Rishi Tradition:** The *Rishi* tradition had a deep impact on Sufism. Although the tradition of *Pir* and *Khalifa* was already prevalent in Sufism, some *Sufi* saints in India called themselves *Rishis*. They used to give their speeches in common language.
- **(iii) About the Soul:** According to Alberuni, the ideas related to the soul of *Sufi* saints were like the *Yoga Sutras* of Patanjali. The idea expressed in *Sufi* writings is that "the body is the embodiment of the soul for the purpose of receiving retribution." Gorakh Panthis also had an impact on this

opinion. Nijazuddin Auliya believed that the part below the navel is related to power and the part from navel to the head is related to spirituality.

To coclude the whole topic, it could be said that when Hinduism and Islam came in contact with each other, one was labelled a winner and the other a loser. There was an atmosphere of fear and uncertainty in the society. *Sufi* and *Bhakti* ideologies taught the lesson of love instead of fear and tied people in the thread of unity. Forgetting religion, differences, caste, untouchability, people got bound in the bond of love and got absorbed in the devotion of God. In this way, both the religions were propagated and brotherhood also increased. Hindu and Muslim religions were only the means to attain the same God.

14

Marathas, Third Battle of Panipat, George Thomas and East India Company

During the eighteenth century many developments happened in Haryana. In these periods Haryana witnessed Battle of Karnal, Third Battle of Panipat, rise of Marathas and establishments of many princely states. In later half of the eighteenth century Marathas and George Thomas were leading Haryana and finally, in nineteenth century the East India Company established its rule over the whole of Haryana.

Marathas attacked Haryana five times. The third attack was the Third Battle of Panipat, in which the expansion of Marathas was halted for some time. Marathas again became powerful and their chieftains established their rule in most parts of Haryana. The British defeated the Marathas and established their rule over Haryana and established a solid administrative system.

Rise of Marathas in Haryana

Marathas were the descendants of Shivaji and were ruling the whole of South India under the Peshwas. Inspired by the anarchy of the Mughal Empire, they also entered Delhi and Haryana. The Marathas arrived in Delhi in 1750 when the feuds between the

Iranian and Turani nobles in the Mughal court were at their peak. Marathas also started taking keen interest in these conflicts.

First Maratha Invasion 1753

In 1753, Malharrao Holkar and his son Khanderao first entered Delhi with their army. At this time there was a fight going on between Wazir Intezamuddaula and Mir Bakshi Imadulmulk. The Wazir wanted to form a confederacy against external powers with the Nawab of Awadh, Surajmal Jat of Bharatpur, and Rajputs. Mir Bakshi wanted to maintain his influence on the emperor Ahmad Shah by allying with the Marathas. In this conflict, the Marathas supported Mir Bakshi Imadulmulk. The Marathas dashed to Delhi and made Alamgir II the emperor in place of Ahmad Shah and Imadulmulk the Wazir in place of Intazamuddaula. In 1754, the emperor was pleased with the Marathas and granted them the area of Kurukshetra, but the Marathas took control over many areas of Haryana. By 1754-55, the Marathas captured large parts of Haryana and looted and damaged crops and finally, returned to the south.

Second Maratha Invasion and Third Battle of Panipat

During 1759-60, the Marathas once again came to Delhi. This time the main reason for their arrival was not only the chaos in the north but also to control the attack of Ahmad Shah Abdali. The Marathas wanted to establish a single rule over the whole of India by fighting Abdali to the finish. They first captured and looted Delhi and the whole of Haryana afterwards. They attacked the Abdali supporter ruler of Kunjpura—Najabat Khan and killed Najabat Khan and his two sons along with his 20,000 soldiers. The whole of Haryana was terrified by such a terrible massacre. They no longer had any sympathy for the Marathas. The news of the killing and slaying of the Marathas reached Kabul, the capital of Ahmad Shah Abdali. The ruler of Afghanistan, Ahmad Shah Abdali immediately rushed towards Haryana and encamped to the plains of Panipat to deal with the Marathas.

Third Battle of Panipat 1761

Third battle of Panipat was fought between Afghans under Ahmad Shah Abdali and Marathas under Sadashiv Rao Bhau in 1961. In this battle over 1,25,000 troops involved and ended with much loss of both sides. The Afghan army ultimately emerged victorious from the battle after successfully destroying several Maratha flanks. The extent of the losses on both sides is heavily disputed by historians, but it is believed that between 60,000 and 70,000 troops were killed in the fighting, while the numbers of injured and prisoners taken vary considerably.

After the Marathas moved from Kunjpura to Panipat, Diler Khan Marwat, with his father Alam Khan Marwat and a force of 2500 Pashtuns, attacked and took control of Kunjpura, where there was a Maratha garrison of 700-800 soldiers. On 1st November, 1760, both the armies camped in Panipat. The Maratha army was led by Peshwa's cousin Sadashiv Rao Bhau and Peshwa Bajirao's son Vishwas Rao was his ally. At that time Atai Khan Baluch, son of the Shah Wali Khan, the Wazir of Abdali, came from Afghanistan with 10,000 cavalry and cut off the supplies to the Marathas. The Marathas at Panipat were surrounded by Abdali in the south, Pashtun Tribes in the east, Shujauddaula, Atai Khan and others in the north and other Pashtun tribes in the west. Marathas were surrounded from all sides and their supplies was cut and reached in a position of starvation. Maratha chiefs began to pressurize Sadashiv Rao Bhau, to go to battle rather than perish by starvation, on 13 January, the Marathas left their camp before dawn and marched south towards the Afghan camp in a desperate attempt to break the siege.

Sadashiv Rao Bhau, with the Peshwa's son Vishvas Rao and the royal guard, was in the centre. The left wing consisted of the artillery under Ibrahim Khan Gardi. Holkar and Sindhia were on the extreme right. The Maratha line was formed up some 12 km across, with the artillery in front, protected by infantry, pikemen, musketeers and bowmen. The cavalry was instructed to wait behind the artillery and bayonet-wielding musketeers, ready to be thrown in when control of the battlefield had been fully established. Behind this line was another ring of 30,000 young Maratha soldiers who were not battle-tested, and then the civilians. Many were ordinary men, women and children on their pilgrimage to Hindu holy places and shrines. Behind the civilians was yet another protective infantry line, of young, inexperienced soldiers.

On the other side the Afghans formed a somewhat similar line, a few metres to the south of today's Sanauli Road. Their left was being formed by Najib and their right by two brigades of troops. Their left centre was led by two Wazirs, Shujauddaula with 3,000 soldiers and 50-60 cannons and Ahmad Shah's Wazir Shah Wali with a choice body of 19,000 mailed Afghan horsemen. The right centre consisted of 15,000 Rohillas under Hafiz Rahmat and other chiefs of the Rohilla Pathans. Pasand Khan covered the left wing with 5,000 cavalry, Barkurdar Khan and Amir Beg covered the right with 3,000 Rohilla cavalry. Long-range musketeers were also present during the battle. In this order, the army of Ahmad Shah moved forward, leaving him at his preferred post in the centre, which was now in the rear of the line, from where he could watch and direct the battle.

After a long wait Marathas started the combat. They emerged from the trenches, pushing the artillery into position on their prearranged lines, some 2 km from the Afghans. Seeing that the battle was on, Ahmad Shah positioned his 60 smooth-bore cannon and opened fire. On 14 January, 1761, the Marathas were defeated due to lack of supplies, non-co-operation of the local populace and inexperience of their army generals. On the other hand, Abdali had both numeric as well as qualitative superiority over Marathas. The combined Afghan army was much larger than that of Marathas. Though the infantry of Marathas was organized along European lines and their army had some of the best French-made guns of the time, their artillery was static and lacked mobility against the fast-moving Afghan forces. The heavy mounted artillery of Afghans proved much better in the battlefield than the light artillery of Marathas. The farmers of Haryana also looted a lot of the fleeing soldiers.

Almost all 27 chieftains including Vishwas Rao and Sadashiv Rao Bhau were killed and the soldiers could not even be counted. There was huge massacre in this war. According to a report about half a million Marathi people were present there in Panipat town and it is said that 40,000 prisoners as executed by Afghans. Qutub Shah's son slaughtered 4,000 fugitives near Sonipat and Abdus Samad Khan's son killed 5,000 near Bahadurgad, to avenge their father's death. Some 22,000 women and children were driven off as slaves. According to Jadunath Sarkar, there was no house in Maharashtra which did not have to mourn some member of its family.

The bodies of Vishvas Rao and Bhau were recovered by the Marathas and were cremated according to their custom. Jankoji Sindhia was taken prisoner and executed at the instigation of Najib. Ibrahim Khan Gardi was tortured and executed by enraged Afghan soldiers. The Marathas never fully recovered from the loss at Panipat, but they remained the largest empire in the Indian subcontinent and managed to retake Delhi ten years later.

While leaving, Abdali handed over Northern Haryana and Sirhind to his governor Jaina Khan and left the rest of Haryana under the control of the Mughals. Abdali returned to Kabul after making Najibuddaula the Wazir in Delhi. Najib also killed Surajmal, the most powerful ruler of that time. During the Haryana campaign itself, Najibuddaula fell ill at Hisar and appointed his son Jabita Khan as his successor in front of all the chieftains. Thereafter Najibuddaula died in 1770.

Third Maratha Invasion 1770-71

After the death of Rohela Sardar Najibuddaula, anarchy again spread in Delhi and Haryana. Maratha Peshwa Madhav Rao had also strengthened his position in the south. In such a situation, Peshwa sent Malhar Rao Holkar and Mahadji Sindhia to attack Delhi and Haryana again and establish their influence on the Mughals. The Maratha generals became successful in establishing

Maratha influence on Delhi and were successful in recapturing the Haryana region.

However, Marathas could not last long in Haryana and Delhi because Mughal chieftain Mirza Najaf Khan drove them out of Haryana and Delhi. Praising Najaf Khan, Jadunath Sarkar has written that "When we look at the life of Najaf Khan, we do not know which of his qualities to praise. Of his military skill, statesmanship, foresight or his human qualities." After the death of Najaf Khan on 26 April, 1782, the whole of Haryana again came out of the hands of the Mughals and came under the control of the old chieftains.

Fourth Maratha Invasion 1785

After the death of Najaf Khan, due to anarchy and conspiracy, the old emperor Shah Alam invited Maratha chieftain Mahadji Sindhia and appointed him as the commander and administrator of the state. Maratha chieftain Mahadji Sindhia took control of his assignments but due to his ability and quality the Mughals, Rajputs and Ruhela chieftains became his enemies. Finally, Mahadji Sindhia was forced to return to Gwalior in 1787.

Fifth Maratha Invasion 1789

As soon as the Marathas withdrew from Delhi, taking advantage of the power vacuum and anarchy in Delhi, a Rohela chieftain, Ghulam Qadir Rohela, attacked Delhi and established his supremacy. Mahadji Sindhia, who was very fond of Mughal emperor Shah Alam, attacked Delhi with an army in 1789. Rohela was defeated and fled. Ghulam Qadir was caught and brutally murdered. Sindhia again established his dominance over Delhi and Haryana. He defeated Najaf Quli Khan, the ruler of Gurgaon, Rewari, Narnaul and Konode. Sindhia defeated the Bhattis and also captured Fatehabad, Sirsa and Rania. After the death of Mahadji Sindhia in1794, his incompetent nephew Daulatrao Sindhia failed to hold the position in Haryana. Another Maratha Sardar Khanderao strengthened his position over entire Haryana. The reason for his success was his commander George Thomas.

George Thomas's Rule over Haryana

George Thomas, who had established his rule over a large part of Haryana, was a resident of Ireland. He reached Madras in 1782 in search of a job. He took up the job of a gunner with the Nizam of Hyderabad. He came to Delhi in 1787. He took up a job with Begum Samru, the ruler of Sardhana in Meerut, who had converted from a Muslim to a Christian after marrying a German Samru. Begum Samru was so impressed with George Thomas and married him her adopted daughter. Begum Samru appointed Thomas the collector of Tappal near Aligarh. But due to some political conspiracies, Thomas was retired by the Begum.

Thomas's Rule in Haryana under the Marathas

George Thomas formed an army of 250 soldiers in Anupshahr in 1783 and met Maratha Sardar Appa Khanderao and joined his army along with his men. Khanderao entrusted him with the responsibility of managing Mewat in Haryana. The Meos of Mewat were very brave and courageous but paid taxes with much difficulty. Thomas forcibly collected taxes from the Mewatis and punished those who did not pay taxes.

In 1794, Thomas plundered Gurgaon, Badshahpur, Bahadurgarh, Jhajjar and the estate of Begum Samru. Pleased with bravery of Thomas, Khanderao appointed him the Jagirdar and manager of areas like Jhajjar, Pataudi etc. apart from Mewat, where he worked till 1797. Khanderao also sent Thomas to fight the Sikhs in Saharanpur, where he was successful. Now his army had 2000 infantry, 200 cavalry and 16 cannons. For such a large army, apart from Mewat, Thomas was given the parganas of Panipat, Sonipat, and Karnal. After Khanderao's death in 1797, Thomas was relieved from Maratha service in 1798.

George Thomas as Independent Ruler

Due to deteriorating relations with the Marathas, Thomas was retired from service and by forming an army of soldiers and robbers, he established an independent state in the southern regions of Rewari, Delhi, Karnal, Patiala. His state included Jhajjar, Beri, Mandothi, the area between Pataudi and Badli, Gurgaon, Rohtak, Sonipat, Bhiwani, Fatehabad, Tohana etc. He also established a city which was known as Georgegarh (Jahajgarh). The capital of George Thomas was Hansi.

Thomas established a farmer-friendly state and also settled many villages. According to a table given by K.C. Yadav, he populated 950 old villages and established 253 new villages in 14 parganas of his state, whose total annual income was Rs. 3,47,000. In his capital Hansi, Thomas established a mint in which coins were minted. These coins were called "*Sikka-e-Sahib*". George himself prepared his cannons, guns and gunpowder.

To expand his kingdom, he attacked Jaitpur, which was under Bikaner state. Raja Suraj Singh of Jaitpur saved his life by giving one lakh rupees to Thomas. Later he attacked and captured the Maratha state Gokulgarh. In 1798, as soon as Afghan ruler Shahjamal attacked Punjab, Thomas attacked Jind's Sikh kingdom Bibi Saheb Kaur and took control of Jind. Bibi Saheb Kaur, the sister of Patiala ruler Saheb Singh, succeeded in driving away Thomas from Jind with the help of the Sikh forces of Patiala, Nabha, Kaithal, Ladwa, and Thanesar. The Sikhs pursued Thomas till Hansi but near Narnaul Thomas suddenly attacked the pursuing army and was successful. Later there was a treaty between Sahib Kaur and Thomas. Due to this treaty, Raja Saheb Singh of Patiala became angry with his sister Saheb Kaur and put her in jail. As soon as Thomas heard this news, he attacked Patiala in 1800 and plundered the city and also attacked Sirsa and captured it.

The League Against Thomas and its Fall

Despite the treaty between the Sikhs and Thomas, enmity among themselves continued. Mansingh, the ruler of Jind, lured the French general Paron of Daulatrao Sindhia, who was the commander-in-chief of the Maratha army in North India, to his side by paying him money. Hence, both Marathas and Sikhs became enemies of Thomas. They formed an alliance against Thomas in 1801 and surrounded Georgegarh. On 29 September, 1801, Thomas defeated the army of general Paron. General Paron, with the help of another French general Bogen, attacked Thomas again, but the battle was inconclusive.

Apart from the French generals of the Marathas, many Sikh chieftains joined the anti-Thomas campaign and surrounded Thomas near Jhajjar. Thomas reached Hansi to save his life on 1 November, 1801. The Union also surrounded Thomas in Hansi and finally, due to lack of army and money, Thomas surrendered on 23 December, 1801. Bogen took over all his kingdoms and ordered Thomas to leave India. Thomas was returning home but on 22 August, 1802, Thomas died at Baharampur.

Rule of East India Company in Haryana

Like the Arabs, Portuguese, Dutch and French, the British also came to India for trade. They started their trade and commerce by establishing the East India Company in 1600. Taking advantage of the anarchy spread in India and with the help of military power, the British also became a political power. Like the whole of India, Haryana region was also a victim of anarchy. Here also the British established their supremacy.

General Lake and Maratha

The credit for victory and occupation of Haryana goes to the British commander General Lake. In the last decades of the eighteenth century, the entire Haryana was under the rule of the Marathas, but there was internal discord among their chieftains. Sindhia and Holkar defeated Peshwa Bajirao II near Poona for supremacy. Peshwa sought help from the British and signed the Subsidiary Treaty. However, this treaty was not accepted by Maratha chiefs Sindhia, Bhosale and Holkar. Hence, the second Anglo-Maratha war started. After the victory of the British in this war, the British rule spread over almost the entire North India including Haryana.

The military ability and political ambition of the British commander General Lake is considered responsible for the success of the British in this war. General Lake first opened a front against Sindhia in 1803 and within two months he defeated the Marathas in the battle of Aligarh and destroyed the fort of Aligarh on 1 September, 1803. After this victory, Delhi and Agra were snatched from Daulatrao Sindhia. The most important war against Sindhia was the battle of Laswari on 1 November, 1803 in which Sindhia was completely defeated and on 30 December, 1803, he signed the treaty of Surji Arjun Gaon. According to this treaty, Sindhia handed over entire Haryana including Delhi and Agra to the British.

Metcalf and Ranjit Singh

Ranjit Singh of Lahore was expanding his kingdom and was a big challenge for the British. At that time Napoleon of France was also a threat to India. In such a situation, the British wanted to make a compromise without enmity with Raja Ranjit Singh. For this purpose, C.T. Metcalfe, on behalf of the British, went to Lahore in 1808 with many gifts. A treaty was signed between the two at Amritsar on 25 April, 1809, which is called the Treaty of Amritsar. According to this treaty, Ranjit Singh withdrew all his rights from the south-east of Sutlej. In this way, all the Sikh states of Haryana came under British protection. South Haryana also fell into the hands of the British in 1803 and North Haryana in 1809.

Company Administration in Haryana

Like different regions of Haryana, the British also entered Delhi on 4 September, 1803. They gave protection to Mughal emperor Shah Alam and took control of the entire North India except Delhi. They divided South Haryana into two parts—(i) Assigned Territory, and (ii) Areas under indirect control. After taking control of North Haryana in 1809, the British appointed a Resident in that area and implemented the administration according to their own wishes.

(i) **Assigned Territory:** This area was under the direct control of the company. The highest official of this area was the Resident who used to run the government with the help of his assistants. It included Panipat, Sonipat, Samalkha, Gannaur, Haveli Palampur, Palwal, Nuh, Hathin, Nagina, Tapukda, Sohna, Indri etc.

(ii) **Areas under Indirect Control:** These included the rest of Haryana, conquered in 1803 and 1809, which were governed by princely states. The British gave many areas to their Indian allies and took away the jagirs from those who did not help them. The prominent princely states were—Pataudi under Faizal; Loharu and Jhirka under Ahmad Baksh Khan; Rewari under Rao Tej Singh; Hodal under Murtaza Khan; Palwal under Mohammad Ali Khan Afridi; Rohtak, Meham, Beri, Agroha, Hisar and Hansi were first given to Bambu Khan, then Ahmad Baksh and finally, to Samad Khan. The area of Kunjpura was left with Nawab Diler Khan. Begum Samru of Sardhana was given some parts of Karnal and Gurgaon. The rulers of Jind, Thanesar, Ladwa and Shamgarh were given old jagirs. The princely states acquired from Ranjit Singh in 1809 were also allowed to remain with the old rulers. All these rulers ruled at the behest of the British Resident, but they did not interfere in their internal affairs.

It can be concluded that after the chaos created in Mughal courtiers, the Marathas turned to North India and established their supremacy by defeating the local powers. They also gained influence over the Mughal court and the emperor. Although Abdali caused damage to the Maratha power, the Marathas became prosperous again. They won and also ran the government with the help of George Thomas. But the Marathas had to surrender before the British. The British also cleverly acquired a large part of Haryana region from Ranjit Singh without fighting.

15

The Rise of Nawabi Kingdoms and Entry of Sikhs in Haryana

In the last years of Aurangzeb, there were frequent rebellions in North India and local powers became independent. Nadir Shah's invasion put the last nail in the coffin of the Mughal Empire. Sikhs and Marathas established their kingdoms in Haryana along with other areas.

Fall of the Mughal Empire

Emperor Aurangzeb spent his last twenty-five years away from Delhi, fighting battles with the kings of the south, who were mostly Muslims. Absence of Aurangzeb in Delhi created a kind of power vacuum in North India, due to which rebellion and anarchy spread throughout North India. Jats, Sikhs, Marathas and native princely states became independent and started attacking the Mughal territories. Jat king Rajaram attacked Sikandra, dug up Akbar's grave and burned the bones. The Sikhs revolted and the Marathas also strengthened themselves.

At the time of Aurangzeb's death in 1707, the opponents and rebels who had tasted power wanted to keep themselves independent at any cost. In this way, the condition of Mughal power went from bad to worse. Like other areas of Mughal empire, the hold of the Mughals also remained weak in Haryana region. Local powers emerged and established order in their respective areas. Faujdar Khan in Farrukhnagar, Gopal Singh in Ballabhgarh, Rao Nandram in Rewari, Sahajad Khan in Hisar, Najabat Khan in Kunjpura established order. Rohtak, Panipat, Sonipat and Karnal remained under the Mughals only in name. The Marathas took advantage of such crucial circumstances.

Delhi rulers being subservient to their ministers, ministers becoming emperor makers, incompetence of rulers and princes, Iranian-Turani conflicts in the Mughal court etc. made the Mughal empire in worst condition. The Mughal Empire became even weaker due to foreign and Maratha attacks. Jats and Marathas also jumped into the court fight and started appointing ministers and even the emperors. In this way, Mughal rulers became puppets in the hands of their own feudal lords and feudal lords and ministers established independent kingdoms at different places of their influence. The same situation happened in Haryana also.

Nadir Shah's Invasion

Nadir Shah, the ruler of Iran, invaded India in 1739. At that time India was ruled by Mughal emperor Mohammad Shah and the Mughal Empire was at the peak of its decline. Mughal amirs and provincial governors became more powerful and did not obey their ruler. Taking advantage of the chaos, Nadir Shah first attacked and captured Kabul. From Kabul, Nadir Shah captured Punjab and reached Ambala on 7 February, 1739. After looting Ambala he went to Shahabad. On 10 February, 1739, Nadir Shah captured Thanesar. Even now the local rulers and people were fighting against Nadir Shah and were losing without the help of Emperor Mohammad Shah. Here Mohammad Shah was still confused as to how to counter the Iranian invader Nadir Shah.

Responding the invasion of Nadir Shah, the Mughals, Marathas and other chieftains marched towards Karnal to fight Nadir Shah and camped on the banks of river Yamuna in Karnal on 18 February, 1739. Nadir Shah had an army of 30 thousand, while the royal army numbered 75,000. Both armies fought on 24 February, 1739, and Nadir Shah became victorious in this battle popularly known as battle of Karnal. The Mughal army suffered heavy casualties and about 8,000 soldiers of the royal army were killed. The Mughal army, though large in numbers, was ill-equipped and had outdated artillery compared to Nadir Shah's disciplined and manoeuverable forces. The Persian army's use of firearms and artillery, particularly targeting the Mughal war elephants, played a decisive role in the battle. The defeat at Karnal hastened the decline of the Mughal dynasty.

After Karnal, Nadir Shah marched towards Delhi and captured the emperor. Mohammad Shah was compelled to pay a large indemnity to Nadir Shah, leading to his submission and acceptance of Persian control. This marked the beginning of Mughal vassalage to the Persian ruler of Delhi and looted and massacred a lot. Despite Mohammad Shah's co-operation with Nadir Shah, rumors and discontent spread among the population of Delhi, leading to an uprising. This unrest culminated in a violent massacre in which the city was sacked, resulting in a significant loss of life and turmoil.

On 1 May, 1739, Nadir Shah went back with a lot of wealth and also took the Peacock throne and the Kohinoor diamond with him. Nadir Shah did not establish his kingdom in India but he definitely broke the Mughal empire. After Nadir Shah's departure from Delhi, Mughal nobles declared independence and many princely states were established in Haryana too.

Rise of Nawabi Princely States

Many princely states emerged in Haryana in the eighteenth century. Rewari, Ballabhgarh, Farrukhnagar, Hisar, Rania, Kunjpura etc. were prominent among them. The descriptions of the main princely states and principalities are as follows:

Rewari

Rewari state was established in 1555 by Rupa Singh, a chieftain of Tijara. He belonged to a community called Ahir. Members of this group are linked to the Yadav community. This area was given to Rupa Singh by Mughal emperor Humayun because Rupa Singh had helped Humayun against Suri Afghans. When Rupa Singh's son Ram Singh eliminated the bandits of his area, Akbar was pleased and made Ram Singh the Faujdar of Rewari. According to Abul Fazal's "*Ain-e-Akbari*", Rewari had a total of 12 palaces, 2175 horsemen and 14,600 infantry.

Ram Singh's son Shahbaz Singh fought with Badgujar dacoit Hathi Singh of Dihana (Badshahpur) and was killed. His son Nand Ram killed Hathi Singh in Agra. The then emperor Aurangzeb was pleased and gave Nand Ram the title of "Choudhary" and made him the governor of Rewari pargana. Nand Ram established Nandrampur and Dharuhera villages and built Nandsagar pond in Rewari. Nand Ram's son Bal Kishan (1713-1739) fought with Nadir Shah in the battle of Karnal with 5,000 soldiers and was martyred along with his soldiers. Mughal Emperor Mohammad Shah gave the title of "Rao Bahadur" and a mansab or chieftainship of 5,000 to Bal Kishan's son Rao Gujarmal (1739-1750) .

In the Rewari state of Rao Gujarmal, Dadri, Hansi, Hisar, Mahendragarh and Narnaul were also included. Bahadur Singh, the ruler of Ghasera, wanted to take revenge from Gujarmal for the murder of his father, the dacoit Hathi Singh. Bahadur Singh got Rao Gujarmal killed with the help of his father-in-law Todarmal, the ruler of Neemrana. After that Rao Bhawani (1750-1758), Hira Singh, Tej Singh etc. ruled Rewari state. During Tej Singh's time, his area included Tauru, Sohna, Nuh, Hodal, Palwal, Tapukda, Kot Kasim, Bawal etc. In 1803, Lord Lake attacked Rewari and annexed all the areas except 58 villages to the British kingdom. After the death of Tej Singh in 1823, Rewari was divided between his two sons—Rao Puran Singh and Rao Nath Singh. After him, Rao Tularam and Rao Gopal Dev became rulers and they took part in the revolt against the British in 1857. Ultimately, the British annexed 58 villages to the British Empire.

Ballabhgarh

Taking advantage of Aurangzeb's death, many anarchist elements started raising their heads. Among them, Jat Chaudhary Ram Gopal Singh used to loot in one of the settlements (Ballabhgarh). Mughal ruler Farrukhsiyar appointed Ram Gopal Singh the Chaudhary of Faridabad and gave him the right that he can keep one *anna* out of one rupee of rent collected.

Ram Gopal Singh's son Charandas stopped sending revenue to the Mughals. On this conduct Charandas was arrested and called to Delhi. Charandas's son Ballabh Singh got his father released by meeting the Jat king of Bharatpur. Ballabh Singh's father had made Ballabh Singh wear his own turban during his lifetime. Ballabh Singh built a fort and named it Ballabhgarh. Ballabh Singh had good relations with the Ahirs of Rewari and the Jats of Bharatpur. During the time of Mughal ruler Ahmad Shah, Ballabh Singh was attacked by the royal forces because he did not pay revenue. Ultimately, Ballabh Singh and his sons were killed.

Wazir Imad Khan acquired the estate of Ballabhgarh and Faridabad and assumed the title of Nizamul Mulk. He renamed Ballabhgarh as Nizamgarh. But on the intervention of Jat king Surajmal, Ballabh Singh's successors Bishan Singh and Kishan Singh were appointed as fort commanders. After them Hira Singh and Bahadur Singh ruled the state. In 1829, Raja Nahar Singh became the ruler and there were a total of 101 villages under him. Raja Nahar Singh of Ballabhgarh took part in the revolt of 1857. After the collapse of the revolt, the British hanged him and confiscated the estate of Ballabhgarh.

Kunjpura

Kunjpura state in Karnal district was established in 1739 by Pathan Najabat Khan who came from Kandhar. Najabat Khan had supported Nadir Shah in the Karnal war for which he got this state. In 1748, for supporting Abdali, he received the estate of 149 villages as reward which was completely tax free. In 1750, Nawab Khan built a fort in Kunjpura which was named "Lal Qila". He was murdered in 1760. After Najabat Khan, Nawab Diler Khan (1760-1773) and Gulsher Khan (1773-1801) became the rulers. After them, Nawab Rahmat Khan, Nawab Bahadurjang Khan, Nawab Ghulam Ali Khan were the descendants of Nawab Najabat Khan of Kunjpura. The last Nawab of Kunjpura, Ibrahim Ali Khan, migrated to Pakistan after the partition of India and died in Lahore in 1953.

Farrukhnagar

The state of Farrukhnagar was founded by a Mughal governor named Baloch Sardar Faujdar Khan (Dalel Khan) in 1732. Nawab Faujdar Khan received the area of Hisar from Nawab Shahzad Khan in 1737, over which he had a war with Gujarmal of Rewari and after being defeated, Hisar was merged into Rewari. In 1757, Raja Surajmal of Bharatpur ruled Farrukhnagar for seven years. After the death of Surajmal in 1763, Mughal Wazir Ghaziuddin handed over Farrukhnagar to Musa Khan. In 1850, Nawab Ahmad Ali Khan became the ruler of Farrukhnagar. He took part in the rebellion of 1857. After the suppression of the rebellion, the British sentenced death punishment to Nawab Ahmad Ali Khan and included the Jagir in the British Empire.

Rania

After the return of Nadir Shah to Persia in 1739, Mohammad Hasan Khan, the head of Bhatti clan of Sirsa, laid the foundation of Rania state by taking control of Sirsa, Rania and Fatehabad. But Mohammad Hasan Khan also had to fight with the rulers of Bikaner and Patiala over territorial rights. After the death of Hasan Khan, Mohammad Amir Khan became the ruler of Rania, who was defeated by Kamruddin, the commander of Raja Gaj Singh of Bikaner and Rania came under the influence of Bikaner. In 1774, Raja Amar Singh of Patiala attacked Rania and defeated Amir Khan and took control of Rania. In 1781, Mughal Wazir Najaf Ali Khan, along with the king of Jaipur, attacked the region and got Rania, Sirsa and Fatehabad and handed over these areas to Rania's successor Amin Khan.

After the death of Amin Khan, the Rania state was divided between Amin Khan's two sons Bahadur Khan and Kamruddin Khan who ruled their estate from Fatehabad and Rania. In 1792, Maratha administrator Mahadji Sindhia attacked Rania and brought it under his influence. The British also attacked Rania and Fatehabad in 1810. Khan Bahadur Khan, the ruler of Fatehabad, was given a monthly pension of one thousand rupees and the ruler of Rania, Jabit Khan, was allowed to continue as the ruler after accepting British subordination. But in 1818, the British again defeated him, confiscated his estate and fixed a monthly pension for his living. The pensioner ruler of that place, Noor Samad Khan, took part in the revolt of 1857 and was hanged after the revolt was suppressed.

Ramgarh

Rajput Miyan Khushal Singh (1763-1785), a Chandel lineage of Chanderi, established Ramgarh Riyasat near Panchkula in 1763. There were a total of 125 villages in this state. The successors of Miyan Khushal Singh were Miyan Maldev Singh (1785-1820), Miyan Devi Singh (1820-1854), Miyan Ranjit Singh (1854-1881), Sardar Bahadur Pradyuman Singh (1881-1902), Sardar Sahib Aniruddh Singh (1902-1928), Sardar Sahib Jagjit Singh (1928-1954). They were loyal to the British, so their state remained under the British for a long time.

Pataudi

Pataudi princely state was established in 1806 by Nawab Faiz Talab Khan with the grant of British officer Lord Lake. Nawab had helped Lord Lake in his campaign against Marathas. In the battle of Bhanpura, Faiz Talab Khan was injured while fighting with Holkar and was taken prisoner. After winning the battle, Lord Lake released him and gave him the estate of Pataudi. After the death of Faiz Talab Khan in 1829, his son Nawab Mohammad Akbar Ali Khan became the ruler of Pataudi. In 1857, he helped the British along with his army. After the death of Akbar Ali Khan in 1862, many rulers ruled

Pataudi. Nawab Iftikhar Ali Khan (1917-1952) became the eighth ruler and Nawab Mansoor Ali Khan (1952-2011) became the ninth ruler. Nawab Mansoor Ali had only a title. He also inherited the Bhopal state through his mother Sajida Khan as she was the only daughter of Nawab Hamidullah Khan of Bhopal.

Jhajjar

Jhajjar city, which was settled by Chhajju Jat during the time of Mohammad Ghori, was made a princely state by Nawab Najabat Ali Khan in 1806. In the Anglo-Maratha war of 1803, Najabal Ali Khan supported Lord Lake. His successors Faiz Mohammad Khan in 1813, Faiz Ali Khan in 1835 and later Nawab Abdurrahman Khan in 1845 became the rulers of Jhajjar. The Nawab had supported the rebels in the rebellion of 1857. After the suppression of the rebellion, the Nawab was executed in Delhi on 24 December, 1857.

Loharu

The name Loharu is derived from the Lohar (blacksmith) caste, coins of Jaipur were minted here in Loharu city. The Loharu princely state was established by Ahmad Baksh Khan in 1803. This area was given to him by Raja Bakhtawar Singh of Alwar after being pleased with Ahmad Baksh Khan for mediating with British general Lord Lake. Ahmad Baksh Khan was succeeded by Nawab Shamsuddin, Nawab Aminuddin (1835-1869), Nawab Alauddin Mahmood Khan (1869-1884), Alauddin Ahmad Khan (1920-1926), Aminuddin Ahmad Khan II (1926-1947), the rulers of Loharu.

Dujana

The princely state of Dujana was founded by Abdus Samad Khan in 1806. Abdus Samad Khan first held a high position with Peshwa Bajirao and later joined Lord Lake's army. Lord Lake had given him the kingdom of Dujana in return for his services. After the death of Abdus Samad Khan in 1825, Nawab Mohammad Dunde

Khan (1825-1850), Nawab Hasan Ali Khan (1850-1867), Nawab Mohammad Saadat Khan (1867-1879), Nawab Mohammad Mumtaz Ali Khan (1879-1908), Nawab Mohammad Khurshid Ali Khan (1908-1925), Nawab Mohammad Iqtadar Ali Khan (1925-1947) ruled Dujana estate.

Bahadurgarh

The princely state of Bahadurgarh was founded by Nawab Ismail Khan in 1806. Earlier this city was called Sharafabad, which was founded by Rathi Jats. After the defeat of Sindhia in 1803, Lord Lake gave Bahadurgarh to Nawab Ismail Khan of Jhajjar. In 1808, Nawab Ismail Khan made his son Nawab Jang Bahadur the Nawab of that place. Jang Bahadur took part in the rebellion of 1857. Because of his participation in the revolt against the British, his estate Bahadurgarh was dissolved.

Firozpur Jhirka

Firozpur Jhirka estate was granted by the British to Ahmad Baksh Khan in 1803, in lieu of his services for mediating between Lord Lake and the king of Alwar, Bakhtawar Singh. After the death of Ahmad Baksh Khan in 1827, his son Nawab Shamshuddin Khan (1827-1835) became the ruler of Firozpur Jhirka. But Nawab Shamshuddin did not get along well with the British. Therefore, he got Delhi resident Willian Fraser murdered. The Nawab was tried and hanged in 1835 and the state of Firozpur Jhirka was annexed to the British Empire.

Rise of Sikhs in Haryana

The Sikhs also took advantage of the chaos prevailing in the Mughal Empire. They had an old enmity with the Mughals. They revolted against the Mughals under the leadership of Banda Bahadur and achieved success.

Revolt of Banda Bahadur

Banda Bahadur or Banda Bairagi's real name is not known, but he called himself Banda after meeting Guru Govind Singh in Nanded. He was also called Bairagi because of his Bairagi life and he was also called Bahadur because of his rebellion and bravery. K.C. Yadav believes that Banda was from Rohtak. Anyway, Banda met the Guru in Nanded and he asked Banda to go towards the north. Obeying the Guru's orders, he came to Rohtak and taking advantage of the anarchy in Delhi, raised the flag of rebellion. A large number of Jat and Sikh youth had gathered under him. According to Khafi Khan, "In just two to three months, Banda had gathered 5,000 horsemen and 8,000 infantry."

Banda first attacked the royal ruler of Sonipat and captured Sonipat. After this Banda attacked Kaithal, Thanesar, Kunjpura, Shahabad and was successful. According to K.C. Yadav, "Banda's army looted the cities to its heart's content and cut thousands of people like carrots and radishes." After these initial victory, Banda attacked Sirhind because the governor of that time, Wazir Khan, had killed two sons of Guru Gobind Singh. The war between the two sides took place on 22 May, 1710, in which Banda became victorious and killed Wazir Khan.

Banda made Sirhind his headquarters and prepared an army of 40,000 soldiers. He started ruling from there. Mughal ruler Bahadur Shah sent the chieftains and armies of Jodhpur, Jaipur, Moradabad, Allahabad, Mewat to attack Banda. The army was led by Firoz Khan Mewati of Mewat. On 26 October, 1710, the royal army badly defeated Banda's army between Indri and Karnal. Banda was also defeated in Thanesar and Shahabad and then he was defeated in Panipat too. Later, taking advantage of Bahadur Shah's death and anarchy in Delhi, Banda captured Batala, Jammu and Sirhind.

In 1713, Mughal Emperor Farrukhsiyar again sent his army against Banda. The royal army led by Khidmat Talab Khan defeated Banda and drove him out of Punjab. Banda took refuge in the fort of Lohgarh (Mukhlispur) in Haryana. The royal army again chased Banda and forced him to hide in the mountains. Banda continued to wage guerilla war. Banda was caught along with his

750 companions on 19 December, 1715 in Gurdaspur. He was brutally killed in Delhi on 15 March, 1716. Thus, Farrukhsiyar succeeded in establishing peace in Haryana.

Sikh Princely States in Haryana

During the downfall of the Mughal Empire, the Sikhs in Haryana as well as Punjab started increasing their power by forming Misls. After the last attack of Ahmad Shah Abdali in 1763, the Sikh Misls attacked Sirhind in January 1764 and killed the governor Jain Khan. After this, they captured most of the areas of Punjab and Haryana one by one and established their own states.

Kalsia

The state of Kalsia was established by Sardar Gurubaksh Singh in 1760 after defeating Hakim Adani Beg of Hoshiarpur. Its capital was Chhachhrauli and it had 181 villages and two towns. Gurubaksh Singh Karora belonged to the Sindhia family and named this state after his village Kalsia. His son Sardar Jodh Singh (1785-1818) expanded the state. Maharaja Ranjit Singh also granted it some areas. Sardar Sobha Singh (1818-1857) had helped the British a lot in the rebellion of 1857. Sardar Sobha Singh was succeeded by Sardar Lahna Singh, Bishan Singh, Jagjit Singh and Ranjit Singh who became one by one the chiefs of the state. They were given the title of Raja in 1916. After this Raja Rao Singh, Raja Sher Singh became the kings of Kalsia state or misl.

Kaithal

As per the mythology, Kaithal is known to be the birthplace of God Sri Hanuman Ji, hence its original name was Kapisthal, as the place of Kapi (Hanuman). Thereafter, Kaithal became the short form of Kapisthal. There is a famous place in the name of His mother Mata Anjani Devi, known as "*Maa Anjani Ka Tila*".

The princely state of Kaithal in Haryana was established in 1767 by Bhai Deshu Singh by defeating two brothers named Bhik Baksh Khan and Niyamat Khan, the rulers of Kaithal. Among the successors of Bhai Deshu Singh, Bhai Badal Singh, Bhai Lal Singh, Bhai Pratap Singh, Bhai Udai Singh (1819-1843) were the rulers of Kaithal. When Udai Singh died childless, the British did not allow his wife Mahtab Kaur to adopt a son for succession and annexed the princely state to their empire by giving the pension to the queen.

Ambala

It is surmised that Ambala city to have been founded by Amba Rajput during the 14th century CE. Another version is that the name is made of Amba Wala or the mango-village judging from mango groves that existed in its immediate neighbourhood. Still another version is that the city has taken its name after goddess "Bhawani Amba" whose temple still exists in Ambala city.

After Abdali's last attack on India (1763), Sardar Sangat Singh took control of Ambala. At the time of the death of Sangat Singh in 1768, his commander Gurubaksh Singh became the ruler of Ambala. After that his wife Daya Kaur took over the kingdom. In 1808, Raja Ranjit Singh captured Ambala. But the British signed the Treaty of Amritsar (25 April, 1809) with the king in Lahore Maharaja Ranjit Singh, according to which the king withdrew his forces from Ambala and assured not to attack across the Sutlej river. In this way, the British brought Daya Kaur back to Ambala. After the death of Daya Kaur in 1822, the British abolished the princely state and established a military cantonment in Ambala.

Narayangarh

During the decline of the Mughal Empire, Raja Lakshmi Narain of Nahan (Sirmur) state constructed a fort in Kulsan, which he named Naraingarh after himself. Later on Narayangarh became an important princely state situated amidst the hills near Ambala. The state of Narayngarh was established by Mirza Singh in 1784 by snatching its king at Nahan (Sirmaur). Raja Ranjit Singh captured Narayangarh in 1807. But according to the Treaty of Amritsar, Ranjit Singh had to leave the state and the British returned the state to its ruler Fateh Singh Ahluwalia. After the First Anglo-Sikh War in 1845-46, the British abolished the princely state and annexed it to their state.

Jind

Raja Gajpati Singh (1763-1789), who belonged to the Phulkian Misl of the Sidhu Jat clan of Sikhism, established the Jind State. Gajpati Singh attacked and killed the Afghan Faujdar of Sirhind, Jain Khan, in 1763 and established the Jind State. In 1768, the Mughal Emperor recognized this state. Gajpati Singh expanded his kingdom by defeating the ruler of Nabha. After the death of Gajpati Singh, his son Bhag Singh (1789-1819) became the ruler of Jind. He helped Lord Lake against the Marathas in 1803. He prevented his nephew Maharaja Ranjit Singh from establishing relations with the Maratha chieftain Jaswant Rao Holkar.

After Bhag Singh became disabled, Pratap Singh and Rani Sobrahi became administrators. After his death, Fateh Singh (1819-1822), Sangat Singh (1822-1834) and Sarup Singh (1837-1864) became rulers. Sarup Singh helped the British in the revolt of 1857. His successor Raghvir Singh (1864-1887) helped the British in the Second Afghan War. The last ruler of Jind was Ranveer Singh (1887-1947).

Budhiya

Sikh Sardar Nanhu Singh established Budhiya Riyasat 10 km away from Yamuna Nagar. After him Bhag Singh, Sher Singh, Jaimal, and Gulab Singh became the rulers of Budhiya state. Jeevan Singh helped the British in the revolt of 1857. At the time of partition of India in 1947, the ruler of Budhiya was Raja Anmol Singh who saved the Muslims from the violent people in Budhiya.

Thanesar

Thanesar was an ancient capital of the Pushyabhuti dynasty, whose rulers conquered most of Aryavarta following the fall of the Gupta Empire. The Pushyabhuti emperor Prabhakarvardhana was a ruler of Thanesar in the early seventh century CE. He was succeeded by his sons, Rajyavardhana and Harsha. Al-Biruni, an Iranian scholar and polymath, wrote in his book "*Tahqiq-e-Hind*" that the city of Thanesar is held in high regard by Hindus. The idol worshipped in the city is called Chakrasvamin, which means the owner of the Chakra, a weapon previously described in the book. The idol is made of bronze and is almost the same size as a man.

Thanesar Riyasat was established by Meeth Singh in 1760. There were two forts in Thanesar, the first was under the control of the Shaikhs and the second was under the control of Deshu Singh. Firstly, Raja Meeth Singh got the fort from the Shaikhs. Later his successors Bhag Singh and Bhagga Singh took control of the second fort as well. After Meeth Singh's death in 1791, Bhag Singh (1791) became the ruler but after his death in the same year Sardar Bhagga Singh (1791-1815) became the ruler. After the death of Sardar Fateh Singh (1815-1819), the British took over half of the Riyasat in 1834. In 1850, the British also took over the remaining half of the Riyasat.

In this unit we saw that after the fall of the Mughal Empire, rebellion and anarchy prevailed in the entire Haryana. In Haryana, Mughal Subedars and Sardars were defeated and fled. They were replaced by new princely states. After defeating the Marathas, the British themselves distributed a large part of Haryana as estates to their loyalists. Later, those princely states which supported the British in the revolt of 1857 continued to exist and the rest were annexed to the British Empire.

16

Arya Samaj, Sanatan Dharma Sabha and Development of Education

During the nineteenth century many social and religious movements were started to end the increasing evils in religion and to bring the religious purity. Arya Samaj and Sanatan Dharma Sabha are prominent among them. These movements also developed education to a great extent. Because without education it was almost impossible to come out of the evils. Along with this, the government also indirectly helped these movements by emphasizing on modern education.

Emergence of Arya Samaj in Haryana

Many religious and social evils were prevalent in various regions of India during the nineteenth century. The area of these evils had spread so much that every aspect of human life started getting affected by it. Therefore, to end these evils, the Renaissance movement started in the 19th century. Arya Samaj, Brahma Samaj, Ramakrishna Mission, Singh Sabha, Aligarh Movement, Theosophical Society etc. were important among these movements. As for Haryana, two movements were prominent, first Arya Samaj and second Sanatan Dharma Sabha movement.

Swami Dayanand Saraswati founded Arya Samaj, a Hindu reform movement, on 10 April, 1875 in Mumbai. The philosophy of Arya Samaj is based on the principles of Vedic teachings and seeks to promote values such as truth, righteousness, and social reform. He wrote two important books *Satyarth Prakash* and *Arya Abhinav*. Swami Dayanand came to Ambala in Haryana on 17 July, 1878, but at this time he had to change trains. But, his arrival in the true sense took place in 1880, when he stayed in Rewari in Haryana. In Rewari, Swami Dayanand started preaching by sitting between the *Chhatris* of Rao Mansingh, near the railway station, near a small pond. After some time, Arya Samaj branches were established in Rohtak and other parts of Haryana.

Teachings of the Arya Samaj

Swami Dayanand based his teachings on the Vedas which can be summarised as follows:

1. There are three entities that are eternal:

(i) The Supreme Lord or *Paramatma*.
(ii) The Individual Souls or *Jivatmas*, which are vast in number but not infinite.
(iii) *Prakriti* or Nature.

2. *Prakriti* or Nature, which is the material cause of the creation, is eternal and is characterized by *Sattva*, *Rajas*, and *Tamas*, which tend to be in equilibrium. In every cycle of creation, the conscious Supreme Lord will disturb its equilibrium and make it useful for the creation of the world and its forces and to manufacture the bodies required by the individual souls. After a specific time called the day of the *Brahma* (*Brahma* means great, lengthy etc.), the creation would be dissolved and nature would be restored to its equilibrium. After a period called the Night of *Brahma*, which is equal to the length of the day of the *Brahma*, the creation would set forth again. This cycle of creation and dissolution is eternal.

3. *Jiva* or *Jivatma* or individual eternal soul or self, are many who are different from one another yet have similar characteristics

and can reach the "same level" of happiness in the state of *Moksha* or Liberation. They are not made out of natural particles and are bodiless, beyond all genders and all other characteristics as seen in the world, but they acquire a body made out of Nature and it is known as taking "birth". These souls are subtler than Nature itself but take birth through the body as per the creative principles set by the Supreme Lord based on their past *karmas*, and they put effort into improving themselves. By realizing oneself, Nature, and the Supreme Lord, individual souls are liberated. But this realization depends on their efforts and knowledge. They keep coming to the world, use Nature, obtain the fruits of their actions, and appear taking myriads of lives of different animals (those who have attained higher intellectual bodies can also go back to lower forms based on their *Karmas* or actions), they redo their actions, and are free to choose their actions, learn and relearn, attain liberation. After the long duration of *Moksha* or Liberation, would come back again into the world. Since this period of *Moksha* or Liberation is long, it appears as though they never return or they never take birth again, by the other beings who are still in the world. Since they are eternal and capable of working, these characteristics cannot be destroyed. They are timeless, eternal but are not omniscients and hence cannot be the pervaders of entire space.

4. The Supreme Lord who is one without second like him, whose name is *Om*, is the efficient cause of the universe. Lord's chief characteristics are—*Sat*, *Chit*, and *Ananda*, i.e. "Exists", has "Supreme Consciousness" and is "Eternally Blissful". The Lord and his characteristics are the same. The Supreme Lord is ever present everywhere, whose characteristics are beyond Nature or *Prakriti*, and pervades all the individual souls and the Nature. It is not characteristic of the Supreme Lord to take birth or incarnate. He is ever pure, i.e. unmixed by the characteristics of Nature and the individual souls. The Supreme Lord is bodiless, infinite, hence has no form and hence cannot be worshipped through idols but can only be reached by any being through *Yogic Samadhi* as advocated in the *Vedas* which is summarised in the *Yoga Sutra* of Patanjali. Since

the Lord is bodiless and hence beyond all genders, the Vedas address him as father, mother, friend, cause of the worlds, maker etc. He is the subtlest entity which is subtler than Nature, Pervading and filling the entire existence and space. It is due to his subtlety that he could take hold of Nature to create the worlds and he proposes no difficulty for the motion of the worlds in space. Hence, he is called *Parmatman*, which means "Ultimate Pervader". There exists neither who is equal to him nor completely opposed to him. The ideas of Satans, Ghosts etc. are foreign to the Vedas.

5. He said the names Agni, Shiva, Vishnu, Brahma, Prajapati, *Paramatma*, *Vishva*, *Vayu* etc. are the different characteristics of the Supreme Lord, and the meaning of each of the names should be obtained by *Dhatupatha* or root. And these names do not refer to any Puranic deities. Also, certain names may also refer to the worldly elements which should be distinguished from their contexts.

6. Regarding the notion of *Saguna* and *Nirguna* in explaining the nature of the Lord. *Saguna*, he says, refers to characteristics of the Lord such as pervasiveness, omnipotency, bliss, ultimate consciousness etc. and, *Nirguna*, he says, refers to those characteristics which do not characterize the Lord, for example: of Nature and the individual souls such as different states of existence, taking birth etc.

7. *Moksha* or state of liberation does not refer to any characteristic place but it is the state of individual souls who have achieved liberation. The *Jivas* or individual souls are characterized by four different states of existence which are: (i) *Jagrat* (wakefulness), (ii) *Swapna* (dreaming), (iii) *Sushupti* (deep sleep), and (iv) *Turiya*. It is in the fourth *Turiya* state, that the individual souls exist without contact with Nature but are conscious of their own selves, other individual souls, and the Supreme Lord (or Eternal Truth). This state of *Moksha* or *Turiya* is not seen in the world hence incomparable but can only be realized. In this state, they are free of every tinge of Nature and possess their own minds and experience bliss, the pleasure of their freedom, and the like, which are incomparable with any form of pleasure in the world. They are bodiless in that state and can attain any form of pleasure

by their own will without requiring any external agent such as, for example, they can perform the function of ears on their ownself without requiring material ears etc. In that state they are capable fulfilling of all their wishes, can go anywhere they want right then and there, witness the creation, maintenance, and dissolution of the worlds, they also come in contact with other individuals who are liberated. But in that state, the creative powers remain with the Supreme Lord because the powers of the Lord and the Lord himself are not different things. In *Moksha*, the individual souls remain distinct from one another and from the Supreme Lord. And, by means of their own capability and with the Supreme Lord as their means, they enjoy the bliss. After the period of *Moksha*, they pass on to this world again, in support of which, he quotes *Veda Mantras* and *Mundaka Upanishad*, in his books *Satyarth Prakash* and *Rigvedadi Bhashya Bhumika*.

8. Again, it is the mark of Maharshi Dayanand's wit that he reconciles the notion of unending or Eternal *Moksha*. He says, the "Eternal *Moksha*" or "*Ananta Moksha*", refers to the permanency of pleasures of "*Moksha*" unlike the momentary pleasures of the world, and does not necessarily mean the individual souls will remain in *Moksha* permanently. He clarifies it by saying that the individual souls are permanent and hence their characteristics also, and it is "illogical" to consider that an individual soul would get trapped in one of the moments of the beginningless time, and escape the world for eternity by using the finite time period of his lives in different creature forms. Even if the illogical is accepted then also it means that even before he got trapped in creation, he was in *Moksha*, and hence his *Moksha* period may fail at times is the conclusion that is contradictory to the assumption that *Moksha* is an infinite period of time. Hence, the Vedic teaching that the individual souls should come back after liberation should be considered valid. In a different point of view, he clarifies the same idea by saying that all actions whatever, are done for a finite time period cannot yield infinite results or fruit-of-actions, and after the period of *Moksha*,

the *jivas* or individual should not have the capability to enjoy the bliss of *Moksha* further.

Development and Propagation of Arya Samaj

The preaching of Arya Samaj is centred around the certain principles and teachings. The subject of Swamiji's preaching was the refutation of eight lies. These eight lies included: (1) Eighteen Puranas, (2) Idol worship, (3) Sectarianism, (4) Tantra Granth and Bagh Marg, (5) Use of alcohol and intoxicants, (6) Adultery, (7) Theft, and (8) Deceit and lies. Swamiji also established a branch of Arya Samaj in Rewari.

The Arya Samajists conduct religious ceremonies, prayers, and discourses that focus on promoting the values of truth, morality, and social responsibility. Swami Dayanand considered the knowledge of Vedas important for human life. He gave the slogan to the people to "Return to the Vedas". The land of Haryana was suitable for Swamiji's teachings. The poor farmers here wanted to escape from expensive customs and ostentation. Swamiji's teachings, besides being based on the Vedas, were quite simple which the common man could understand. Therefore, following the teachings of Swamiji and Arya Samaj, the people here considered them very true. Arya Samaj expanded in Haryana in the following manner:

(i) **Spread of National Consciousness:** Swami Dayanand developed the feeling of love for the people of Haryana. In his sermons, Swami explained the importance of patriotism. He believed that dependent people cannot attain happiness even in dreams. According to him, humans should have a feeling of complete dedication for the country.

(ii) **Propagation by Swami Dayanand:** When Swamiji came to Rewari in Haryana, he himself propagated his ideas. Here he was welcomed by Ahir leader Rao Yudhishthir and he became his follower and disciple. People of this region also became members of Arya Samaj. On the request of Swamiji, Rao Yudhishthir also got a cowshed constructed.

(iii) **Contribution in the Field of Education:** Swamiji believed that if we want to save our religion and culture, we will have to accept Vedic and other teachings. Arya Samaj started the Gurukul education system in Haryana which was the centre of pure Indian education. The first Gurukul was built in Gujranwala in 1900. Later it was shifted to Kogdi (Haridwar). In 1911, Swami Shraddhananda established a Gurukul in Kurukshetra. In this way, many Gurukuls were formed all over Haryana, among which the Gurukuls of Rohtak, Hisar and Jhajjar are important. Arya Samaj later also established Dayanand Anglo Vedic Schools.

(iv) **Contribution in the Field of Religion:** Arya Samaj opposed many evils like child marriage and encouraged widow remarriage. The people of Arya Samaj stopped the people from converting to religion and called Arya religion the best religion. Started purification and organization movement to make people Hindu again. He strongly condemned idol worship, useless worship methods and unnecessary ostentation. Orphanages and widows' homes should be built for social welfare.

Contribution of Prominent Persons in the Propagation of Arya Samaj

The credit for promoting Arya Samaj in Haryana goes to many people, the first name among them is of Pandit Bastiram of Sultanpur Khedi village. Born in 1841, Bastiram was first a priest and later he met Swami Dayanand first in Haridwar and then in Rewari and became his disciple. He used to promote Arya Samaj while singing with Ektara. Due to his efforts, Arya Samaj spread in Rohtak and Jhajjar districts. The credit for promoting Arya Samaj in Rewari goes to Rao Yudhishthir.

Lala Lajpat Rai also gets a lot of credit for spreading the Arya Samaj in Haryana. Lala Lajpat Rai was born in Jagraon, Punjab in 1865. His father was a teacher in a government school in Rohtak. Lalaji became the chief propagatorr of Arya Samaj in Rohtak and worked to infuse new life into the society. Local leaders like Choudhary Pirumal, Choudhary Maturam, Choudhary Ranpat Singh etc. supported him in this work. Due to their efforts, Arya Samaj preachers started going to far-off villages and spreading propaganda against the evils. Along with propagating Arya Samaj, he also prepared the background for political and social awakening by giving patriotic lectures. Soon, signs of renaissance started appearing among the people of Rohtak district and especially among the Jats.

In 1886, Lala Lajpat Rai went to Hisar and started practicing law and there he founded the Arya Samaj. Lakhap Rai, Chudamani Vakil, Seth Chandulal and Seth Hiralal gave him a lot of support in this work. In the words of Lala Lajpat Rai, "Chandulal was a philanthropist of high order. He was always ready to serve others day and night. It is my belief that if Chandulal had been more educated, he would have been in the category of great leaders of this country. In fact, he was the most respected person in his field."

The credit for spreading the Arya Samaj in the rural areas of Hisar and Rohtak goes to Dr. Ramji Lal. Dr. Ramji Lal belonged to a Jat family in Rohtak district but he served in Hisar and made the Arya Samaj more popular. He had a lot of influence in the Jat community and in the rural areas. In the words of Lala Lajpat Rai, "He was very unique in his caste. I have never seen an English-knowing Indian in my life like Dr. Ramji Lal, who used to meet people of his uneducated caste without any discrimination. His house in Hisar was like a Jat Dharamshala."

Apart from Hisar and Rohtak, Arya Samaj had spread to the cities and towns of Ambala, Karnal, Gurgaon by the end of the century and its centres had been established. According to the Census report of 1901, "There is only one religious institution of Hindus in Ambala city. Its name is Arya Samaj. Most of its members are English educated." Gurgaon Deputy Commissioner has written in his report that, "There is no religious institution here except Arya Samaj. Only this religious movement is spreading in the last ten years. Many Ahirs follow the principles of Arya Samaj."

Arya Samaj and the British Raj

Arya Samaj was not directly connected to the national movement but due to its members participating in the national movements, the British started associating Arya Samaj with politics. In the reports sent to the British Government by the British officials of Punjab, an attempt was made to prove Arya Samaj to be a political organization. They said that:

(i) The leading leaders in the Rawalpindi riots of 1907 were Arya Samajis. Denzil Ibbstson has written that "Arya Samaj is the centre of treason."
(ii) Dayanand wanted to make India Aryavarta again. Words of patriotism and nationalism were on his lips. He once told the Christian priest that the days of your downfall are coming like the downfall of the Aryans.

Along with these efforts of the British Government, Munshiram and Lala Hansraj kept trying to prove that Arya Samaj is not a political organization. Nevertheless, due to the participation of Arya Samajists in the national movement in Punjab, the cycle of repression by the government continued on the Samajists. The British believed that the principles of Arya Samaj were going to shake the foundation of the British government in India. Showing Arya Samaj's love for its ancestors was the simple solution to drive the British out of India. The British started harassing people belonging to Arya Samaj and confiscated and burned their books and magazines. Following are the details of some such incidents:

(i) In 1889, six students were expelled from Lahore Central Training College on the orders of Sir James Lyall. These students were accused of publishing Arya magazine.
(ii) In the same year 1889, three other students of the Lahore Central Training College were expelled for publishing a magazine in which an attempt was made to prove the importance of Swami Dayananda's commentary on the *Yajurveda*.

(iii) The three jailors of Panipat showed their diary to Munshiram (Swami Shraddhanand) in which it was written that the jailor is very good but he is an Arya Samaji and hence he should be kept under surveillance.

(iv) The British Government had a harsh attitude towards the 10th Jat Battalion because of the Arya Samaj. This battalion had more Jats from Hisar and Rohtak districts. In 1898, the Arya Samaj was also formed in this battalion in which speeches were given every Sunday. Although these speeches were religious, they also had an indirect political touch. For this reason, Colonel Hunter expelled four Jat soldiers from the regiment and burnt their books.

After these episodes, the British officers started specially monitoring the activities of the Arya Samaj and they implemented "Seditious Meeting Act" in Hisar and Rohtak districts and decided that Arya Samaj Jats should not be recruited in the army. But due to opposition in the London Parliament, the government had to withdraw the decision of "Seditious Meeting Act".

Sanatan Dharma Sabha

Influenced by the Arya Samaj movement, orthodox Hindus of Haryana formed the Sanatan Dharma Sabha. The leader of this movement was Jhajjar's Pandit Deen Dayal Sharma, a lecturer. He was born in Jhajjar in 1863. He was well-versed in Persian, Urdu and English. He formed a society named "Rifa-e-Aam" in Jhajjar, whose members were people of both Hindu and Muslim religions. From Jhajjar he also published a weekly newspaper named "Hariyana". After this, he went to Vrindavan and studied Hindi and Sanskrit. Later, he also published a weekly newspaper in Urdu named "Mathura" from Mathura city. In 1897, Pandit Deen Dayal established "Bharat Dharma Mahamandal" in Haridwar. Along with this, he started religious education in Haryana and Jhajjar became the centre of the first Sanatan Dharma Sabha in 1890. After Bhiwani, Sanatan Dharma Sabha was also formed in Hisar in 1891.

Pandit Nekiram Sharma was the main leader of Sanatan Dharma Sabha in Bhiwani and Hisar.

In 1892, Karnal also became the centre of Sanatan Dharma Sabha. In the same year, Sanatan Dharma Sabha was also established in Kurukshetra. Around 1895, Sanatan Dharma Sabha was also formed in Safidon, Rewari, Palwal, Kaithal, Panipat, Rohtak, Beri and Gurgaon. After this, Sanatan Dharam Sabha was established in every small and big town and many big villages of Haryana. Due to this, the faith that people had lost in Sanatan Dharma was re-established. The Sabha established temples, cowsheds and educational institutions at various places throughout Haryana through which Sanatan Dharma was propagated. Even after the partition of Pakistan, the strength of Sanatan Dharma continued to increase.

Development of Education

Most of the population of Haryana region lived in villages, where there were no educational institutions. Therefore, Haryana was very backward in the field of education. In nineteenth century Haryana, the meaning of education was different from today's education. Only a person who was skilled in his traditional system was considered educated. For example, a farmer with more knowledge of agriculture was considered educated, a Brahmin with knowledge of religion was considered educated etc. A very few people used to send their children to educational institutions, because for this they had to be sent to big cities. The "*Government Records*" edited by Sharp shows that in Rohtak, Hisar and Gurgaon districts, there were a total of 70 schools for Hindus, in which 886 students were educated by 70 teachers. There were a total of 27 schools for Muslims, in which 886 students were educated. There were 247 schools in Delhi district, most of them were in Delhi city itself. There were 5-6 schools in Panipat, in which the number of students was very less. Karnal had a population of 20,000 but there was only one school.

These Hindu and Muslim schools running at that time did not get any support from the government. Here education was either given free or the children had to bear it. Teachers were mostly Brahmins or Maulvis, who taught in temples, mosques and in their homes. Whatever limited knowledge the teachers had, they imparted it to the students. Mostly children between 6 to 15 years were enrolled in schools. The school curriculum was also simple and the methods of teaching were quite old and unscientific. Everything was based on rote and memory.

Government's Education Policy Before 1857

In 1813, the government's policy towards education was indifferent. But after the passing of the Act, a change was brought in the education policy and it was decided that "every year a grant of one lakh rupees should be set aside to promote education and literature, to encourage enlightened Indians and to spread knowledge and science among the residents of British India." Unfortunately, these instructions remained buried in government files.

Instead of the government, some government officials, understanding their human responsibility, took some constructive steps in this direction. William Fraser, who was an assistant here, opened schools in two villages in Sonipat Pargana in 1816. Fraser opened the third school in 1820 and the fourth in 1823. He used to give one rupee per month to each child and one rupee per month to each parent, so that the children come to study daily and the parents keep sending their children to school. Fraser did this because Fraser's schools were in the countryside, and the children studying there were farmers. Farmers would have to suffer in sending their children to school, so they generally did not send them to school. Hindi and Urdu reading-writing and accounting were taught in these schools, because there were no resources here to teach English and science.

General Committee of Public Instruction

In 1823, the government formed the "General Committee of Public Instruction" to control and promote education. Fraser also requested this committee to provide financial assistance to his schools so that good education could be provided in the villages. Emphasizing the speciality of his work, he wrote, "It is not so important to open schools in cities and towns, because the residents here are mostly those who can afford to educate their children. But the children of poor farmers and common people of the villages are resourceless. It is very important to help them. They are also more in number and will be benefited from right education." But unfortunately Fraser's request was rejected as it was against their policy and thus Fraser's schools were closed due to lack of funds. It is worth noting here that the government's policy was also to provide education to the resourceful and not to the needy poor, because the foundation of British imperialism also rested on the shoulders of these rich, resourceful and respected class.

(i) **Efforts of James Thomson:** In 1843, James Lieutenant Thomson became the Lieutenant Governor of the North-West Frontier Province (Haryana was a part of this province). Like Fraser, he too was in favour of spending government money on the education of the rural class instead of the education of the upper class. He said, "The majority of our population is farmers. They are cheated by government officials, lawyers, rich *baniyas* due to their ignorance, illiteracy and naivety. If the farmer becomes literate, no one will be able to exploit them." Keeping these things in mind, a detailed plan for opening schools was sent to the Government of India. When the plan was not approved, Thomson sent another plan in 1846. According to this, a school should be opened in every village which had a population of 200 houses. For this, it was recommended to give 5 to 10 acres of land to the villagers for free, so that the expenses of the school master could be met. The government rejected this plan of Thomson as well. In 1848, Thomson again sent a plan. According to this, there was a proposal to open at least one government school in every tehsil, along with this, a system of opening and properly inspecting indigenous schools was also proposed. Fortunately, the government accepted this plan but due to lack of funds, the government could not implement it with immediate effect.

Wood's Dispatch

In 1854, an important change came in the government policy. This time, the problem of money was resolved in the dispatch of Sir Charles Wood. It was also proposed that private institutions engaged in the spread of education should be given financial help, in this way a lot of money will be saved and it can be spent on spreading education in the villages. With this saved money, tehsildar schools were opened in Rohtak and Gurgaon. At the same time, some town schools were also opened like Karnal, Rohtak (1856), Bhiwani, Rewari, Ambala, Jagadhari (1857). At the same time, another scheme was made which is called "Halka Bandi School Scheme". According to this scheme, there was a plan to open a school between every 10-20 villages, but due to the start of the rebellion, the whole plan came to a halt.

Government Education Policy After 1857

In 1858, Haryana was merged with Punjab. After this merger, the situation changed a little. The Education Department of the Punjab Government planned to open a government school at a distance of every six miles for the development of education, but due to lack of financial resources, the plan could not be fully implemented. At that time, most of the students studied in local schools. There were very few government schools at that time.

District	Number of schools	Number of students
Delhi	216	3304
Gurugram	55	659
Karnal	77	1042
Rohtak	99	1184
Sirsa	122	1014
Ambala	138	2090

It is clear from the above table that the number of children going to school was very low. Government's neglect was the biggest reason for this and the villagers also considered education useless. The villagers gave priority to their traditional occupation, because the means of livelihood were very limited. The condition of girls' education was even worse. Schools were opened for girls' education in the 1870s but were gradually closed due to lack of students. For example, in Karnal, ten schools were opened for girls in 1870, the number of which reduced to four in 1900.

In the twentieth century, the government laid great emphasis on education. In 1918, the government made a five-year plan for education. The main objective of this plan was to open as many primary schools as possible in villages. It was provided that there should be a school in every place where there are 50 students. According to the Government of India Act, 1919, the Punjab Government passed the "Punjab Primary Education Act 7" and emphasized on the necessity of primary education. This plan was started in 1922 from Rohtak district. Here 6 schools were selected for this work. After this, it was adopted on a trial basis at other places as well. The main features of this Act were as follows:

(i) Compulsory education was made optional for local administration.
(ii) It was applicable only to children between 6 and 11 years of age.
(iii) This was restricted to an area of two miles from the school.
(iv) This education was provided free of cost.

In 1937, the responsible government elected in Punjab laid full emphasis on the expansion of primary education. The Unionist Government of communist ideology was giving special emphasis on rural areas. This government opened many schools. After 1940, more schools were opened in Haryana region than in Punjab. In 1937-38 alone, 1975 new schools were opened. In 1940-41 this number was 1270, while in 1946-47 it was 1498. Most of these schools were opened in rural areas because there were already many schools in the cities.

Higher Education

There was a lack of higher education and educational institutions in Haryana. Before 1927, there was no college in Haryana. After high school, students had to go to Delhi or Lahore for secondary or higher education. The first government college for classes up to intermediate in Haryana was opened in Rohtak in 1927. The first college for full BA classes was opened in Ambala in 1938 in the name of S.A. Jain College. Three years later, the college in Rohtak also became of BA level. In 1944, the second private college All India Jat Heroes Memorial College was opened in Rohtak. Ahir College was opened in Rewari by the Mahasabha. In 1946, the Vaishya community built Vaishya College in Rohtak. Thus, by 1947, the number of colleges in Haryana was 6 in number.

It has been seen in this whole chapter that Arya Samaj spread widely in Haryana. Mainly Jats and other farmers were most influenced by Arya Samaj. Arya Samaj denounced idol worship which had become an integral part of Hindu religion. Some people considered it a threat to Hindu religion and formed Sanatan Dharma Sabha. This Sabha called Hindu religion Sanatan Dharma and justified idol worship. It denounced Arya Samaj as well as Islam and called upon all Sanatanis to remain attached to their religion. We have also studied that Haryana region which was completely illiterate, became the most educated with the help of the government and many schools and colleges were opened.

17

Revolt of 1857

During the British rule, the people of entire India including Haryana were troubled by their policies. The ruling class was feeling humiliated day by day and the people were getting crushed under the burden of taxes and debt. The East India Company, which was a trading company, could not think of anything other than increasing its profits. It was following the *dharma* of trade forgetting the duty of the king. The company had also started playing with the society and religion of the Indians for its own benefit. In such a situation, when the rebellion was started by the sepoys, the fire of rebellion spread in almost all the parts of North India including Haryana, which took a lot of time for the British company to pacify.

Reasons for Discontent Against the British in Haryana

The East India Company, which had established its power in Haryana in 1803, had by 1856 harassed the people with its ignorant administrative system, social and religious interference and deadly economic policy. That is why when the rebellion took place in 1857, the entire public including most of the princely states took part in it. The reasons for the rebellion of 1857 are as follows:

Economic Exploitation

The system of British administration was based on economic exploitation. In the rural state of Haryana, from 1803 to 1857, the Company officials exploited the poor people very badly. Farmers had the highest tax burden. Farmers had to pay about 80 per cent of their produce as tax in the form of various taxes. Farmers were always harassed for not paying taxes because it often happened that due to famine and lack of good rainfall, farmers were not able to pay taxes on time. Apart from farmers, artisans and craftsmen were also victims of the policies of exploitation of the British. Cottage industries were destroyed when every small and big item was imported from abroad. In this way, the atmosphere of rebellion against the British rule was heated up everywhere. The Revolt of 1857 provided an auspicious opportunity to the people of Haryana to quench the fire of their discontent and take revenge from the British.

Excess Land Tax

Haryana is an agricultural region. The Company used to collect too much taxes from the farmers that their economic structure had deteriorated badly. According to K.C. Yadav, "The land tax system implemented by the British ruined the farmers of Haryana. This system was not implemented with the consent of the people. When the settlement was implemented, if the village head objected, he was put in jail." The timing of collecting land tax was also very wrong. Government employees used to reach the farmers even before the harvest. They were more strict while collecting taxes. Therefore, the farmers who were unable to pay the taxes would leave the village and ran away. These types of statements are often recorded in the then government documents related to land tax, "This village is completely empty and hence land tax cannot be collected." "Half the farmers of this village left the village and ran away."

Devastation by Famines and Epidemics

In those days, the land of Haryana was completely dependent on rain. When there was very little or no rain, there used to be famine. By 1857, there were five-six major famines, which devastated the lives of the people in Haryana. People did not get any government assistance during famines. People became weak and sick due to malnutrition, i.e. not getting enough food. The diseases were so terrible that they often took the form of epidemics. Thousands of citizens died in Haryana due to the contagious epidemic of 1841. In 1843, there was an epidemic again and thousands of people died in that too. The government did not provide any help in all these famines and epidemics. Due to this, hatred against the government kept increasing among the people. In the words of Maulana Fazle Haq Khairabadi, "The economic crisis and epidemics had made people the ultimate enemies of the British. Half-fed, helpless and defeated by helplessness, the people of Haryana used to wish day and night for the end of the exploitative government."

Destruction of Village Biradaris and Village Panchayats

In Haryana region, village biradaris or communities and panchayat administration were important for centuries, through which people used to resolve their minor issues voluntarily. They used to consider themselves safe with this system. The British ignored these institutions and imposed their own law and order and imposed police-court on them, due to which people became afraid. With the establishment of the revenue department, the importance of these panchayats decreased with the establishment of tehsil and district level courts. This spread discontent among the people. R.C. Dutt has written, "Village biradaris and village panchayats were formed according to the needs of the people and people used to feel safe and happy under their protection. Their destruction led to social instability and people started feeling insecure."

Faulty Judicial System

The Judicial System of the British Government took a lot of time and a lot of money had to be paid in the British courts. These courts had become a means of exploitation of the poor people in the hands of rich and deceitful persons. False witnesses could be bought and false documents could be prepared. Justice was delivered on the basis of corrupt lawyers and absurd arguments.

Dissatisfaction among Native Kings and Nawabs

There were 40 princely states in Haryana at the time of British Company rule. The British had a harsh attitude towards those princely states which did not flatter them. Hence, the Company Government seized Rania in 1818, Ambala and Shahabad in 1823, Ladwa and Thanesar in 1845-46, Kaithal in 1843, Ferozepur Jhirka in 1835 and some areas of Rewari in 1803. Apart from this, the British Company had started undue interference in the internal matters of Jind, Chhachhrauli, Kunjpura, Karnal and Loharu. Hence, in the revolt of 1857, most of the princely kings supported the revolt directly and indirectly. Since the people of these princely states were emotionally attached to their rulers, the people also participated in the revolt to the fullest.

Discontent among Soldiers

The British army, due to which the British were able to capture the whole of India, included about 80 per cent Indians. These Indian soldiers were commonly called Sepoys. Thay were recruited mostly on lower positions and despite their qualifications, they were not promoted to higher positions. Their salaries and allowances were much less than that of British soldiers. They did not get any separate allowance for their foreign expeditions and their religion was also corrupted. Indian soldiers used to think that if they could conquer the whole of India and hand it over to the British, then they could also drive away a handful of the British from the country. Therefore, the greased cartridge case of 1857 gave practical shape to their thinking.

Religious Reasons

All the people of Haryana, especially the rural people, were of the view that the British wanted to convert them into Christians and the greased cartridge had confirmed their suspicions. It was also proved by the fact that those who accepted Christianity were given high positions in the services and ranks. This fear of Hindus and Muslims made them intent on revolting in 1857.

Immediate Cause

In 1856, a new Enfield rifle was introduced in the British army and to use this rifle the greased cartridges were used by cutting it with teeth. In 1857, the news spread that cow and pig fat was used in these cartridges. Due to these rumours, people of both Hindu and Muslim communities got angry and refused to use these cartridges. The first rebellion against the British on issue of greased cartridges took place in Barrackpore on 29 March, 1857. Mangal Panday and his companion were hanged for their revolt. On 10 May, 1857, the military rebellion was suppressed in Ambala. On the same day, on the evening of 10 May, 1857, a fierce rebellion took place in Meerut, the spark of which spread throughout North and Central India including Haryana.

Progress of the Rebillion

Even before the rebellion broke out in Meerut on 10 May, 1857, the 60th native platoon in Ambala Cantonment rebelled but made a compromise with the British. In the afternoon of the same day, the 5th Indian Army again mutinied but they too had to compromise. On the same day, on 10 May, 1857, in the evening, the soldiers revolted in Meerut and after killing some British, marched towards Delhi through the night and reached Delhi in the morning on 11 May, 1857. In Delhi, rebel soldiers declared the deposed Mughal Emperor Bahadur Shah Zafar the Emperor of India and established their power. Native kings and rebel soldiers from every corner of North India started gathering in Delhi. Here the soldiers gathered in Delhi started establishing their control over the surrounding areas.

Revolt in Gurgaon and Mewat

On 13 May, 1857, about 600 soldiers attacked Gurgaon but the Deputy Commissioner William Ford defeated them at a place called Vijvasan. The next day the revolutionaries again attacked and defeated William Ford and looted a lot. Defeated William Ford fled towards Delhi. The revolutionaries got hold of Rs. 78,000 from the Gurgaon treasury. As soon as the news of the rebellion reached Mewat, all the Mewatis became united against the British. One by one the Mewatis captured places like Sohna, Nuh Tauru, Firozpur Jhirka and started ruling in the name of the Emperor Bahadur Shah Zafar. When the British again took control of Delhi in September 1857, they also tried to capture Mewat region, but here they had to face defeat at several places. The Mewatis gave a tough fight to the British at places like Ghasera, Roopraka, Rewasan, Mahu etc. In the end, after the loss of a lot of money and people, the British succeeded in capturing Mewat region also.

Revolution in Rohtak

Revolution broke out in Rohtak district in the third week of May. Here the Ranghars and Rajputs liberated the entire Rohtak from the British control. The people of Rohtak accepted Bahadur Shah Zafar as their leader and started ruling in his name. The British sent the 60th Desi Battalion from Ambala to suppress the Rohtak rebellion, but the soldiers themselves rebelled on 10 June, 1857. After the revolt of the sepoys, Hodson came to Rohtak with a large army, but at the place of Kharkhoda, Subedar Virasat Ali gave him a tough fight. According to Hodson, "The villagers of Rohtak fought like demons, but in the end the revolutionaries lost." Moving ahead, Hodson attacked Rohtak where the revolutionaries fought bravely, but Hodson had the upper hand after getting help from Jind state. However, as soon as Hodson returned to Delhi, the revolutionaries again captured Rohtak.

After the fall of Delhi, the British sent an army under Cortland to attack Rohtak. But the revolutionaries, frustrated by the fall of Delhi, surrendered and Rohtak finally came under the control of the British.

Revolt in Hisar

Like Rohtak, the revolt broke out in Hisar district also in the third week of May. Here the soldiers of Haryana Light Infantry located in Hisar, Hansi and Sirsa rebelled and the entire public supported them. Prince Mohammad Azam led the revolutionaries of Hisar. The British sent an army under the leadership of General Van Cortland, Deputy Commissioner of Firozpur, to deal with them. On the way, revolutionaries under the leadership of Nawab Noor Mohammad of Rania attacked them. The Nawab was defeated, captured in Ludhiana and hanged.

On 18 June, 1857, residents of Chatrawan village killed a British officer, Hillard, and his brother-in-law. The people of Sirsa village also revolted but the British burnt both the villages and killed several hundred people. After conquering small villages, Van Cortland reached Sirsa. After two weeks of struggle in Sirsa he was able to get control of the entire pargana. Van Cortland reached Hisar on 17 July, 1857. In Hisar also he carried out a massacre and imprisoned the wife of Prince Mohammad Azam. The revolutionaries were defeated at Hansi. In this way, the British rule was re-established over the entire district.

Revolt in Panipat and Thanesar

The flames of revolution also flared up in Panipat and Thanesar districts. The Gujjars settled on the banks of Yamuna; the Jats in Kaithal, Assandh, Jalmana; the Ror people of Kol, Pipli and Amin; the soldiers of Kurukshetra and the Sikhs and other castes of Ladwa chased away the British and established their own kingdom. Since the road to Delhi passed through these areas, the British wanted to crush the rebellion of that area quickly. When the British asked for help from the native kings, the king of Patiala sent 1500 soldiers and four cannons. The king of Jind sent 400 soldiers; the rulers of Kunjpura and Karnal also helped the British with 350 and 150 soldiers respectively. But all of them failed in their boast.

In the last days of May, the British again sent an army from Delhi. They faced the revolutionaries at Panipat. A fierce battle took place and the British commander General Anson was killed. Many soldiers were also killed and the rest fled. But with the arrival of more troops from Punjab, the British succeeded in liberating the main road. The leader of the revolutionaries, Imam Bu Ali Shah Kalandar, was hanged by the British. Still the revolutionary flame was alive in the villages, which could be extinguished only after the fall of Delhi.

Revolt in Ambala

Ambala was the first area in Haryana where the flame of revolution first broke out on 10 May, 1857. Here the native soldiers, i.e. the constables had rebelled but the rebellion was crushed by threatening them. But the public was with the rebels. Ambala's Deputy Commissioner Forsyth has written that, "The entire public in his district is sympathetic to the rebels." He further writes, "The businessmen of Jagadhri, who have always been benefiting from our government, could not show loyalty towards us in these difficult times. But despite such sentiments, the people of Ambala could not revolt openly due to strict military surveillance."

Failure of the Revolt

Although the Hindus and Muslims of Haryana fought together against the British, the revolt failed due to poor leadership, military weakness and lack of organization. The fall of Delhi on 20 September, 1857 had destroyed the morale of the revolutionaries. Almost the entire army of Delhi was ready to crush the revolution in entire Haryana. With the help of the armies of the native princely states, the British started taking control of all the regions one by one.

War in Rewari, Jhajjar and Narnaul

After the fall of Delhi, Brigadier General Showers left Delhi with 1500 soldiers and artillery on 2 October, 1857 to suppress the rebellion in Haryana. He first attacked Rewari, but the revolutionary leader Tularam Rao had already left Rewari and fled to Rajasthan. After his first victory Showers attacked Jhajjar on

12 October, 1857. Nawab Abdurrahman here was friendly with both the emperor and the British. When the Nawab got the news of Showers's attack, he came to Chhuchhakwas and took shelter under Showers. He was arrested by Showers and sent to Delhi. Similarly, rebel Nawab Ahmad Ali of Farrukhnagar and rebel Raja Nahar Singh of Ballabhgarh were also taken prisoner and sent to Delhi by Showers. In Delhi they were hanged.

When Showers went to Delhi, Rao Tularaam formed a coalition of revolutionaries. It included Prince Azam of Hisar, General Samad Khan, son-in-law of Nawab Jhajjar and Rao Tularaam of Rewari. Later, a rebel group from Jodhpur of Rajasthan also joined them. All of them gathered in Narnaul. The British sent an army to Narnaul on 16 November, 1857 under the leadership of Colonel Gerard. The number of revolutionaries was 5000 and there were 12 cannons. A battle took place between the two sides near the village of Nasibdur. In the words of Malleson, "It was a heroic battle. The enemy had never fought with such bravery and courage before. He neither hesitated nor was afraid. We had never been attacked so fiercely before."

Rao Kishan Singh died first in this war, which broke the morale of the Indians. But when Gerard was killed, the courage of the Indians increased again. But British Commander Coalfield took charge and started firing artillery. Luck was with the British and the worthy Rao Ramlal, Prince Mohammad Azam, son of General Samad Khan were martyred. In this way, the British became victorious.

War in Gurgaon or Mewat

Mewat was a region of Gurgaon district. The people of this region were very brave and fighters. The Chaudharys of this region had taken power under the Emperor Bahadur Shah Zafar as soon as the rebellion started. Even after the fall of Delhi, the Mewati people did not want to lose their independence. Therefore, after conquering Delhi, the British had to set out to conquer Mewat. The British army under the leadership of Brigadier General Showers first attacked Gurgaon and captured it on 2 October ,1857. Rebel leader Bakhtar Singh was hanged. The Deputy Commissioner William Ford again started his work in Gurgaon from 13 October, 1857.

General Showers headed towards Mewat with Gurgaon's Assistant Collector Wilgram Clifford. On 31 October, 1857, a war took place between the two sides in Raisina village. Many British soldiers including Clifford were killed in this battle. The rest of the British army ran away. But Showers again launched a fierce attack on Raisina and burnt the entire village. Showers handed over the entire area to the Gurkha Regiment under the leadership of Captain Drummond and went to Farrukhnagar.

After Showers' departure to Farrukhnagar, Lieutenant Grant attacked Ghasera village on 8 November, 1857. Initially, Ali Hassan Khan Mewati defeated the British. But the British were victorious in the second attempt and set many villages on fire. Similarly, the Mewatis of villages and towns like Nuh, Sohna, Tauru, Rupraka, Mahun, Tigaon etc. gave a tough fight to the British. But later due to lack of modern weapons, the Mewatis finally faced defeat. In this way, the entire Mewat and Gurgaon again came under the control of the British.

Nature of the Revolt

1857 is the first such event in history which has been written about the most, but even now there is disagreement among historians as to what this event actually was. The British consider it a military revolt or mutiny. Indians call it the first war of independence. While some scholars try to link it to a mass revolt and some to religious discontent.

Mutiny

Imperialist historians and contemporary British officials consider the incident of 1857 to be a military mutiny. Among these scholars, the names of John Key, John Seeley, Colonel Malleson, Ibbitson, Charles Rex etc. are prominent. They believe that Indian soldiers had adopted the path of rebellion many times before for their caste problems, salary hike, allowances etc. At the time of the Sindh conquest, Charles Napier had also said that "There is so much dissatisfaction among the Indian soldiers that they will definitely revolt in the future."

They are of the opinion that revolt of 1857 was also fought by the soldiers because of greased cartridges. The cartridges of the new infield rifle were kept wrapped in greased paper, which had to be bitten with the teeth before use. The rumour was spread that the fat was of cow and pig and the British wanted to corrupt the religion of Indians. Following the greased cartridges issue, there were revolts among the soldiers first in Damdama, then in Barrackpur and later in Ambala and Meerut. These soldiers reached Delhi and gave a wider scope to the rebellion.

Seeley has written that "The rebellion of 1857 was a selfish sepoy rebellion devoid of patriotic spirit, which had no leadership and no popular support." Indian historians write that this was not just a military rebellion but the result of 100 years of misrule by the Company.

War of Independence

The historians and scholars like V.D. Savarkar, Disraeli, Ashok Mehta, Pandit Jawaharlal Nehru, Dr. Tarachand etc. have confirmed that this was the result of dissatisfaction of military and civilian Indians towards the British rule. Every revolutionary had only one desire to free India from the British and to create a large and independent India. In a manifesto from Delhi it was said that, "Young and old, educated and uneducated, citizens and soldiers, all Indian brothers should come to the field to free themselves from the foreigners."

Pandit Nehru says that, "It was much more than a military revolt. It spread quickly and assumed the form of a popular revolt and the Indian freedom struggle." Dr. Tarachand has written, "For the first time in history, the whole of India became aware of the antagonism between its own and the other, the Indian and the foreigner. The initial development of this consciousness of Indianness found expression in the form of revolt." But some historians like Dr. Sen and Majumdar do not confirm this notion. They believe that at that time there was a lack of nation and nationalism.

Religious War

James Outram, William Taylor and modern historian William Dalrymple have described the revolt of 1857 as a joint conspiracy of Hindus and Muslims on the basis of religion. Sir Syed Ahmad Khan has also described religion as the second basis of this revolt. The policies of the British and the work of Christian missionaries had awakened the Pandits and Maulvis from their slumber. The social reforms of the government were also an attack on religion among Hindus. The fat of cow and pig also incited the soldiers religiously. That is why when the revolt took place, the Hindus raised slogans of *Jai-Jai* and the Muslims *Ali-Ali* and entered the capital Delhi saying *Din-Din*. Appearing in the court of the emperor, the soldiers said, "We have joined hands with each other to protect religion." If the number of rebels is seen, more Muslim *Jihadis* participated in the revolt without any greed than the number of soldiers.

People's Uprising

Many historians and scholars like Maulana Abul Kalam Azad, R.C. Majumdar, Bipin Chandra, Irfan Habib etc. have described it as a mass revolt. They believe that even though the revolt was started by the soldiers, the common people, which included farmers and labourers in large numbers, took it forward. The common people were spreading the spirit and message of revolt by distributing *chapatis* in every village and used to say, "Everything will turn red."

Historian George Dodd believes that the distribution of *chapatis* was going on from Sutlej to Patna and the entire population was involved in it. This is the reason that when the rebellion was suppressed, the atrocities committed by the British on Indian farmers, landowners and artisans are unparalleled in history. Entire villages were burnt down. Properties were confiscated and thousands of people were hanged on the basis of suspicion.

It could be concluded that countless Indians sacrificed their lives and property for their country. They opened the path of nationalism for their future generations. This was the first time that Hindus and Muslims came together and accepted a slogan and a flag. This was a signal for the future generations that they too can unite and liberate India and bind the whole of India in the thread of unity by creating Hindu-Muslim unity.

18

Political Consciousness and National Movement in Haryana (1885–1919)

Although the people of entire Haryana took part in the rebellion of 1857, this armed movement could not stand long against the trained British army equipped with modern weapons. After the failure of the revolt, the educated middle class took the responsibility of leading the movement in India. These educated people started the movement against the British in a well-organised manner. The Indian National Congress was established and under its flag all the people of Haryana once again came forward in a new way to oust the British. Mahatma Gandhi was their popular leader and following his ideals the people of Haryana were taking part in all the national movements.

Political Consciousness

Until the second half of the nineteenth century, people did not have political or national consciousness. Everyone was busy in their professions. But when their professions and interests were attacked, they jumped into the rebellion of 1857. The rebellion of 1857 failed but political consciousness arose among the people. Everyone understood that the British Government can never be a well-wisher of Indians. There were many reasons for political consciousness and nationalism in Haryana. Some of the main reasons are as follows:

Policies of the British Government

The British being foreigners and continuing to be foreigners and exploiting the Indians was a big reason for national consciousness among Indians. The British kept sending their earned money to England and kept exploiting the Indians. This created hatred for the British in the hearts and minds of Indians and this hatred led to love for their countrymen and they started thinking that all Indians are one and India belongs to Indians.

The British Government developed means of transport for its colonial interests. Construction of railways is important among these means. Railways were used to transport raw materials like jute, cotton, indigo, tea etc. from villages, markets and cities to ports. In Haryana region, the first railway line was laid between Delhi, Rewari, Bhiwani and Hisar in 1862-63. After this, Hisar-Sirsa railway was constructed in 1884, Delhi-Ambala-Kalka in 1891 and Narwana-Kaithal railway in 1898. People of entire Haryana and the entire country got connected to each other through railways and they realized that India is a great country and everyone's interests are the same and the British are exploiting the wealth of India.

Apart from railways, the British started providing Western education to Indians. They wanted cheap clerks to run their administration. Apart from this, they believed that Indians who received English or Western education would be Indians by colour but English by mind and would be loyal to the British. But their education policy made Indians aware of their rights. Many Indians, by reading their literature and becoming aware of Western knowledge and science, made themselves capable of taking their rights and attaining independence.

Role of Literature and Newspapers

The merger of Haryana in Punjab in 1858, literature and newspapers started developing in Haryana as well, which were the powerful medium for national consciousness. Sardar Dayal Singh Majithia of Lahore was the first to publish a newspaper called "*The Tribune*" in Punjab in 1885. This newspaper became very famous not only in Punjab but also in Haryana. This newspaper was a source of inspiration for the people of Haryana in the freedom struggle.

Pandit Deendayal Sharma Vyakhya Vachaspati from Jhajjar started two newspapers named "*Rifa-e-Aam*" and "*Haryana*" which could not run for long. In 1889, a newspaper "*Khair Andesh*" started getting published from Ambala. Apart from this, the people of Haryana received a lot from the literature and newspapers coming from other states. These literature and newspapers were "*Kohinur*", "*Rahbar*", "*Bharat Pratap*", "*Akhbar-e-Chunar*", "*Zamana*", "*Azad*", "*Hindi Bangvasi*", "*Hindustan*", "*Bharat Mitra*", "*Sudarshan*", "*Vaishyopkarak*", "*Saraswati*" etc.

Babu Bal Mukand Gupta of Rewari was a poet of high order. He was the pioneer of nationalism in Haryana. Following are his two lines showing the influence of the British Raj and his helplessness:

> "*Bahut Din Beete Ram Prabhu Khoya Apna Des,*
> *Khowat Hain Ab Baith Ke Bhasha, Bhojan, Bhesh*"

(It has been a long time since Ram Prabhu lost his country, now I am looking for language, food and garment.)

According to K.C. Yadav, Balmukand created anger among the people towards the British Government through his writings. Apart from Balmukand, Babu Muralidhar, Pandit Madhav Prasad Mishra etc. also awakened political consciousness among the people of Haryana through their literature and made people aware of the exploitation and atrocities of the British.

Contribution of Middle Class

The development of education and employment opportunities gave birth to a new class, the middle class, in Haryana. This included engineers, doctors, teachers, businessmen, moneylenders etc. People of the middle class could explain their views well to the general public. They formed many organizations to unite and keep people safe. Through these organizations they gathered and started speaking against the atrocities of the British. Due to their efforts, national consciousness developed and the base of the national movement was strengthened.

Babu Muralidhar, Madhoram in Ambala; In Hisar Lala Lajpat Rai, Pandit Lakhpat Rai, Lala Choodamani etc. were prominent in awakening national consciousness. In 1884, Surendra Nath Banerjee, the founder of the "Indian Association", came to Ambala and here also established the "Indian Association". These organizations also spread national consciousness very rapidly in Haryana.

Role of Social and Religious Reform Movements

Social and religious organizations had a great influence in Haryana. Arya Samaj first gave the slogan of "Swarajya" to the people of the country. Almost all the workers of Arya Samaj were involved in politics and were awakening national sentiments among the people. Lala Lajpat Rai, Dr. Ramji Lal, Pandit Lakhpat Rai, Lala Choodamani, Lala Chanduram etc. were prominent among them. They established Gurukuls, Dayanand Anglo Vedic Schools and Colleges in the entire Haryana region and taught the students the lesson of patriotism and national awareness.

Apart from Arya Samaj, "Sanatan Dharma Sabha" also tried to awaken national sentiment among the people. The Sabha also tried to save the mythology of Hindu religion. Muslim organizations also made a major contribution to national consciousness. Branches of "Central Mohammedan Association" were opened in Ambala in 1886 and in Hisar in 1888. Its members were in almost every city and major villages in Haryana. Other similar organizations like "Anjumane Islamia", "Anjumane Insha" etc. tried to bring national consciousness among the Muslims.

During the 19th century, the Sikhs had also organised themselves and established the "Singh Sabha". Though it was a religious gathering, this organisation developed political and national consciousness among its people against the British.

Role of Indian National Congress

In December 1885, A.O. Hume founded the Indian National Congress. Although it was itself a result of the national consciousness growing throughout India, yet this organization propagated the most national unity, integrity and political consciousness in India. The objective of this organization was that all the conscious leaders of India should come together, leave behind caste and religious discrimination and create national unity and solve all social and political problems.

Among the Seventy two members who attended the first session of the Congress in Mumbai in 1885, one was Rai Bahadur Murlidhar, a nationalist leader of Ambala in Haryana. He had participated as a representative of the newspaper "*The Tribune*". After returning from Mumbai, he opened a branch of the Congress in Ambala in 1886. But soon he was jailed for some political crime. K.C. Yadav says that Muralidhar was the first Indian to be made a political prisoner in national politics.

In the second session of the Congress (1886 Calcutta), Pandit Deendayal Sharma and Babu Balmukund Gupta also attended from Haryana. They created a wave of nationalism in the whole of Haryana and awakened the people politically. On 12 October, 1888, a public meeting of the Congress was called in Rohtak which was presided over by Turrabaz Khan. In this meeting, Lala Lajpat Rai presented the programmes of the Congress to the public through his speeches. This had a great impact on the Hindus and Muslims of Haryana.

National Movement (1885–1919)

The Indian National Congress was founded on 28 December, 1885 in Mumbai by A.O. Hume, a retired I.C.S. officer. Its establishment created a new enthusiasm in Indian politics. In the initial period of Congress, its members were mainly upper and middle class educated Indians. Their main leaders were Womesh Chandra Bonerjee, Dadabhai Naoroji, Badruddin Tayyabji, Gopal Krishna Gokhale, Surendranath Banerjee, Govind Ranade, Balgangadhar Tilak etc.

Some leaders of Haryana like Raibahadur Muralidhar opened a branch of Congress in Ambala in 1886. Apart from this, a public meeting of Congress was also organized in Rohtak on 12 October, 1888. Apart from Muralidhar and Lala ji, the prominent people from Haryana region who participated in the initial sessions of Congress were Balmukand Gupta, Pandit Deendayal, Gauri Shankar, Choodamani Vakil, Dunichand Ambalvi, Chhabildas, Shadilal etc.

Swadeshi Movement

For the British Government, it could tolerate everything but not Hindu-Muslim unity. The unity of these communities was the biggest threat to the British Government. The then Viceroy Lord Curzon told the Muslims that they should get a Muslim majority province like Bengal, in which they could form their own government and rule. Curzon divided Bengal into two parts, Hindu Bengal and Muslim Bengal, in 1905. The nationalists considered this a trick of Curzon and started protesting against the partition. The Congress also launched the Swadeshi and Boycott Movement against the Bengal partition.

Babu Murlidhar started the Swadeshi Movement in Haryana. He inspired people to boycott foreign sugar and clothes. As a result, the sale of foreign goods decreased. According to a statistic, the sale of foreign goods in Hisar in 1907 was Rs. 4,000, whereas it was Rs. 10,000 in 1905. Similarly, in Karnal, this figure came down from Rs. 8,000 to Rs. 6,000.

Punjab Provincial Congress

While the Swadeshi movement was going on, a meeting of the Punjab Provincial Congress was held in Ambala city of Haryana in October 1907. People from all over the province came to attend this meeting. Lala Lajpat Rai's speech impressed the people a lot. The following resolutions were passed in it:

(i) Congress branches should be established in every district.
(ii) District Congress Committees should make efforts to solve local problems like high taxes, government atrocities, forced labour etc.
(iii) Hindu-Muslim unity should be promoted.

Sir Fazle Hussain and Muslim League gave their support to Congress on this proposal of Hindu-Muslim unity. Arya Samaj also gave its support because of Lala Lajpat Rai. In this way, the Swadeshi movement spread to every village of Haryana.

Expulsion of Lala Lajpat Rai

During the period when the Swadeshi movement was going on, a massive plague epidemic spread throughout Punjab and Haryana. Lord Minto wrote in a letter to his wife that in one week more than 54,000 people died of plague in Punjab. During the period of epidemic, the British Government also increased the land tax. In such a situation, fearing that a major movement or rebellion might break out, Lord Minto exiled Lala Lajpat Rai and Ajit Singh and sent them to Mandalay (Burma).

The newspapers like "*Janaratna*" and "*The Tribune*" published from Ambala protested strongly against the exilement of Lala Lajpat Rai and Ajit Singh. Arya Samaj was scared and it severed ties with Lala. Apart from this, there was a lot of opposition at the national level too and the government was forced to call back Lala Lajpat Rai and Ajit Singh on 14 November, 1907. In this way, the Swadeshi movement was revived in Haryana.

Revolutionary Activities

In 1905, following the partition of Bengal, there were two factions among the nationalists which were known as the "Naram Dal" or Moderates and the "Garam Dal" or the Extremists in the Congress. The Extremists group was being guided by Lal-Bal-Pal (Lala Lajpat

Rai, Bal Gangadhar Tilak, Vipin Chandra Pal). In view of their revolutionary and radical activities, the extremist group was expelled from the Congress in 1907 in the 23rd session of the Congress in Surat. Now only Moderates or liberal leaders were left in Congress.

But after the partition Congress in Surat, the leaderless and aggressive youth started on the revolutionary path. They wanted to bring the British to their knees or weaken them. Haryana's Pandit Nekiram Sharma wrote an article "Disaster on Disaster" in which the British land tax system was criticized. The revolutionaries had carried out a major attack in Ambala. On 29 December, 1909, a bomb was burst at the residence of Ambala Deputy Commissioner Sykes. Sykes survived but his servant was injured. This incident was the first revolutionary incident in Haryana.

Ambala bomb incident was also seen to be linked to "Minto-Morley Reforms 1909", because this Reform or Act was strongly opposed by the militants. K.C. Yadav writes an article of Balmukand, "For about a year now, Mr. Morley has been singing the praises of improving India's governance, but what has he done? After digging the mountain, a little mouse was taken out. The essence of your whole complex talk is that the number of landlords and Muslims should be increased in big estates and provincial councils... all these have been created to enhance the prestige of the government like the army of princes."

Revolt of 10th Jat Platoon

The 10th Jat Platoon of Haryana youth was stationed in Kanpur and was imbued with the ideas of Arya Samaj. The soldiers of this platoon started participating in political meetings. Sensing the defection in this platoon, it was sent to Alipur in Bengal, away from the influence of Lala Lajpat Rai. There too, the Jats found a revolutionary atmosphere. The Subedar of the Jat platoon, Sahi Ram, met the extremist leader Vipin Chandra Pal at his residence. Apart from this, many soldiers went to pay homage to the revolutionary leader Khudiram Bose of Midnapur.

The proximity between the soldiers and the revolutionaries was warning of a big incident. About 145 soldiers of 10th Jat Platoon along with some revolutionaries planned to loot the government treasury at Diamond Harbour, but a traitor named Lalit Mohan Chatterjee informed the police. All the revolutionary soldiers were caught. All of them were dismissed from their jobs and sentenced to one year of rigorous imprisonment. The rest of the platoon was transferred to Hyderabad in Sindh.

Contribution of Kashiram Joshi

Pandit Kashiram Joshi was a resident of Modauli Kala in Ambala district of Haryana. Joshi went to United States of America in 1902 in search of work. There Joshi, along with some friends, founded the "Indian Independence League". Because of this organization which worked for the independence of India, Joshi established relations with revolutionaries spread all over the world. After coming in contact with Lala Hardayal, Joshi along with Hardayal and other comrades founded the "Gadar Party" in San Francisco in 1913. Sohan Singh Bhakna became its president, Lala Hardayal became its minister and Kanshiram Joshi became its treasurer.

Kanshiram Joshi returned to India in 1914 and along with his revolutionary comrades planned to loot the government treasury in Moga. While carrying out the task, he was caught and put in Ferozepur jail. After various kinds of torture in jail, Kanshiram Joshi was hanged on 27 March, 1915. The government also confiscated Kashiram Joshi's property worth Rs. 4,000. In this way, martyr Kanshiram Joshi was the first martyr of Haryana.

First World War

The intensity of the Swadeshi movement and the opposition of Indians forced the government to cancel the partition of Bengal in 1911. Apart from this, the British government made Delhi its capital instead of Calcutta. In this way, the Swadeshi and Boycott movements ended. After this, the First World War started in 1914 and in this war almost all sections of Haryana joined the army and supported the government. But in return the government did not give any concession to the Indian people. The public was hopeful that at the end of the war they would definitely receive a gift from the government. But Indians got a severe slap in the form of Rowlatt Act.

Home Rule Movement

The national movement had cooled down significantly during the First World War. In such a situation, Mrs. Anne Besant and Bal Gangadhar Tilak started the Home Rule League movement in 1916. They believed that the British could easily accept the demand in this difficult situation. This movement did not take a huge form but was successful in keeping the anti-British wave alive.

Home Rule movement was started in Haryana in 1917 by Pandit Nekiram Sharma. It was propagated from Rohtak to Bhiwani and it was said that the aim of this movement was Home Rule or Swaraj. Deputy Commissioner of Rohtak scolded Nekiram Sharma for this work and lured him for 25 *Murabba* land to keep away from this movement. But Neki Ram Sharma said, "I want the land of entire India which you people have illegally occupied."

Rowlatt Act

Indians had supported the British during the First World War and were hoping that they would get rewards for it after the end of the war. But Indians did not get any such concession, except the Indian Act of 1919 in which the departments were divided into two protected and transferred subjects. The protected subjects were to be under the governor and the transferred subjects were to be administered by Indian ministers. A provision was also made for 80 per cent non-official or Indian members in the provincial legislative councils.

After the War, while the liberals got the 1919 Act, the "Rowlatt Act" was passed to deal with the extremists or revolutionaries brutally. Under this, anyone could be arrested on the basis of suspicion and sent to jail for treason. There was no lawyer in this

Act and there was no scope for argument or appeal. It was passed as a bill and implemented in India in 1919. Actually its name was "Anarchical and Revolutionary Crimes Act", but it is commonly known as the Rowlatt Act after the name of Sydney Rowlatt, the chairman of this committee.

Mahatma Gandhi, who gave a new form to the national movement of India, gave a befitting reply to the government in the form of a movement on the Rowlatt Act. Gandhiji formed the "Satyagraha Sabha" in February 1919 and everyone there took an oath that they would oppose these black laws by following the path of truth and non-violence. Gandhiji called for a countrywide strike on 30 March, 1919, which was later postponed to 6 April, 1919.

Meetings were held at various places in Haryana from 30 March to 19 April, 1919. In these meetings, 2,000 to 10,000 people used to attend with black bands tied on their hands. When they were asked why they were doing so, they would say that the king had died and they were mourning for him. K.C. Yadav narrates the incident of the death of a Christian priest, Kerry Lone that neither any carpenter was ready to make his coffin nor any labourer was ready to dig his grave. After several hours, this work could be completed by the government machinery.

Jalianwala Massacre

Arya Samaj was also very active in protesting against the Rowlatt Act and spread hatred against the British from village to village. In this way, Arya Samaj's religious guru Swami Shraddhanand and Punjab's public leaders Dr. Saifuddin Kichlu and Dr. Satyapal fanned the flame against the Rowlatt Act in Punjab and Haryana. The government arrested both the leaders, Dr. Saifuddin Kichlu and Dr. Satyapal and put them under house arrest. The people of Punjab and Haryana went out of control due to this action of the government. Gandhiji left for Punjab to take charge of the situation but on 10th April he was taken out of the train at Palwal and sent back to Mumbai. Punjab again lit up on the news of Gandhiji's arrest in Palwal. The government had to impose Section

144 over this uproar. On 13 April, 1919, on the day of *Baisakhi*, during the fair in Amritsar, General Dyer opened fire on a meeting in Jalianwala Bagh. After the Jallianwala massacre, instead of improving, the situation worsened.

The revolutionaries attacked Bahadurgarh railway station in Haryana on 14 April. On 15 April, telegraph lines were cut in Rohtak. The post office in Gohana was attacked. Kaithal railway station was attacked. The government was also running a cycle of repression and putting everyone in jails. Due to the government's cycle of repression, the enthusiasm of the people gradually cooled down. Another reason was that Gandhiji was against violence.

In this unit we studied that the feeling of nationalism became popular among the upper class and middle class and then among the lower class. The people of Haryana were ready to sacrifice everything in the name of their beloved leaders and the nation. In Haryana, the leaders took the nationwide movements to every village and every house. For the first time after 1857, Hindus and Muslims were fighting shoulder to shoulder against the British only for the benefit of the country. Mahatma Gandhi, Swami Shraddhanand and Saifuddin Kichlu gave further impetus to Hindu-Muslim unity and nationalism.

19

Unionist Party and Sir Chhotu Ram

Punjab and Haryana region was an agrarian population dominated area. However, unfortunately, there was no one in this region to take care of these agrarian people. Farmers suffered the most during famines and epidemics. In such a situation, the establishment of the Unionist Party for the interests of farmers, landlords and common people, was no less than a boon. After forming the government, the Unionist Party did a lot for the revival of farmers and landlords. New farmer-friendly laws were made, schools were opened for their children and employment opportunities were also created. Many policies were made for the upliftment of Jats and Muslims who were more backward than other communities in Haryana and Punjab.

Formation and Ideology of Unionist Party

The Unionist Party was formed in 1923 by Mian Sir Fazl-e-Hussain with the help of Sir Chhotu Ram. This party had revived the farmers of Haryana and Punjab. The founder of this party was Mian Sir Fazl-e-Hussain, son of retired District Judge Mian Hussain Baksh of Gurdaspur. He was associated with the Muslim League and was very influenced by Jinnah's secular ideas. Sir Fazl-e-Hussain supported Jinnah's idea of giving more representation to Hindus in

1916. But Mian Mohammad Shafi resigned from the League on this issue.

After the end of the non-cooperation movement, there were riots in the entire Punjab-Haryana and in such a situation, Fazl-e-Hussain left the League and planned to form a secular party. In 1923, with the help of Sir Chhotu Ram, he formed the Unionist Party. In the same year, in November 1923, elections were held for the Punjab Legislative Council in which this party got a lot of success. In the new government, Sir Fazl-e-Hussain got the ministry of education and local government.

Sir Fazl-e-Hussain and Sir Chhotu Ram of the Unionist Party were considered protectors of the interests of Hindus and Muslims. Both were in favour of Hindu-Muslim unity. The Unionist Party, which worked for Hindu-Muslim unity, the interests of the lower class or farmers, and took together Hindus, Muslims and Sikhs, became very popular in Haryana and Punjab. The ideology and main objective of the Unionist Party was to work for the welfare of the village farmers and backward poor people. By joining the people of the villages and rural areas, the support base of this party increased tremendously. The programmes of this party influenced farmers, Hindus, Muslims and Sikhs. This was the reason that it got tremendous success in the Punjab Legislative Council elections of 1923.

Contribution of Sir Chhotu Ram

Sir Chhotu Ram was born on 24 November, 1881 in Gadhi Sampla, a small village in Jhajjar of Rohtak district in Haryana. His real name was Rai Richpal. Being the youngest in the family, everyone called him Chhotu, hence his name became Chhotu Ram. His father's name was Sukhi Ram. He did his graduation from Delhi and got a law degree from Agra and practiced law in Rohtak. Chhotu Ram was a staunch supporter of Arya Samaj. He formed the Jat Sabha. In 1913, Jat Arya Samaj held a meeting and on 7 September, 1913, a Jat school was established in Rohtak. In 1915, Chhotu Ram started a newspaper named "*Jat Gazette*" which is the oldest newspaper in Haryana. In 1916, Congress Committee was formed in Rohtak and Chhotu Ram became the first head of Rohtak Congress Committee. He increased his mass base and became a popular leader of farmers in the entire Haryana region.

Sir Chhotu Ram left the Congress in August 1920 because his views on non-cooperation were different from Gandhiji. He believed that if the farmers stop paying taxes, the government will take away their lands and in the end the farmers will have to bow before the government. Chhotu Ram left Congress and adopted the policy of cooperation with the British Government. At the same time in 1923, Sir Chhotu Ram met Sir Fazl-e-Hussain. Both were farmer-friendly and supporters of Hindu-Muslim-Sikh unity. At the same time, Sir Fazl-e-Hussain, with the advice of Sir Chhotu Ram, formed the Unionist Party in 1923. Due to the interests of farmers, this party came to be known as "Zamindar League". This party was a party of farmers, labourers, Sikhs, Muslims and exploited people.

Sir Chhotu Ram was made the Agriculture Minister of Punjab after the Unionist Party's success in the 1923 elections. Sir Chhotu Ram also became a minister in the 1937 government. While in the government, he did a lot of work for the farmers. He also published articles in his newspaper "*Jat Gazette*" to make farmers aware, such as "*Thug Bazaar Ki Sair*", "*Bechara Kisan*" etc. Sir Chhotu Ram died in 1945.

Election of 1923

Following the Reform Act of 1919, elections for the Punjab Legislative Council were held in November 1923. Almost all political parties except Congress participated in this election. The Unionist Party under the leadership of Sir Fazl-e-Hussain got 38 seats out of total 71 seats. According to the data of "*The Tribune*" of 4 January, 1924, Unionist Party got 38 seats, Independent Members got 11, Swaraj Party and Shiromani Gurdwara Parbandhak Committee got 10 seats and others got 3 seats.

The Lieutenant Governor of Punjab made the Unionist Party leader Sir Fazl-e-Hussain, the Minister of Education and Local

Administration. Raibahadur Lalchand of the same party was made the Finance Minister but he had to resign due to a court case. Sir Chhotu Ram of this party was made the Agriculture Minister. Both these ministers did a lot of work in their respective fields. Due to the works of both the Unionist Party leaders, this party became very popular among farmers, backward classes and labourers. By this time, the influence of Muslim League was negligible while Congress was limited to cities only.

Sunahri Qanoon

Sir Chhotu Ram did a lot of good to the farmers as the Agriculture Minister. He demanded reservation in government jobs for helpless farmers and raised his voice in the Legislative Council for their each and every right. He got a law passed to reduce the interest rates on the loans taken by the farmers. This law freed the farmers from the cruel clutches of moneylenders, *mahajans* and usurers. Farmers got a lot of relief from this law and this law came to be known as "Sunahri Qanoon" or Golden Law. According to this law, moneylenders could not snatch their land from the farmers on the basis of loan. Sir Chhotu Ram and the Unionist Party got a lot of popularity from this law and their support base strengthened among the general public.

Election of 1937

In 1935, a law was passed according to which it was talked about establishing autonomous governments in the provinces. Under this law, the governance of the provinces was handed over to the ministers representing the people. This cabinet was made collectively responsible to the provincial legislature. Following to this Act of 1935, elections were held in 1937. Unfortunately, the party's founder Sir Fazl-e-Hussain died before the elections. But before his death, Fazl-e-Hussain had handed over the reins of the party to Sir Sikandar Hayat Khan. Sir Sikandar Hayat Khan was made Revenue Minister by the Lieutenant Governor in 1937 on behalf of the Unionist Party.

The election of 1937 was fought under the leadership of Sir Sikandar Hayat Khan. In this election, influential Hindus formed the National Progressive Party and supported the Unionist Party. The Sikh party Khalsa National Party also supported Sikandar in government formation. Sir Sikandar handed over the responsibility of election campaign in Haryana region to Sir Chhotu Ram. During the election campaigning Sir Chhotu Ram visited every village and informed the people about the policies of the party. As a result, this party won this election with a huge majority. Jagdish Chandra's "Freedom Struggle in Haryana" contains the statistics of 1937 elections—out of total 175 seats, Unionist Party got 99 seats, Congress won 18, Independent members had 16, Khalsa Nationalist Party got 13, Hindu Mahasabha got 12, Akali had 11, Ahrar got 2 seats, Muslim League won 1 seat, Congress Nationalist won 1 seat, and 2 seats were of Ittehade Millat.

Sir Sikandar Hayat Khan became the Premier (Chief Minister) of Punjab. In his government, Sir Chhotu Ram became Development and Revenue Minister, Chaudhary Tika Ram was made Parliamentary Secretary. Despite the Unionist Party having a clear majority, it formed the government by taking everyone along. Among them, Sunder Singh Majithia of the Khalsa Nationalist Party and Manohar Lal of the fundamentalist Hindu Nationalist Progressive Party were also made ministers. A poet has written beautifully about the formation of this unique unity government:

"*Kai Din Me Yahaan Phir Daur-e-Akbar Aane Wala Hai,*
Sikandar Hai Abul Fazal, Manohar Lal Todar Mal"

[The age of Akbar is going to come here again after many days (years), now the Sikandar Hayat Khan is Abul Fazal and Manoharlal is Todar Mal.]

Congress-Unionist Confrontation

In 1937 elections, three Congress members from Haryana region—Lala Dunichand, Lala Deshbandhu and Pandit Shriram Sharma were elected. Later, Congress won a seat through by-election as well, because Congress was increasing its support base in Haryana region. In such a situation, Sir Sikandar and Sir Chhotu Ram visited major cities of Haryana like Panipat, Rewari, Hisar, Rohtak etc. in 1939 and organized meetings. In these meetings, the Unionist Party ran a public relations campaign and directly attacked the Congress policies. In Rohtak, there was a violent fight between Congress and Unionist workers.

Just as there was conflict between these two parties in cities and villages, similarly there was conflict within the Legislative Assembly as well. Sir Chhotu Ram was the messiah of the farmers, but when Pandit Shri Ram Sharma talked about land tax waiver for the farmers in the House, Sir Chhotu Ram opposed it. When asked by a Congressman, Sir Chhotu Ram said, "Even if the landlord goes to heaven with the help of his opponents, I will not let him go. If the landlords want to get well then it will happen only through us."

Jinnah-Sikander Pact

It was really an irony that despite the entire Punjab being a Muslim majority province, the Muslim League got only one seat in the 1937 elections. Therefore, like Congress, Muslim League was also trying to increase its support base in Punjab and Haryana. For this purpose, Jinnah started making inroads into the Unionist Party. For this, Jinnah met Sikandar Hayat in 1937 and an agreement was reached between the two. This agreement is called "Jinnah-Sikander Pact". There were two reasons for this agreement, one was that Jinnah wanted to increase his support base through this party and second, Sikandar Hayat saw his future in the Muslim League or rather wanted to capture Muslim League.

Sikandar Hayat was in a mood to capture the Muslim League through Jinnah-Sikander Pact. Knowing the intentions of Sikandar, Allama Iqbal wrote that he would not allow this to happen. Overall, this caused a lot of loss to the Unionist Party. Chhotu Ram strongly criticized this agreement and Gopichand Narang resigned from the party in protest because the party suffered a lot due to this agreement. Many Muslim leaders came under the influence of Jinnah and started joining the Muslim League.

Farmer Friendly Works of Unionist Party

The Unionist Party did a lot of work in favour of the common people and farmers. Following are the farmer and people friendly laws passed before and after the formation of the government in 1937.

Punjab Debt Waiver Act, 1934 or Sunahri Qanoon

This law was passed to free the farmers and labourers from the clutches of moneylenders. It is also known as "Sunahri Qanoon". Under this law, if double the loan amount has been paid, then the debtor will be considered debt free. Under this law, debt waiver boards were also formed which had a chairman and two members. The rule of "Daam Dupatta" was also implemented, under which there was a provision of not auctioning the means of livelihood like milch animals, calves, camels, carts, *Gher*, *Gitwads* etc.

Moneylender Registration Act, 1938

Under this law, every moneylender had to get himself registered. Without registration, no moneylender could give loans under this law nor could he file a case against the farmer in the court.

Free Return of Mortgaged Lands Act, 1938

Through this Act, all the lands that were left unconfiscated after 8 June, 1901 and were mortgaged for 37 years were returned to the farmers. This Act had a provision to give the farmer ownership of the entire land if he paid double the loan taken on the land.

Agricultural Produce Market Act, 1938

Under this law, market committees were formed in certain areas. These committees worked to ensure that farmers got a fair price for their crops. Any kind of deductions like commission, weighing, rolling, accountant, *palledari* etc. were banned. In this way, people got relief from the exploitation of commission agents.

Occupational Labourers Act, 1940

This law prohibited bonded labour. Workers could not be made to work for more than 61 hours a week or 11 hours a day. Children below the age of 14 could not be made to work. According to this law, shops and commercial facilities were kept closed on Sundays. Wage deduction for minor mistakes was prohibited and there was a provision to spend the fine amount on workers' welfare. Labour inspectors were appointed to check these abuses.

World War II and the Unionist Party

World War II broke out when Germany attacked Poland in September 1939. England supported Poland in this war and also included and indulged India and its resources in this war. But no advice was taken from Indian political parties and provincial governments for Indian participation in the war. There began a reaction all over India against British Government against Indian participation into the war. Congress said that how can a slave country take part in any war? He said that if England wanted India's support, it would first have to liberate India. To put pressure on the government, Congress got the resignations of its provincial governments in all nine provinces.

The Unionist Government of Punjab and Haryana region was loyal to the British and hence the British had their back on it. This party and government supported the British Government in the war efforts. The Unionist Party announced to recruit soldiers for the war and contribute to the war fund. For this purpose, Punjab Premier Sir Sikandar Hayat Khan got a resolution passed from the Assembly. In September 1939, Sir Chhotu Ram organized a conference of the Jat Mahasabha in Rohtak, of which he himself was the president. In this conference, he inspired all the Jats to take part in the government's war efforts. Lakhs of rupees were deposited in the fund from the rural areas of entire Haryana and thousands of villagers joined the army.

Election of 1946

While the Second World War was going on, Punjab Premier Sir Sikandar Hayat Khan died in 1942. This was a difficult time because at this time the Quit India Movement of Congress had started. In the same circumstances, in 1942, Malik Khizr Hayat Tiwana became the Premier or Chief Minister of Punjab. He ran the government facing opposition from both Congress and Muslim League. But, unfortunately, Sir Chhotu Ram was also died in 1945. With the death of Chhotu Ram, the whole of Haryana passed out of the hands of the Unionists. On the other hand, Muslims were also influenced by the Pakistan propaganda of the Muslim League and were getting attracted and influenced towards the League.

In this difficult situations, elections for the Punjab Legislative Assembly were held in 1946. In this election, Muslim League won the majority seats in Punjab but could not gather the absolute majority. Out of total 175 seats, Muslim League got 75 seats, Congress got 51, Akali got 22, Unionist got 20, and independents got 7 seats. The Unionist Party was not even ready to provide its support to the Muslim League in the government formation. Therefore, Khizr Hayat formed the government with the help of Congress, Akali and some independent MLAs. From the Congress side, Chaudhary Lahiri Singh and Bhimsen Sachar were included in the cabinet. But this government had to face strong opposition from the Muslim League in the Assembly House.

Fall of the Unionist Party

The party was shocked by the death of Sir Sikandar Hayat in 1942 and Sir Chhotu Ram in 1945. Hindus started moving towards Congress, Muslims started moving towards Muslim League and Sikhs started moving towards Akali Party. The biggest threat to the Unionist Party was from both the Muslim League and the Congress. After the immense success of 1946, the Muslim League intensified the pace of its Pakistan movement and made Punjab the centre of the movement.

The whole of Punjab got burnt in the fire of Pakistan. Communal riots started happening not only in Punjab and Haryana but all over India. A lot of uproar started inside the Punjab Legislative Assembly and it became very difficult for Khizr Hayat to run the government. The pressure and opposition of the Muslim League became so strong that Khizr Hayat's government had to resign in March 1947. As soon as the Unionist Party resigned, this party completely collapsed. At the time of partition of India and Indian independence in 1947, there was an atmosphere of complete anarchy in Punjab and Haryana.

We studied in this unit that Punjab and Haryana region was a completely Muslim majority region in which Hindus and Sikhs lived together with Muslims with great love. The main occupation of all was agriculture and their common enemies were moneylenders and the British Government. The Unionist Party united all religions and castes and formed a government of goodwill. This government never discriminated on the basis of religion or caste. Because of Sir Chhotu Ram, laws were made for farmers and labourers and the downtrodden society of this region could also get justice. In the end, the poison of religion overpowered goodwill and the Unionist Party fell for ever.

20

Mass Movements

Non-Cooperation, Civil Disobedience and Quit India Movement

During the beginning of his Indian politics Gandhiji realized that no movement could be successful without the participation of the poor and exploited people of every religion, caste and class. By involving people of all classes and religions in politics, Gandhiji united the whole of India against the British and became the unifying leader of all. In this Gandhian era or from 1917 to the independence of India, almost every decision of national movement had Gandhi's seal of approval except partition. He put challenges before the government like Non-Cooperation Movement, Civil Disobedience Movement, Quit India Movement and finally liberated India from British control. His biggest weapons were non-violence and truth, for which even the guns and cannons of the British had no answer.

Non-Cooperation Movement

The Non-Cooperation Movement of 1920 was India's first nationwide movement, which was an experiment and also the key to success against the British. Gandhiji knew that the British would be in India only as long as they had the support and cooperation of the Indians. If cooperation ends then British power ends. This non-cooperation of the Indian people shook the roots of British power.

Causes of Non-Cooperation Movement

The Non-Cooperation Movement, which was launched by Gandhiji and Indian National Congress in 1920, was the first nationwide mass movement in which people of every caste, class and religion took part. This kind of unity was seen for the first time in India after 1857, which gave sleepless nights to the British. There were many reasons for this movement which are as follows:

Effects of World War I

During the First World War, the British Government had promised administrative reforms in India after the war. On this basis, the whole of India including Haryana had fully supported the British in their war efforts. A total of 74,001 youth from entire Haryana had joined the British Army. According to a record, 8,341 youth from Ambala, 6,553 from Karnal, 17,580 from Gurgaon, 22,144 from Rohtak, 15,461 from Hisar and 14,322 youth from Native States had joined the British army for the First World War. For their recruitment, recruitment offices were opened at places like Rewari, Bhiwani, Jhajjar, Delhi etc. Despite such a big sacrifice by the people of Haryana and the country, they got nothing after the war.

During the war, a lot of India's food grains and essential goods were sent abroad, which led to a huge increase in inflation in India. Every section of Haryana was affected when almost every item became expensive during the war. Countless people died out of hunger. Many natural calamities like plague, epidemic, flood etc. also hit them. The public held the government responsible for all these problems. Finally, on the call of Gandhiji, every section of Haryana jumped into the Non-Cooperation Movement.

Khilafat Movement

The British had promised during the First World War that they would not harm the Caliph and Muslim religious places. But when they got victory, they deposed the Caliph and divided Turkey among themselves. Due to these activities, Muslims of Haryana and India along with the Muslims of the whole world became angry with the British. Indian Muslims started the Khilafat Movement against the British in 1919. Their demand was that the institution of Caliph should be kept as before and religious places should be freed. An "All India Khilafat Committee" was formed in Lucknow in September 1919. Its main leaders were Maulana Mohammad Ali, Maulana Shaukat Ali, Maulana Abul Kalam Azad, Hakim Ajmal Khan, Maulana Abdul Bari, Dr. Mukhtar Ahmad Ansari etc.

A Khilafat Conference was called in Delhi on 23-24 November, 1919, in which Mahatma Gandhi was the President of the Conference. Madan Mohan Malviya and Motilal Nehru also participated in this Conference. In this Conference, the resolution of non-cooperation with British was passed. Gandhiji himself returned his title of "Kaiser-e-Hind" and proved himself as the first non-cooperator under the banner of Khilafat Movement. Khilafat leaders appealed to the public to adopt the policy of non-cooperation against the British.

There were approximately 15,000 active soldiers of Khilafat Movement in Haryana alone. Among them were Abdul Rashid, Ghulam Beg Naurang, *Sufi* Iqbal of Ambala, Chaudhary Mohammad Yasin Khan of Mewat, Yakub Khan from Gurgaon, Bashir Ahmad Khan from Jhajjar, Zaman Ali and Haji Alauddin of Rohtak, Abdul Aziz of Mohana, Mohammad Shafi of Bahadurgarh, Mohammad Usman of Bhiwani, Nazir Beg and Mohammad Ismail of Hisar etc. were prominent Khilafatist in Haryana. Gandhiji used Khilafat Movement and its policies for the country and against the British. In 1920, he himself started a Non-Cooperation movement and raised the issue of Khilafat in it and included all the Muslims in the national movement against the British.

Rowlatt Act of 1919

During the First World War, the government had promised to reward the Indians for their cooperation in war efforts. But the

British slapped Indians hard by passing the Rowlatt Act in 1919. Under this law, anyone was put in jail on the basis of suspicion and they were not allowed to have a lawyer, appeal or argument. Gandhiji called it a black law and carried out Satyagraha against it. There were nationwide strikes against this Act on 30 March and 6 April, 1919. On April 10, while going from Mumbai to Punjab, Gandhiji was taken off the train at Palwal in Haryana and sent back to Mumbai. This increased the movement further.

Jallianwala Bagh Massacre

Many public protests, strikes and *dharna* were going on at many places against the Rowlatt Act. Its main leaders were Dr. Satyapal and Dr. Saifuddin Kitchlu. The government turned a blind eye to them. The movement against this Rowlatt Act increased further due to which Gandhiji planned to come to Punjab but he was imprisoned in Palwal and sent back to Mumbai. This treatment of Gandhiji further agitated the agitators.

On 13 April, 1919, some people were holding a meeting in Jallianwala Bagh of Amritsar during the Baisakhi fair. Since Section 144 was imposed at that time, General Dyer opened fire on that meeting. According to the government report, the number of people killed in this massacre was 379 while the actual number of dead was not less than 1000. When the non-cooperation movement started, this issue was made the main issue of the movement.

Disappointment with the 1919 Act

An Act was enacted in India in 1919. Many liberal and extremist leaders were dissatisfied with this Act because the issue of colonial Swaraj was not included in it. The people of India were not going to be satisfied with the expansion of dual governance system and communal electoral system. Therefore, in the upcoming movement, everyone gathered whole-heartedly for their rights.

Beginning and Progress of Non-Cooperation Movement

After Jallianwala Bagh massacre Britishers honoured General Dyer with a sword and 26,000 pounds in London. This shameful act of the British people showed that there was no place for Indians in their hearts. Pained with Jallianwala Bagh massacre, honouring General Dyer, Rowlatt Act and issue of Khilafat forced Mahatma Gandhi to start a new movement which could unite the entire people of India. Although the Khilafat Movement was in great progress but it was limited to the Muslim community and a handful of few rashional people of other communities. But, undoubtedly, Khilafat Movement and its workers worked as torch bearer to the new movement launched by Mahatma Gandhi. Gandhiji also found a fare chance to engage entire Muslim community in favour of national movement by adopting the issue of Khilafat and the programmes of its movement. The new national movement of Gandhiji and Congress was Non-Cooperation Movement which was started on 4 September, 1920. In this way, the non-cooperation issue which was going on under the Khilafat Movement on 1 August, 1920 became a movement on 4 September, 1920. The programmes of the Non-Cooperation Movement were mainly as follows:

- (i) All titles and honorary posts conferred by the British Government should be given up and nominated members of municipalities etc. should resign.
- (ii) Not to participate in Darbars called by the British Government and other government or semi-government functions etc.
- (iii) Children should be removed from government-run schools and colleges and admitted into national schools and colleges.
- (iv) Lawyers should boycott government courts and in place of government courts, Panchayats should be established for settling mutual disputes.
- (v) Elections to the councils should be boycotted.
- (vi) Foreign goods should be boycotted and indigenous clothes should be used.

The resolution presented by Gandhiji was passed in the special session of Congress on 4 September, 1920 in Calcutta under the chairmanship of Lala Lajpat Rai. Later, in the annual session of the Congress in December 1920, it was again approved and all responsibility to run this movement was handed over to Gandhiji. Thousands of people in Haryana jumped into this movement. Rohtak Congress Committee formed a five-member campaign committee, its president was Shriram Sharma. This Committee visited Sonipat, Jhajjar, Beri, Kosli, Gudiani etc. in February 2021. The second committee which was under Roopram visited Mhow Madina, Meham. The third committee under Ramlal and Daulatram Gupta visited villages like Kalanaur, Kelgaon, Kharak, Kaahnaur, Sundana etc. Apart from this, Nekiram Sharma, Dunichand, Shyamlal, K.A. Desai etc. visited Hisar, Karnal and Ambala districts and fully campaigned for the Non-Cooperation Movement.

After launching of the Non-Cooperation Movement on 4 September, 1920, many efforts were made to make the movement successful. In October, 1920, a conference was organized in Panipat city of Karnal district. Both Hindu and Muslim communities participated in this conference. Maulana Takaullah Khan was the president of the welcome committee and Lala Lajpat Rai presided over the conference. In this conference, thousands of people took an oath to make the non-cooperation programme successful.

"Ambala Divisional Political Conference" was organized in Bhiwani on 22 October, 1920. Leaders like Mahatma Gandhi, Maulana Azad, Mohammad Ali, Shaukat Ali, Dr. Ansari, Lala Dunichand, Devdas Gandhi etc. participated in this conference. The president of this meeting was Babu Muralidhar. About 2,000 delegates and 8,000 spectators were present in this conference. Using the term "*Shaitani Sarkar*" to the British Government, Gandhiji in his speech appealed to non-cooperate with the government, leave government jobs, give up law practice and make students leave schools and colleges.

On 8 October, 1920, a big rally was organized at Ramlila Maidan in Rohtak. Mahatma Gandhi was the chief guest in this rally. Maulana Mohammad Ali and Shaukat Ali also participated along with Mahatma Gandhi. Gandhiji appealed for non-cooperation with this dishonest government. Another conference was organized in Rohtak from 6 to 8 November, 1920. Sir Chhotu Ram, Lala Lajpat Rai, Swami Satyadev etc. participated in this conference. It was presided over by Chaudhary Rambhaj Dutt and Lala Shyamlal was the chairman of the welcome committee. In this meeting, farmer leader Sir Chhotu Ram gave a speech against farmers not paying taxes and leaving their jobs. On this speech of Chhotu Ram, a cry of "shame-shame" came from the pandal and a fight broke out and even a scuffle broke out. Chhotu Ram did not attend the conference the next day and thus Chhotu Ram separated himself from Congress and the non-cooperation movement.

The Non-Cooperation Movement in Haryana became much successful and in each and every place in Haryana there was a competition to give up posts and titles. After Gandhiji returned "Kaiser Hind", "Zulu War Medal" and "Bower War Medal", most of the people of Haryana returned their titles. Lala Muralidhar returned the title of Rai Bahadur. Mirza Nazir Beg, Ganpat Rai, Gokul Chandra, Nainsukh Das etc. returned the "Kursi Nashini" medals and certificates. Akheram of Meetathal in Hisar returned his recruiting badge and Sanad to the government. Many Zaildars and Lambardars of Hisar and Rohtak also left their posts.

On Gandhiji's call, many students also jumped into this movement. At that time there was no college in Haryana for higher studies. Therefore, the students here used to go to Delhi, Lahore and other places for studies. These students promoted Swadeshi and Non-Cooperation Movement in those colleges. The president of the college's student union and Jhajjar resident Mouli Chandra Sharma left the college along with his friends and asked other students to do the same. The same happened in Sanatan Dharma College Lahore. Ayodhya Prasad and Lala Ramswaroop Sharma also left the college. Shriram Sharma and Ramphal left Hindu College, Delhi. Gaud

High School and Jat School of Rohtak were also closed due to the boycott. The same happened in government and aided schools of Hisar, Bhiwani, Sonipat, Bahadurgarh, Jhajjar etc. In place of these schools, Gandhiji established national schools at various places. The establishment of Jamia University of Delhi was also a result of the Non-Cooperation Movement.

Similarly, lawyers also left their established practice of law. About 25-30 lawyers boycotted the courts across Haryana. The main lawyers among them were Lala Shyamlal of Hisar, Abdul Rashid of Ambala, Gulambeg Naurang, Ram Chandra Vaidya of Karnal, Dwarkadas, Mohammad Abdul Majeed and Jugal Kishore. On 18 May, 1921, the National Court was established in Bhiwani and many National Panchayats were established.

All the people of Haryana boycotted foreign goods and pledged to use Swadeshi. Around 7,000 Muslims of Hansi held a panchayat and decided not to wear foreign clothes. A similar event was organised by the cloth merchants of Hisar, Jhajjar, Bahadurgarh, Beri, Sirsa and Bhiwani and they pledged not to sell foreign clothes. Cloth began to be made on the spinning wheel and it became a symbol of independence. People also protested at liquor shops and boycotted the council elections as well. The people of Haryana boycotted the Delhi Durbar of the Prince of Wales on 17 November, 1921.

Repression and End of the Movement

In response to the nationalists' non-cooperation policy, the government started a cycle of repression. Almost all the big leaders were put in jails and were given severe torture. In total, about 500 people were arrested from all over Haryana. But despite the arrests, this movement did not stop. The more efforts were made to stop this Satyagraha movement, the more enthusiastically people participated in it.

According to a data presented by K.C. Yadav, 40 political gatherings were held in Haryana in 1920. In 1921, this number increased to 110 and in the next year 1922, the number of *Jalsas* reached 118. Like Haryana, there was frenzy in the entire country. People were happily going to jails and enduring torture. It seemed that they will attain *Swaraj* very soon.

Everything was going well in a non-violent movement when on 1 February, 1922, a violent incident occurred in Chori Chaura village of Gorakhpur. The police opened fire on a peaceful crowd. The crowd went out of control and attacked the police station and set it on fire. Total 22 policemen were burnt to death in this violence. After this incident Gandhiji felt that now this movement will turn violent. Hence, he declared the end of the Non-Cooperation Movement. The government intensified the repression. Congress was declared illegal and almost all the leaders were put in jail.

Civil Disobedience Movement

After the end of the non-cooperation movement in 1922, no movement took place in India for about eight years. In the meanwhile many incidents happened. In 1923, all parties except Congress took part in the elections in entire Haryana and Punjab. Gandhiji stayed away from politics and did many positive works like weaving *khadi*, spinning *charkha*, Hindu-Muslim unity, *Harijan* liberation etc. During these days, the government's ignoring attitude towards some Indian affairs forced Gandhiji to start a new movement, called the Civil Disobedience Movement.

Causes of the Civil Disobedience Movement

Before this movement, many political activities took place which the government did not pay much attention to. These activities were the demand for *Poorna Swarajya*, bringing Simon Commission to India etc. Following were the main reasons for this movement:

Arrival of Simon Commission

On 8 November, 1927, the British Government constituted a commission under Sir John Simon. Out of seven members there was no Indian member in this Commission. It was an all white commission and its function was to review the Act of 1919.

Congress passed a resolution to boycott the "Simon Commission" at the Madras session of December 1927. It was boycotted everywhere in India and in Haryana and the slogans such as "Simon go back" were raised and processions were taken out. A resolution was passed in Jhajjar against Simon Commission. There was a strike in Rohtak district and a huge meeting was organised, whose president was Lala Lajpat Rai.

Death of Lala Lajpat Rai

The Simon Commission reached Lahore Railway Station in Punjab on 30 October, 1928. There was strong opposition to the Simon Commission in Lahore. The protesting leaders were Lala Lajpat Rai, Dr. Satyapal, Lala Dunichand and Abdur Rahman. They showed black flags to the commission and raised slogans of "Simon go back". There was lathi charge on the crowd in which Lala Lajpat Rai was badly injured. In this, Lala Lajpat Rai had said in a meeting, "Each blow of the stick on my body will prove to be a nail in the coffin of the British Empire." Lala Lajpat Rai died on 17 November, 1928 due to lathi injuries. To avenge Lalaji's death, Bhagat Singh and his comrades killed police officer Saunders.

Nehru Report

Simon Commission was opposed because no Indian was included in its members. Nationalists believed that how can British living abroad make a universally accepted constitution for India. On this objection, India Secretary Lord Birkinhead said that no Indian can make a constitution which is universally accepted and undoubtedly it was a challenge to the Indian political parties. All Indian parties accepted this challenge and formed a constitution making committee whose president was Pandit Motilal Nehru. Pandit Motilal Nehru presented his report in the Calcutta session in 1928 which is known as Nehru Report. It said that India should be given the dominion status. But many young leaders like Pandit Jawaharlal Nehru etc. did not accept this constitution and demanded complete independence.

Demand of Complete Independence

In December 1929, a Congress session was held on the banks of the Ravi river in Lahore, which was presided over by Jawaharlal Nehru. In this session, at 12.00 midnight on 31 December, 1929, a proposal for India's early independence was passed. The tricolour flag was also hoisted in this session. After passing of complete independence resolution by Indian National Congress, 26 January, 1930 was celebrated as Independence Day and same practice was followed in the later years. Pandit Shriram, Lala Shyamlal, Captain Bali etc. from Haryana participated in this Lahore session in large numbers. After passing of this resolution, a civil disobedience movement was also considered in this session.

Growth of the Civil Disobedience Movement

The Civil Disobedience Movement was started on 12 March, 1930. Sitting in his Sabarmati Ashram, Gandhiji placed 11 demands before the Viceroy. When the Viceroy did not pay attention to them, Gandhiji started Civil Disobedience Movement. Gandhiji marched 240 kilometres on foot from Sabarmati Ashram with 78 followers. Gandhiji reached Dandi after a journey of 124 days. It is popularly known as Dandi Yatra. Kept a fast on the first day and on 16 April, 1930, Gandhiji broke the salt law by making salt from sea water. Since salt could not be produced everywhere, people boycotted foreign goods, gave up government jobs and boycotted schools and colleges.

National leaders of Haryana encouraged the common people to join this movement. On 10 April, 1930, the law was broken by making salt by taking water from a well in Rohtak. On 13 April, 1930, the law was broken by making salt in Jhajjar. Similarly, people of other places of Haryana like Beri, Sanghi, Sonipat, Hisar, Rewari and Gurgaon participated in this movement by breaking the salt law. Holi of foreign goods was burnt.

The government unleashed a repression on the agitators. People were arrested and beaten up. According to a data, 380 people from Rohtak, 90 from Hisar, 40 from Gurgaon, 67 from

Ambala and 33 from Karnal were jailed. Meanwhile, elections were held in September 1930 in which the Unionist Party formed the government in Punjab and Haryana. Meanwhile, the first Round Table Conference was called on 12 November, 1930 in which the Congress did not participate. On 5 March, 1931, an agreement was reached between Mahatma Gandhi and Viceroy Lord Irwin, which is known as the "Gandhi-Irwin Pact". It was decided that political satyagrahis would be released and the Congress would participate in the Second Round Table Conference. Hence, Gandhiji participated in the Second Round Table Conference in December 1931 but returned empty-handed as none of his demands were accepted.

After returning back from England, Gandhiji again started the Civil Disobedience Movement on 4 January, 1932. The government showed strictness. Approximately 1,20,000 people were put in jails. Many leaders including Gandhiji were arrested. Under such circumstances, the Third Round Table Conference was held, in which Dr. Ambedkar was given a separate electoral system for *Dalits* like Muslims. Gandhiji considered it a ploy by the British to divide the Hindus and fasted for 21 days in Poona jail against the grant of separate electorate. In such a situation, Gandhi-Ambedkar Pact or Poona Pact was reached, in which Ambedkar abandoned the separate electoral system and accepted reservation for *Dalits*. Gandhiji came out of jail and ended the Civil Disobedience Movement on 7 April, 1934.

Quit India Movement

World War II broke out in 1939 and in this war, without the consent of the Indians, the British again pushed India into the war. Pushing India and Indian resources into the war was opposed everywhere in India. It seemed that after centuries of British slavery, India would now become a slave of some other country after defeat of the Britain. In such a situation, Gandhiji started the Quit India Movement on 8 August, 1942.

Reasons for Quit India Movement

Launching of the Quit India Movement in 1942 shook the roots of the British Government and it was undoubtedly a major achievement of Mahatma Gandhi and the Congress. There were the following reasons for Quit India Movement:

Second World War

The Second World War had started in 1939 and the British used India's army and resources in this war. In this way, India started having the status of a partisan on the British side. For using the Indian army and resources, the British did not consult any Indian political party. Indians felt that if England lost the war, then it was certain that India would again become a slave of a victorious country. Therefore, Gandhiji opposed the British and started the "Quit India Movement" to drive the British out of India.

Individual Satyagraha and August Declaration

Gandhiji was so angry at India's involvement in the war that he called for individual Satyagraha. Thousands of people broke laws and were arrested as part of individual Satyagraha. By May 1941, about 14,000 Satyagrahis went to jail, of which 516 people were from the Haryana region alone. The government made an announcement in August 1940 that if Indians cooperated in the war efforts, India would be given the status of Dominion and given the right to make a constitution after the war. But this announcement could not influence any party or agitator. On 2 March, 1941, Hisar leader Jugal Kishore was jailed. Apart from this, leaders like Abdul Ghaffar from Ambala, Syed Mutawali from Gurgaon, Dr. Madhoram and Dr. Krishna from Karnal were arrested for participating in Individual Satyagraha.

Muslim League's Proposal for Partition of India

The Muslim League had demanded reservation in government jobs for Muslims in 1940. But on 23 March, 1940, the Muslim League passed a resolution demanding an independent nation for Muslims in its Lahore session. The Congress opposed this demand of independent nation for Muslims. Sir Chhotu Ram of the Unionist Party also opposed this move of Muslim League.

Azad Hind Fauj

Lord Linlithgow's announcement that India would get Dominion Status after the war was nothing but a hoax. Gandhiji called it a "Post dated cheque of a bankrupt bank". Meanwhile, on 17 March, 1942, Japan captured Andaman Island and then Manipur too. Japan's next target was Assam and Bengal. Congress began to feel that India might slip out of the hands of the British and become a slave of Japan. In such a situation, the demand to drive out the British began to gain momentum.

On 17 February, 1942, the Japanese handed over 50,000 Indian war-defeated soldiers in Singapore to Mohan Singh, who was earlier the captain of this contingent under the British. Mohan Singh formed Azad Hind Fauj which was reorganized by Subhash Chandra Bose in 1943. This army marched towards India along with the Japanese forces. This included 398 officers and 2317 soldiers from Haryana.

Progress and End of Quit India Movement

In the unusual situation of war, Congress met in Mumbai and passed the resolution of "Quit India Movement" on 8 August, 1942. Gandhiji gave the slogan of "Do or Die", meaning we will liberate India or we will sacrifice our lives in this effort. Immediately after launching this movement, the British Government arrested big leaders including Gandhi on the very first day. This was the first movement which ran successfully without central leadership. People were fired upon, lathicharged and arrested. The people of Haryana destroyed the railway station, post-telegraph and property belonging to the government. According to K.C. Yadav, 4 railway stations were damaged, 11 post offices were attacked, 45 wire cutting incidents took place, 8 police stations and government buildings were attacked, 6 railway track uprooting incidents took place.

Hundreds and thousands of people were arrested and locked in jail cells. Still, people were so enthusiastic that the movement was not stopping. Farmers, labourers and socialists were mostly involved in the sabotage. Their main leaders in Haryana were Lakshman Das, Mangeram Vats, Radhakrishna, Ramkumar Vidyath, Comrade Shishupal Singh, Vaidya Lekh Ram etc. Total 525 people were arrested from many districts of Haryana—61 from Ambala, 49 from Karnal, 111 from Gurgaon, 228 from Rohtak and 76 from Hisar. Due to violent repression by the government, this movement gradually went underground and also turned violent. When the movement became violent, Gandhiji observed a 21 days fast from 10 February, 1943. In this way, this movement ended by the end of 1943. The government realized that now they would not be going to survive in India for long.

Elections of 1946 and Partition of India in 1947

The strongest party in Punjab and Haryana was the Unionist Party. But due to Pakistan issue of Muslim League and death of Sir Chhotu Ram and death of Sikandar Hayat Khan, Muslim League became more powerful. In 1946 elections, the League got the maximum of 75 seats while the Unionist Party got 20 seats. Except the League, all the parties formed the Unionist Party government but it had to face opposition from both Congress and Muslim League.

In the midst of communal tension, riots and looting, Unionist premier Khizr Hayat Khan had to resign in March 1947. Jawaharlal Nehru and Sardar Patel accepted the partition of Bengal and Punjab and gave their approval for the separation of Pakistan. Gandhiji was against this partition but he too had to remain silent in the last. India was partitioned on 14 August, 1947 and India got independence the next day on 15 August, 1947. Punjab and Haryana suffered the most loss of life and property in this partition of India.

In this chapter we studied that the people of Haryana and Punjab participated in all the national movements with great enthusiasm. Despite the pro-government Unionist Party being in power in Haryana and Punjab, people of almost all religions, castes and classes participated in the national movements. On Gandhiji's call, the entire public was ready to fight and die. On the instructions of their leaders, leaving their personal work, the people of Haryana were always in the forefront to make India independent. On Gandhiji's call, people left their jobs, left their studies and sacrificed everything and these freedom-loving people were happily facing the bullets, sticks and jails of the British Government.

21

Prajamandal Movement

Due to the national movements and political activities of the Indian National Congress and Azad Hind Fauj, there was awareness among the people of the princely states also. Although the rulers of these princely states were Indians, still they were cruel towards their subjects and their subjects wanted independence from them. The Princely States collected huge amounts of taxes and forced labour from the people and mercilessly suppressed any voice raised against them. Influenced by the national movements, the people in their states formed Prajamandal Movement. The national leaders sympathized with these people and fully supported them as they could.

General Condition of Princely States and Subjects in Haryana

After conquering North India from the Marathas, the British had divided the areas around Haryana and Delhi among their loyalists. These were the kingdoms and states against which the people launched movements in the first half of the twentieth century.

Princely States

In 1803, British Army Commander Lord Lake defeated the Marathas and captured a large area of North-West India. He distributed some of that territory among his loyalists who had helped him in this war against Marathas. There were some regions or states which existed even before the British and the British had given them their protection because of their loyalty. In the first half of the twentieth century, influenced by the movements of Congress and Gandhiji, Prajamandal Movement was started in almost every princely state. The princely states in Haryana where the movement broke out were—Dujana, Pataudi, Loharu, Jind, Narnaul and Bawal.

People and their Economic Condition

Most of the princely states in Haryana were rural and the main occupation of the subjects was agriculture. The subjects were poor due to lack of any other means. Due to frequent famines and crop failure, the farmers were dying of hunger. In such a situation, the princely states were not helping them at all and the burden of taxes and forced labour were taking away their livelihood. The subjects held their kings responsible for all this misery and sufferings. Arya Samaj and Congress fuelled the disappointment of the subjects. And it was true that there were no canals, no irrigation, no other means, no roads and no industrial development. Despite all of this, there was no dearth of luxury and comfort of the native kings.

While emphasis was being laid on development and education in many parts of India, these princely states were like frogs in the well, ignorant of education and development. The native kings believed that if the people became educated then they would start agitating. Still, some people came out of the small schools of the princely states, obtained higher education and started the Prajamandal Movement. The rulers of the princely states used to act arbitrarily due to the absence of any written law and the people were unhappy with their exploitation and atrocities. The people there could not even think of civil liberties.

Creation of Prajamandal

When the people of entire India were participating in the Congress movements, Haryana was also not untouched by it. It also affected the princely states. However, in Princely States the pressure was less because of the Unionist Government in Haryana and Punjab. When the educated people of these Princely States returned after completing their education from Delhi and Lahore, the spirit of patriotism was overflowing in them. Arya Samaj also united the people of these Princely States against the kings. The people of Arya Samaj linked the exploitation and atrocities on the people with religion and incited the Hindu people against the Muslim kings. The educated people and the people of Congress and Arya Samaj suggested the people to form an organization or Prajamandal.

Following the suggestions of Congress, "All India State People's Conference" was formed in 1927. This organization worked to inspire the people of the Princely States. The very next year in 1928, "Punjab Riyasati Provincial Prajamandal" was established in Mansa. Branches of this organization were opened in entire princely states. These organizations made a commendable contribution in uniting the people of the Princely States and preparing them for the movement. Congress was also working with the Prajamandal Movement. When Jawaharlal Nehru became the President of the Congress in 1929, he said that "the princely states cannot be kept separate from the rest of India." Due to his efforts, Congress included the wars of native states in its policies.

In 1938, the Prajamandals of Punjab gathered in Ludhiana and held a conference, which was presided over by Jawaharlal Nehru. It was decided that the Prajamandal Movement should be carried out vigorously in every Princely State. This conference also brought enthusiasm and awareness among the people of the princely states of Haryana and this movement was carried out with full vigour.

Prajamandal Movement in the Princely States of Haryana

Prajamandal was a movement carried out by the people of Princely States. In these movements, ordinary farmers fought against the atrocities of the king and forced him to accept their demands. Prajamandals started being formed in princely states after 1927 and by 1938-39, Prajamandals were fully formed. Thereafter, the struggle for a responsible government began. Congress also included Prajamandal issues in its policies and Prajamandal Movements were taken forward. There were the following princely states in Haryana where Prajamandal Movement was carried out:

Dujana State

Dujana was a small Princely State. Its area was 91 square kilometres and its population was 30,666. Its annual income was Rs. 2,31,000. This princely state was established in 1806 by Yusufzai Pathan Abdus Samad after the Second Anglo-Maratha war. This Princely State included two tehsils Nahar and Dujana and 24 villages. In 1945, when the Prajamandal Movement was going on here, the ruler of Dujana was Iqtadar Ali Khan, who was an illiterate person. Iqtadar Ali Khan had made Naib Diwan Nawab Umardaraz Khan from a school master, and himself was a puppet in his hands. Naib Diwan Nawab Umardaraz Khan used to loot the people of Dujana a lot and had imposed heavy taxes. In the name of making the life of the people happy, there was one dispensary and one school in the entire Princely State.

In 1945, the dissatisfied people of Dujana established Prajamandal and made its centre in Nahar. The head of Prajamandal was Rao Devkaran Singh and the secretary was Rao Sardar Singh. Among other prominent workers, Rao Neki Ram and Hariram Arya were prominent. In 1946, people launched a massive agitation and the people stopped paying taxes and the rest of the classes did not cooperate. This infuriated the Nawab Iqtadar Ali Khan. He imposed a ban on Prajamandal and imprisoned the major leaders like Devkaran Singh, Rao Sardar Singh, Pandit Hariram, Ramji Lal etc. He issued warrants against other workers and started arresting them.

But the Nawab's repressive policy further fuelled the fire of the movement. The people threatened that if their leaders were not released, a mass satyagraha would be started in Dujana. The agitators also got a resolution passed on 19 November, 1946. Apart from the release of the leaders, they also demanded reduction of land tax, abolition of forced labour, holding of Panchayat elections and opening of a middle school in Nahar. The Nawab was frightened by these threats and released the leaders on 8 December, 1946 and accepted most of the demands. Nawab promised to provide schools, roads, hospitals and other facilities. But before all the demands could be met, India became independent and the Dujana Princely State was merged with Rohtak district. The Nawab himself went to Pakistan.

Pataudi

Pataudi was a small town, which was founded during the time of Jalaluddin Khilji by a Mewati chieftain named Pata and after him the town was named Pataudi. The Princely State of Pataudi was established by Nawab Faiz Talab Khan in 1804. This princely state was given to the Nawab in return for helping the British in the Second Anglo-Maratha War. There were 40 villages in this state and the area was 40 square kilometres. Their population was 21,520 of which 90 per cent were Hindus. Its annual income was three and a half lakh rupees. There was one dispensary and five primary schools in the state.

Due to its proximity to Gurgaon, political consciousness came to the people Pataudi very quickly and in the 1930s itself, the people of Pataudi had put forward the demands of ending forced labour, reducing land tax, building roads, schools and hospitals in front of the Nawab. Prajamandal was established here in Pataudi on 1 June, 1939. Roop Chandra became its president and Mogelal its secretary. At this time, the ruler of this princely state was Mohammad Iftakhar Ali Khan, who was also a famous cricket player.

Due to day-to-day opposition, Nawab declared Prajamandal illegal and started crackdown. In August 1939, Prajamandal launched a mass Satyagraha, due to which 200 Satyagrahis were arrested. The Nawab was forced to compromise with the Satyagrahis and released the prisoners. But when the Quit India Movement of 1942 was going on, Prajamandal workers like Gauri Shankar Vaidya, Pandit Babu Dayal Sharma, Thakur Ram Singh, Nand

Kishore, Chhotelal etc. started a powerful movement in Pataudi. Many leaders were arrested. After the end of Quit India Movement, Pandit Jawahar Lal Nehru made a compromise with the Nawab and got the Satyagrahis released.

After the end of the Second World War, the Prajamandal Movement again gained momentum in Pataudi in 1945. The nationalists of the British India and Congress leaders also came out in support of the agitators. At this time, the leader of the movement was Rao Gajraj Singh. The Nawab had to bow down and he released the political prisoners and also assured to reduce the land tax. After India's independence, Pataudi was included in Gurgaon district.

Loharu

The area of Loharu state was 226 square miles and its population was 27,892. Pleased with the services of his lawyer Ahmad Bakhsh Khan, Raja Bakhtawar Singh of Alwar gave Loharu state to him. In this way, Loharu state was established in 1803 by Ahmad Bakhsh Khan, the lawyer of Mughal Sardar and Bakhtawar Singh. It was named Loharu because at one time this area used to be the mint of the Princely State of Jaipur and most of the coin minting blacksmiths used to live here in Loharu. When the people's movement became active in 1940, Nawab Alimuddin was the ruler of this state. Due to differences between the Nawab's brother Shahzad Miyan and the Arya Samajists, the Arya Samajists started a movement by calling the Nawab a fanatic. Many economic issues were also included.

It is true that Arya Samaj had started a religious movement in Loharu like the other Muslim ruling Princely States of Haryana region. If the Nawab of a state was a Muslim, the first issue of Prajamandal and Arya Samaj was religion. In 1935, the people of the state protested against the rule of the Nawab. The local people started a movement by forming "Jat Sabha". All of them started a "Civil Disobedience Movement" very similar to Gandhiji's Civil Disobedience Movement. In this way, religious and political movements together took a terrible form. On 8 August, 1935, about

1200 people were gathering and holding a meeting in Singhani village. Nawab Loharu's army opened fire on this crowd. In this firing, a total of 22 people were killed and 30 people were injured. After this incident, the movement was suppressed for some time.

After the Second World War, Prajamandal was established in Loharu state in 1945, in which the prominent leaders were Subedar Dilsukh, Thakur Bhagwant Singh, Chaudhary Mohar Singh, Nathuram, Chandiram, Shankarlal etc. He raised the slogan "Merge the Princely States with India". They launched a powerful movement by including leaders from other areas. The agitators of Hisar supported this movement. Nawab's brother Shahzad Mian and Diwan Bhure Khan supported the Nawab. Again a meeting was held in Sinhani village in which 700 people attended. Everyone had only one demand to merge the Princely State with British India. Nawab started the repression cycle and arrested Prajamandal Secretary Krishnadutt and one member Bhagat Bhujjan Ram. Meanwhile, India became independent and the Princely State was merged into Hisar district on 1 March, 1948.

Jind State

Modern Dadri tehsil and Jind district were part of the Princely State of Jind. The area of this Princely State was 1026 square miles and it included 346 villages. The population of this princely state was 2,19,248. The state of Jind was established in 1763 by Sardar Swaroop Singh of Phulkia Misl. During the Prajamandal Movement, the King of Jind was Ranbir Singh (1879–1948). The king had imposed heavy taxes on his subjects and forced them to do forced labour. In the First World War, the king helped the British with Rs. 11,50,000 and also with his army.

"All India State People's Conference" and "Punjab State Riyasati Prajamandal" in 1927 and 1928 inspired the people of Jind State to fight for their rights. Under the influence of these institutions, some conscious people of Jind established "Jind State Prajamandal" in Narwana. Among the founders of this institution, the names of Hansraj Rahbar, Pandit Devidayal, Banarasi Das Gupta, Rajendra

Kumar Jain etc. are prominent. Other leaders like Ramkishan, Pandit Shivkaran, Mahtab Singh, Mangeram, Chiranjilal, Baba Indra Singh, Baburam, Sadhuram, Mangalram etc. made important contributions in taking the Prajamandal movement forward.

In 1940, the first public meeting was organized in Dadri which was presided over by Dr. Satyapal. Nekiram Sharma was the special guest in this meeting. Everyone demanded to reduce land tax, end corruption and end the influence of chief minister Gangadas Kaul. The king resorted to repression and arrested most of the people of the meeting. Meanwhile, the king accepted their demands and released the prisoners.

After the Second World War, the Prajamandal Movement gained momentum again. Prajamandal president Banarasi Das Gupta was put in jail for threatening to launch a movement. Many other Satyagrahis were also imprisoned. A public meeting was held in Dadri on 1 November, 1946 against the arrest in which 500 people participated. Due to this threat, Raja Ranveer Singh got scared and accepted most of the demands of the Satyagrahis and released the prisoners. But despite the agreement, there was no reduction in exploitation and atrocities.

The members of the Prajamandal formed a 17-member action committee under the leadership of Hira Singh Chinariya and the committee started public satyagraha and civil disobedience movement from 8 August, 1946. The king, out of fear, again made a compromise and under this compromise, prime minister Ganga Ram Kaul was removed and Mohammad Sadiq was appointed as the prime minister in his place. Apart from this, a new cabinet of eight members was formed to run the people's representative government. In this new cabinet, apart from the prime minister, two members were appointed by the king, two were members of Akali Dal, one member of Muslim League and two were members of Prajamandal. The king was given veto power on any decision against his cabinet. This system continued in the state till independence.

Narnaul Area (Patiala State)

The area of Narnaul in the Haryana region was under the Patiala Princely State of Punjab. Patiala State was founded by Maharaja Bhala Singh in 1752. In 1764-65, Ahmad Shah Abdali gave recognition to the state by giving the title of Maharaja to Bhala Singh. At the time of Prajamandal Movement, Maharaja Bhupendra Singh (1900–1938) and Maharaja Yadvinder Singh (1938–1948) were the rulers of Patiala. The people of Narnaul were victims of the Maharaja's atrocities and exploitation. The subjects had to pay heavy taxes and forced labour.

1945, the people here tried to draw attention towards the people by establishing Prajamandal. The people put forth their demands before the king but instead of listening the king started threatening the people. According to K.C. Yadav, the king threatened the people that this is not an English state where the excesses of Congress are tolerated. Here, those doing anti-state activities will be taught such a lesson that future generations will also remember it. The Maharaja again threatened the people, "I am a soldier, my words are blunt and my bullets fire straight."

However, the king's threat had no effect on the people. Many leaders like Ram Kishore, Matadin, Ayodhya Prasad, Kamla Devi, Banwari Lal, Rao Madho Singh, Rao Ishwar Singh Azad, Chaudhary Dulichand, Ramsharan Chandra Mittal, Shriram Kaushik etc. started a strong movement. The whole of Narnaul jumped into this movement. In the end, the Maharaja had to bow down before the people and accept all their demands and ended the exploitation and atrocities. Fortunately, at the same time India became independent and Patiala state was merged with Punjab.

Bawal Area (Nabha State)

The Bawal region in Haryana was a part of the Nabha Princely State of Punjab. The Princely State of Nabha was established in 1755 by Raja Hamir Singh. At the time of Prajamandal Movement, Nabha was ruled by King Maharaja Pratap Singh (1923–1948). Like other princely states, exploitation and oppression were prevalent in Nabha too. More taxes and forced labour were taken from the public and there were no facilities for the public. There was dissatisfaction among the people of Bawal towards the king. After the Second World War, like other princely states, Prajamandal was established here in 1945. Prajamandal launched a mass movement here. Its main leaders were Master Shyam Manohar, Rameshwar Dayal, Matadin Bhagat, Rameshwar Singh, Ishwar Singh Azad etc.

In 1946, Raja Pratap Singh tried to suppress the movement and imprisoned many leaders. The people got angry with the oppressive actions of the king and started a movement. They raised the slogan "*Nabha Wale Bawal Chhodo*" and urged all the people to join the movement. Finally, Raja Pratap Singh bowed down to the public and released the prisoners. He also promised to reduce taxes and abolish forced labour. But in 1947 India became independent and Bawal and Nabha were merged in Punjab.

In this chapter we studied that like the British Government, the native Princely States also exploited their subjects. When Congress and Gandhiji launched a movement all over India, the people of the Princely States also became aware and the people of the states established Prajamandal in their respective states. A mass movement was launched by Prajamandal against exploitation and oppression in the entire Princely States. Congress and Arya Samaj supported the people in these movements. The kings tried to suppress the movement but ultimately had to bow down to the movements of the people. The kings accepted the demands of the people. But during the time of Prjamandal Movement, India became independent in 1947 and like the Princely States of other regions, the princely states of Haryana and Punjab were also merged into Indian Union.

Bibliography

Ahmad, Aijaz (2017). *History of Mewat*, K.K. Publications, New Delhi.

Ahmad, Aijaz (2017). *Mewati Rebellion of 1857*, Fiction House, New Delhi.

Ahmad, Aijaz (2020). *Cultural Heritage of Mewat*, Concept Publishing Co., New Delhi.

Ashraf, K.M. (1983). *Life and Conditions of the People of Hindustan,* Pearl Publication, Calcutta.

Buddh Prakash (2012). *Haryana Ka Itihas: Ek Sarvekshan*, Granth Academy, Haryana, Panchkula.

Buddha Prakash (1962). *Haryana Through the Ages*, Kurukshetra University, Kurukshetra.

Buddha Prakash (1969). *Glimpses of Haryana*, Kurukshetra University, Kurukshetra.

Das Gupta, K.K. (1974). *Tribal History of Ancient India: A Numismatic Approach,* Navbharat Publishers, New Delhi.

Datta, Monika (1999). *Formation of An Identity: A Social History of Jats*, Oxford University Press, New York.

Devahuti, D. (1970). *Harsha: A Political Study*, Oxford University Press, New Delhi.

Dwivedi, H.N. (1973). *Dilli ke Tomar (736–1193),* Vidya Mandir Prakashan, Gwalior.

Goyal, J.B. (1966-edited) *Haryana-Puratattva, Itihas, Sanskriti, Sahitya evam Lokwarta,* Delhi.

Gupta, Hari Ram (1961). *Marathas and Panipat*, Punjab University, Chandigarh.

Gupta, S.P., Rama & Chandran, K.S. (1976). *Mahabharata: Myth and Reality*, Agam Prakashan, New Delhi.

Irfan Habib (1982). *Cambridge Economic History of India*, Cambridge University Press, Cambridge.

Jagdish Chander (1982). *Freedom Struggle in Haryana*, Vishal Publication, Kurukshetra.

Kadian, Arjun Singh (2021). *Land of Gods: The Story of Haryana*, Rupa Publications, New Delhi.

Kenneth, W. Jones (1976). *Arya Dharam*, Manohar Book Service, New Delhi.

Mittal, S.C. (1986). *Haryana: A Historical Perspective*, Atlantic Publishers, New Delhi.

Phadke, H.A. (1990). *Haryana: Ancient and Medieval*, Harman Publication House, New Delhi.

Phogat, S.R. (1978). *Inscriptions of Haryana,* Kurukshetra University, Kurukshetra.

Pradaman Singh & S.P. Shukla (1985-edited). *Freedom Struggle in Haryana and the Congress, 1885–1985*, Haryana Pradesh Congress (I) Committee, Chandigarh.

Prem Chaudhary (1995). *Punjab Politics: The Role of Sir Chhotu Ram*, Vikas Publishing House, New Delhi.

Puri, B.N. (1968). *History of Gurjar-Pratiharas,* Munshiram Manoharlal, New Delhi.

Ranjeet Singh (1976). *Haryana Ke Arya Samaj Ka Itihas*, Arya Pratinidhi Sabha, Rohtak.

Sen, S.P. (1979-edited), *Sources of the History of India,* Vol. II, Munshiram Manoharlal, New Delhi.

Sharda, Sadhu Ram (1978). *Haryana—Ek Sanskritik Adhyayan,* Bhasha Vibhag, Haryana, Chandigarh.

Shukla, S.P. (1985). *India's Freedom Struggle and Role of Haryana*, Criterion Publication, New Delhi.

Singh, Fauja (1997–2000-edited). *History of the Punjab,* Vol. I-III, Publication Bureau, Punjabi University, Patiala.

Singh, R.B. (1964). *History of Chahamanas,* Nand Kishor and Sons, Varanasi.

Suraj Bhan (1975). *Excavations at Mithathal (1968) and other Explorations in Satluj-Yamuna Divide,* Kurukshetra University, Kurukshetra.

Tripathi, R.S. (1964). *History of Kanauj*, Munshiram Manoharlal, New Delhi.

Verma, D.C. (1981). *Sir Chhotu Ram: His Life and Times*, Sterling Publication, New Delhi.

Yadav, K.C. (1975). *Rao Tula Ram and Revolt of 1857*, S. Pramod & Co., Jallandhar.

Yadav, K.C. (1994). *Haryana: Itihas Avam Sanskriti,* Vol. 1, Manohar Publications, New Delhi.

Yadav, K.C. (1994). *Haryana: Itihas Avam Sanskriti,* Vol. 2, Manohar Publications, New Delhi.

Yadav, K.C. (2002). *Modern Haryana: History and Culture, 1803–1966*, Manohar Publications, New Delhi.

Yadav, K.C. (2012). *Haryana: Itihas Ke Jharokhe Se,* Haryana Academy of History and Culture, Gurgaon.

Yadav, K.C. (2023). *Revolt of 1857 in Haryana*, Manohar Publications, New Delhi.

Index